Staging Lives in Latin American Theater

Staging Lives in Latin American Theater

Bodies, Objects, Archives

✦

Paola S. Hernández

NORTHWESTERN UNIVERSITY PRESS
EVANSTON, ILLINOIS

Northwestern University Press
www.nupress.northwestern.edu

Printed in the United States of America

10 9 8 7 6 5 4 3 2 1

Library of Congress Cataloging-in-Publication Data

Names: Hernández, Paola S., author.
Title: Staging lives in Latin American theater : bodies, objects, archives / Paola S. Hernández.
Description: Evanston, Illinois : Northwestern University Press, 2021. | Includes bibliographical references and index.
Identifiers: LCCN 2020046523 | ISBN 9780810143364 (paperback) | ISBN 9780810143371 (cloth) | ISBN 9780810143388 (ebook)
Subjects: LCSH: Historical drama, Latin American—History and criticism. | Spanish American drama—21st century—History and criticism. | Theater and society—Latin America.
Classification: LCC PQ7082.D7 H47 2021 | DDC 862.70998—dc23
LC record available at https://lccn.loc.gov/2020046523

CONTENTS

ACKNOWLEDGMENTS

This book was made possible through the generosity and collaboration of numerous scholars, institutions, and friends, to whom I am indebted and deeply grateful. The University of Wisconsin–Madison provided the leave time and funds to concentrate on my research. The UW-Madison Institute for Research in the Humanities and its director Susan Friedman invited me to participate in a semester-long scholarly residency. The Vilas Associate Fund at UW-Madison funded the field research and two years of summer support necessary to complete this project as well as the Summer Humanities Research Fellow program (2018) directed by Steven Nadler, through which parts of the book were workshopped by theater scholars Jean Graham-Jones, Brenda Werth, Sarah Misemer, Ana Puga, and Mary Trotter. I am honored to have worked with all of you.

Because I believe in collaborative work and feedback, I know that this book could not have been produced without engaging dialogue with colleagues and friends in the field and beyond. At the University of Wisconsin, my colleagues Mercedes Alcalá-Galán and Steven Hutchinson have participated in long conversations about theater and art over wonderful dinners that continued late into the evening. Many thanks to Rubén Medina, Luís Madureira, and Guillermina De Ferrari for being great colleagues with insightful comments; to Laurie Beth Clark and Michael Peterson for teaching me about generosity; and to Falina Enriquez and Jill Casid for always engaging with my work. I am grateful to all of you for providing me with constant support and intellectual conversations. A special mention goes to my friend and colleague Marcelo Pellegrini for always believing in my book and everything related to theater. I am also thankful to the many graduate students who have shared their thoughts and ideas in seminars and have traveled to Chicago with me to see plays, especially Christina Baker, Marin Launfenberg, Megan Bailon, Laissa Rodríguez Moreno, Carlos Ortiz, Alex Leme, Isabel Martín Sánchez, Sabina Madrid Malloy, and Anna Gerbaski. To my theater-loving students who participated in many of our own productions of plays at the Play Circle: thank you!

Ever since I completed my PhD at the University of Kansas, I have been fortunate to build a circle of colleagues who have either worked with me on projects or conference sessions or have given me insightful comments on my work. I am most indebted to my friends and colleagues Brenda Werth, Sarah Misemer, Camilla Stevens, Michelle Warren, and Pamela Brownell for their commitment to scholarship, their generous input on my work, their friendship, and their camaraderie. My deep appreciation goes to "las tertulianas," a group formed by Eugenia Afinoguenova, Sarah Davies Cordova, and Vicky Unruh—thank you for all the trips to the theater, all the conversations about many of the plays in this book, and, most of all, for your ongoing friendship and support. I am grateful to Jeffrey Coleman for meeting once a week to write and making the writing process less solitary, and to Paul A. García for his productive comments on draft versions of this book. Portions of chapter 4 appeared in "Remapping Memory Discourses: *Villa* and *Discurso* by Guillermo Calderón," in *South Central Review* 30, no. 3 (Winter 2013). I have presented excerpts of this book at conferences (American Society for Theatre Research [ASTR], Association for Theatre in Higher Education [ATHE], Latin American Studies Association [LASA], Hemi) where colleagues have provided excellent feedback: Analola Santana, Jimmy Noriega, Katie Zien, Marcela A. Fuentes, Sarah J. Townsend, Jorge Dubatti, Milena Grass, Cristián Opazo, Grisby and Gisela Ogás Puga, and Adam Versenyi. I also appreciate Diana Taylor and the Hemispheric Institute of Performance and Politics for inviting me to design working groups related to my research.

At Northwestern University Press, I thank Trevor Perri and Patrick P. Samuel for believing in this project and helping to make it a reality. Thank you also for your careful selection of readers; their comments helped me strengthen this book.

I would especially like to thank all the artists whose work is included in this book, for their determination, time, and dedication: Vivi Tellas, Lola Arias, Teatro Línea de Sombra (especially Jorge Vargas, Alicia Laguna, and Eduardo Bernal), Guillermo Calderón, and Federico León. To producers Sol Sañudo, Sofía Medici, Lucila Piffer, Laura Cecilia Nicolás, I am indebted for giving me access to material important to this book.

During the years of writing this book I lost my best friend, Silvina Di Stéfano and my dad, Roberto Blanco, to cancer. Sil, thank you for your friendship and for all the laughter. Dad, thanks for all the life lessons. You both left too soon. Finally, my dear family in Argentina and the United States has been a source of inspiration and love. Thank you, Todd, for being my constant companion, for inspiring me to do my best, and for always coming to every play I wanted to see (no matter how late it was). And to our two daughters, Camila and Sofía, for daily joys and for keeping me grounded. This book is for you.

Introduction

✦

The Real Onstage

New Modes of Documentary Theater

On a large white wall in a small theater in Bogotá, Colombia, a graffiti artist draws the lines of someone's face. With sharp, quick, black strokes, details begin to emerge. We watch silently as we take our seats. The sound of the paint being applied at the end of the long pole he uses to reach to the top of the high wall, along with the movements of his artistic, careful hand, mesmerizes us all. No one seems to be interested in reading the program notes; no one is making small talk. The effect of a face slowly revealing itself onstage makes us aware that whatever we are about to watch already has the air of a live event. It is 2016 and the play, *Baños Roma* by Mexican collective Teatro Línea de Sombra, envelops us in theater, document, and event.[1] We will eventually learn the name of the person whose face has emerged, José Angel "Mantequilla" Nápoles, and that the story behind that face documents a perspective on the life of an old boxer who then lived in Ciudad Juárez, Mexico, long forgotten by society. Photographs and other documents of his past reveal the highs and lows of an athlete once revered as a hero, but it is his painted face that gives us a sense of presence.

At the turn of the twenty-first century, and a few years before *Baños Roma*, Argentine theater artist and curator Beatriz Catani identified a turn or a shift in how artists understood their work in relation to the political context of an acute economic crisis, specifically the one in 2001 that left many Argentines below the poverty line.[2] Similarly, and in reference to the end of *Menemism*, a decade-long government characterized by adherence to the neoliberal ideals of the Washington Consensus and material excess, another Argentine director, Vivi Tellas, stressed that after two decades of simulations and simulacra, "art needs to find a new way to relate to the real."[3] Artists thus employed documentary techniques as a way to explore issues stemming from real events. In doing so, they destabilized fictional settings, and highlighted the possibilities of how the theater could engage with real events in a more direct way, relying less on traditional realism. Catani and Tellas took this moment to explore how to use real events to envision and stage their work, taking advantage of the fact that theater, as a live event, already has the privilege of presenting documents in situ. Groups such as Teatro Línea de Sombra and independent artists like Tellas and Catani found provocative ways of working with the real in the imagining and creation of live events.

In his celebrated 1968 manifesto about documentary theater, Peter Weiss contends that "documentary theatre shuns all invention."[4] Twenty-first-century documentary theater could not fall further from this declaration. Contemporary artists seek to fuse fiction and facts, personal and public narratives, creating a new approach to both official archives and documents. *Staging Lives in Latin American Theater: Bodies-Objects-Archives* analyzes the role of the real in contemporary theater and performance of the twenty-first century in Argentina, Chile, and Mexico, as exemplified by the Argentine artists Vivi Tellas and Lola Arias, the Mexican collective Teatro Línea de Sombra, and the Chilean playwright and director Guillermo Calderón. Here I explore the real through the stories, objects, and personal artifacts that performers (both trained and untrained) bring to the stage. In part, the real is evoked by the performers who tell their own stories of the past, using their bodies as documents or as mediums through which other stories get retold and reenacted. This exploration of the real also urges us to rethink how theater's personal objects-turned-props—such as letters, videos, clothing, and photographs—generate a sense of authenticity, inviting audiences to discover new perspectives or interpretations of the past. The stories I discuss here are either autobiographical or biographical, and some are more testimonial than others, but they all engage the real in retelling personal life stories. I propose that the affective hold of the real, orchestrated through site specificity, autobiography, the innovative use of people with no formal acting training, personal documents, video, and photographs, may affect spectatorship, transform private and public memories, modes of participation, and the kinds of truth claims theater can make. Consequently, I argue that playwrights, performers, and artists use the real to highlight the liminality between fact and fiction, and question discourses of authenticity as well as the veracity of the "archive" as an object of truth.

Scholars Alison Forsyth, Chris Megson, Carol Martin, Jenn Stephenson, Cecilia Sosa, Jordana Blejmar, and Brenda Werth, among many others, have identified a renaissance of documentary practices in Europe, the U.S., Canada, and Latin America. I link this renaissance to both the affective turn and the emergence of the autobiographical in contemporary documentary theater. Specifically, I study the ways in which staged biography or autobiography produce affective bonds with audiences, taking as my case studies stages across Latin America. In my analyses, I show how the staging of personal stories resonates with audiences in a uniquely powerful way. Throughout the book I recall Tellas's explanations of the emergence of the real on Latin American stages, and I elaborate on their formulations to argue that the need to examine the "real" or the authentic is a way to respond to many other forms of simulacra and virtual experiences of our times.

I use the term "archive" to refer to how material objects—photographs, videos, and documents such as witness reports, legal briefs, and letters—come to life on Latin America's documentary stages. I explore how these material archives are recodified by live performance in the present; how the dimension of an object's meaning can be expanded and reinterpreted onstage; and how onstage interpretations of physical objects help to generate an affective relationship between actor and the audience. The idea of the archive is not just what remains, but rather what can be reshaped and even reenacted. I am less interested in the notion of the archive as an inventory of the past and am more interested in understanding how archives themselves help us rethink a performance. In this respect, documentary theater introduces objects from the past and turns them into props and manipulates those objects through the experience or immediacy of performance. It is, perhaps, in Peggy Phelan's perception of performance as "a strict ontological sense [that] is nonreproductive" that *Staging Lives* finds a productive field to dialogue, because documentary theater always seems to credit or at least function with the archive, making a strong commentary on the role of what remains. Phelan's assertion that "performance's being . . . becomes itself through disappearance" is central when thinking about performance's ephemerality.[5] In other words, how do documents persist despite the ephemeral sense of performance? How does the weight of these objects-turned-props help us understand that while performance maybe ephemeral, documentary theater inhabits the lines between fact, fiction, and the material and the ephemeral, prompting scrutiny and rethinking of their value in the present time?

Yet my attention shifts toward the life of objects as agents that blur that binary between animate and inanimate, and how objects become central *actants*. As Jane Bennett defines it, an actant is "a source of action; an actant can be human or not, or, most likely, a combination of both."[6] I am particularly interested in envisioning how objects as *actants*, as archival objects that bring in the weight of historical meaning with them, possess "particular frequencies, energies, and potentials to affect human and nonhuman worlds."[7] In documentary theater, where objects become props, questions about authenticity, affect, relationality, and history arise. Thus, exploring objects-turned-props as actants, with their own agency, allows me to delve deeper into the meaning of documentary theater as an archival space that performs. In this respect, I concur with Rebecca Schneider's concept of new materialisms and "the agency of objects and the forces of materialization [that] have increasingly blurred the borders modernity had built up between the animate and the inanimate."[8] Documents and objects become part of the script and are actants in themselves as well as in the hands of the actors that use them. Theater practitioners have relied on this live relationship between objects and props, the real and the staged. It is precisely within this tension that objects-turned-props become their own entities, with agency and historical value that put forth the documentation of the play at stake.

What is at stake, however, when documentary theater revives the archive? How is the past entwined with the present? The relationship between performance and archive, as Diana Taylor states, is indeed between the two entities she defines as "the archive of supposedly enduring materials . . . and the so-called ephemeral repertoire of embodied practice/knowledge."[9] Her point of view deals directly with the political, cultural, and juridical consequences of evidence and information that gets lost due to the lack of documentation. If a large part of the evidentiary archive in Latin America has been lost or disappeared, she asks, and if performance's ephemerality is not credited with transmitting vital knowledge, then whose stories, memories, and traditions get retold?[10] While her study does not refer specifically to documentary theater, she underscores how the manipulation of the archive, along with its mediation, reinterpretation, and embodiment, can shed new light on understanding the past.[11] This is precisely where the new documentary theater of the twenty-first century positions itself: at the crossroads between fact and fiction and through the possibilities of creating and rethinking documentary materials. It is not the fact that this theater revisits historical characters with a fresh perspective. The artists studied in this book do not just examine historical figures with a new lens; they search for meaning beyond the importance of well-known names and instead turn to everyday stories—often retold by witnesses such as war veterans or children of the disappeared—that illustrate history's lost, forgotten, or unacknowledged experiences.

Within the study of documentary theater, it is also helpful to consider Rebecca Schneider's formulations about the archive in relation to performance. The archive, consisting of objects such as records, legal documents, and even bodies, also produces a sense of loss or confusion. She challenges the binary between the remains (what the archive constitutes) and the disappearance of performance (theater), with a provocative observation: "The archive itself becomes a social *performance* of retroaction."[12] In documentary theater, artists and playwrights borrow the objects from the past to bring new understandings to present life and expose the ways in which testimony, reenactments, and embodiment onstage transform the archive, which in turn might lead to new rules or conditions in the present: for instance, a lifting of previous amnesties, new prosecutions on state-sponsored torture, or more humane treatment and policies that protect rather than persecute migrants.

The central importance of objects-turned-props relies on how objects from the past contain their own meaning and are reimagined in the present. It is because of the potential of the stage and the intervention of the actors and people not formally trained in the theater that objects become documentary, and as such, they establish specific links between memory, community, and historical context. As Andrew Sofer contends, "Stage props become a concrete means for playwrights to animate stage action, interrogate theatrical practice, and revitalize dramatic form."[13] Props, then, are tools "acquir[ing] independent signifying force."[14] As they are triggered by actors, props become alive. However, what type of different meaning does an object that carries a certain sense of authenticity from the past outside of the theater relay? The presence of authentic objects used as props indicates a different relationship to the stage. In a recent study about how documentary objects are their own entities of the past and present, Shaday Larios introduces the theory of catastrophe as a way to underscore the semiotic value of the objects' representation and their resignification through the creation of a "third poetic space."[15] In this new reformulation of objects, some have survived catastrophic events, such as dictatorial governments, disappeared people, or the remains of dead migrants, but they are all part of a material culture that allows for theater to engage with the spectral connection of what they carry. All the chapters in this book relate to the existence and reliability of objects onstage. In some cases, as with Lola Arias, actors wear the clothes that once belonged to their now disappeared parents. Or, in the case of Vivi Tellas, her plays allow for people with no formal training in the theater to build their stories through a close, affective connection to personal objects. After all, documentary theater relies on the materiality of archives and objects that bring in their own sense of participation. The goal of introducing objects onstage is not to make the object look alive but, rather, to understand the logic of the object within the nature of the story onstage.

Documentary Theater and Its Precedents

The new conception of the real in twenty-first-century Latin American theater that I examine in this book departs from a twentieth-century tradition of European and Latin American documentary theater. Taking into account the historical trajectory of the European-style of this genre is important for understanding how documentary theater evolved and was received in Latin America in the twentieth century. With the creation of the short-lived Proletarian Theater in the early 1920s, Erwin Piscator endeavored to "aim to forget about 'Art' and build an ensemble on the basis of common revolutionary convictions."[16] Piscator's technological innovations were central to the beginnings of what would become documentary theater. He used moving images, photographs, and projections to denounce police repression and to make his audience aware of the political context of the time. In other words, Piscator adapted what was called an "elastic montage" by which he used images (posters, news clippings, and manifestos) through different projectors so that the visual impact of political events could be brought in to the theater.[17] His pursuit of what was known as "Total Theatre," designed by Walter Gropius but never built, envisioned a theater in the round surrounded by acoustic and mechanical devices. His documentary technique, with heavy political overtones, was to be directed at the bourgeoisie so his theater would be considered revolutionary. The legacy of his "epic dramas," which Bertolt Brecht would later develop further as epic theater made use of episodic scenes, montage, projections, and a lack of method acting. Piscator decried a Stanislavskian acting method, claiming that the actor was part of a team or collective, "one who draws his whole strength from his involvement in the common cause. In course of time, his attitude will produce a new form of acting."[18] However, as Meyerhold pointed out, Piscator's ideas about acting never came to fruition, and it was not until Brecht that "the concept of epic, 'gestic acting' evolved."[19]

Piscator's pioneering documentary techniques paved the way for Brecht's epic theater. Brecht viewed Piscator as a "master builder" and "a contributor to that 'great epic and documentary theatre.'"[20] Moreover, Piscator's innovative approach to technology, his conception of the role of politics in the theater, and thus the creation of a revolutionary theater marks the beginning of what Brecht would further develop in his epic theater. In 1968, influenced by Piscator and Brecht, Peter Weiss wrote "Fourteen Propositions for a Documentary Theatre," in which he stipulates the goals of documentary theater, what constitutes this type of genre, and how it can awaken society to understand the hidden political agendas of the media. Committed to the political and the need to document global sociopolitical events, such as the assassinations of President John F. Kennedy and Che Guevara, massacres in Indonesia, and preparations for the Vietnam War, documentary theater revealed itself to be a powerful genre.[21] For Weiss, documentary theater both denounced and made use of the political nature of theater and served as a venue for keeping the public well-informed. For him, manipulation of the archive was less central; the goal was to utilize the documentary mode to fulfill a specific political function, mainly that of denunciation of the mass atrocities of the twentieth century.[22] His use and theorization of documentary theater held media accountable for ignoring certain events while highlighting others. This is evident in *The Investigation* (1965), a play where his predilection for employing the tribunal structure to re-create documentary theater is prevalent. Here the audience could understand the dramatic tension as well as the authentic nature of the documents.

Later, Hans-Thies Lehmann argues that the theater of the latter half of the twentieth century and beginning of the twenty-first is "post-Brechtian," by which he means a "theatre which knows that it is affected by the demands and questions for theatre that are sedimented in Brecht's work but can no longer accept Brecht's answers."[23] Lehmann coins the now-acclaimed term "postdramatic theater" to describe a theater that inherited Brecht's "consciousness of the process of representation" but makes a point to leave behind "the political style, the tendency towards dogmatization, and the emphasis on the rational."[24] Certainly, Lehmann's description of postdramatic theater has been a productive contribution to considering how theater can reclaim and reconceptualize the real, by "treading the borderline . . . by permanently switching . . . between 'real' contiguity (connection with reality) and a 'staged' construct."[25] In line with Lehmann's postdramatic theater, new approaches to the real onstage are less interested in engaging the political and are more focused, instead, on studying the nuances of historical reinterpretation through a new lens.

Even as Lehmann refers to how documentary theater can be considered a predecessor of postdramatic forms by enhancing its dramatic techniques with authentic legal documents and court proceedings as props, he contends that documentary theater nevertheless falls into the trap of the dramatic. He notes that in "documentary theatre little depends on the outcome of the process of investigation or that of arriving at a verdict."[26] I would argue, however, that many playwrights and artists in Latin America have found a way to make documentary practices be more than just dramatic plays. Depending on how playwrights engage documentary practices in their work, plays have the potential to become more than theater, and the mere dramatic. For example, Argentine playwright Lola Arias, Chilean playwright Guillermo Calderón, and the Mexican theater collective Teatro Línea de Sombra develop methodologies to documentary theater that transcend the dramatic, have a concrete social impact, and sometimes even result in changing the law.[27] This book shows the significant ways in which new documentary theater of Latin America has departed from the European documentary tradition, showcasing how artists in Latin America have brought about a profound way to postulate new ideas about their own documentary practices and beyond.

In Latin America, a more traditional documentary theater creation in the collective reached its peak during the 1960s and '70s as Augusto Boal developed the foundations of what would later become the "Theatre of the Oppressed," a theatrical doctrine that proposed a more personal and revolutionary look toward theater.[28] Historical reflection in documentary theater was also promoted by Vicente Leñero in Mexico, who wrote his highly acclaimed play *Pueblo rechazado* (*Rejected People*) in 1968. The playwright states that theater provided an ideal vehicle for him to document the violent events that took place that same year.[29] It is worth noting that this particular piece premiered only three years after *The Investigation* (1965) by Weiss, calling attention to possible connections, or influences, that European theater had on Latin American productions.[30] During this period, there was also an increase in the number of collective groups that sought to interrogate their surroundings by means of documentary theater. Works such as those produced by the Teatro Experimental de Cali (TEC), directed by Enrique Buenaventura (1955); the group La Candelaria, founded and directed by Santiago García (1966); the Peruvian groups Yuyachkani, directed by Miguel Rubio (1971); Cuatrotablas, directed by Mario Delgado (1971); the Teatro ICTUS in Chile (1955); and el Escambray in Cuba (1968), among others, encouraged the development of a theater rooted in the collaborative expression of social concerns.[31] This theater attempted to create a space from the margins, offering seldom-heard voices a way to express themselves through a critically engaged dramaturgy. Pedro Bravo Elizondo notes that the documentary theater of the 1960s and '70s intended to establish a place for collective forms of testimonial theater.[32] This genre was also highly concerned with the historical and accurate representation of facts. However, as Silka Freire claims, some of these collective groups that worked with documentary techniques saw their work as an alternative way to promote information that the media was not providing, allowing for a change in perspective and knowledge of history.[33] The groups above had a strong political commitment and worked tirelessly to achieve a theater that resisted commercial interests, one that would allow for experimental and creative approaches to flourish.

New Pathways of Documentary Theater

The long history of documentary theater shows that it is clearly not a new genre; however, younger generations of theater practitioners draw on the ambiguities present in this long tradition to reflect critically on the process of production and reception of their work. As Jenn Stephenson claims, "The core distinction between millennial theatres of the real and their more traditional documentary predecessors lies in profound postmodern, post-structuralist doubt."[34] Today, the use of documentary techniques has proven to be both contagious and prolific in Latin America. It has provided artists and theater collectives with a new creative paradigm for exploring a wide array of topics, from private and personal issues to charged political and traumatic public events. The "theater of the real," in Carol Martin's words, is indebted to the documentary theater that emerged in the 1920s, expanded in the 1960s, and reached enormous popularity in the U.S. in the aftermath of 9/11. *Staging Lives* turns the lens to Latin America—where the strategies of truth-telling as an effective intervention in the present have been developed to their full potential through the manipulation of technology and new access to media. Latin American theater and performance have had a major impact in reshaping, through the manipulation of the document, what truth-telling means, and thus have demonstrated how our perception of the present is shaped by the ways in which we recount and document history. Martin stipulates that the study of this type of theater of the real, or documentary theater of the twenty-first century, goes beyond the document and its historical referent. It provides a new approach to the reinterpretation of history—one with the potential to expose the "truth that many times conflicts with other narratives."[35]

Staging Lives demonstrates how documentary theater of the twenty-first century analyzes political issues through the use of creative and imaginative new strategies. I draw on Martin's approach to this theater as one that both "acknowledges a positivist faith in empirical reality and underscores an epistemological crisis in knowing truth."[36] *Staging Lives* proposes that Latin

American artists who engage with documentary theater push the connections between the judicial system and the stage in a more direct way, using a tribunal method onstage to question what or how documents have influenced people's lives. Lola Arias and Guillermo Calderón's works examine the fictional and political dimensions of testimony onstage while showing, too, examples of staged testimony that have real legal implications outside of the theater in recovering the truth about the past. They each present personal stories as archives that later become instrumental in influencing the law. In Arias's example her work allows one of the performers to make a legal case against a father who was a perpetrator during the Argentine military dictatorship. For Calderón, the law and its interpretation are essential to his vision of documentary theater.

The archive possesses the "unknowable weight" of the past, as Jacques Derrida suggests, and casts doubt on the future as a ghostly image. He explains that the "archive is only a notion, an impression," and he considers it the very concept of the future of the conditions of the archive.[37] How does the theater, in presenting an archive of the past, grapple with this "unknowable weight"? How do witnesses of atrocity contend with the political and traumatic past, and how do second-generation children remember and retell their stories? Contemporary Latin American documentary theater reflects on the notion famously put forth by Jean Baudrillard that simulation has replaced truth and the referent.[38] These artists reassess the role of documentary theater by turning the lens toward an ironic, sometimes even humorous perception of how the real is just another strategy for destabilizing the archive. Documentary theater artists, then, create their own aesthetics, their own fluid relationship to how archives are and may not be part of the repertoire. Taken collectively, and as detailed in this book, these Latin American theater practitioners pose questions about the value of the archive by appropriating new practices that blend fact and fiction. How can witness testimony both become more persuasive in this new theater of the real and at the same time more subject to scrutiny as fiction and fact blend in the telling of stories onstage? How do artists find new ways to revive and energize the past in the present?

Staging Lives explores how this new approach to theater addresses the fragility and imperfection of memory deriving from traumatic experience. It also focuses on the provocative use of real archives to understand history and the present through the manipulation and interpretation of documents. In the works of the playwrights and artists, I am interested in analyzing the communion between the notion of Derrida's "authorized deposit" and theater, as well as the blurry lines between the concrete and historically situated with the ephemeral art of performance, imagination, and creation. While the idea of the real is foundational for this type of artistic genre that draws from interviews, videos, hearings, and photographs, also central to this research is a consideration of how the process of editing, selecting, and organizing this material develops into artistic practice. Thus, even though documents appear to demand factual legitimacy, the editorial process of selection undertaken by these artistic practitioners is not always transparent, thereby emphasizing the duality between what is real and what is represented as such. Broadly speaking, in these works, the impact of the archive lies in its liminality between factual and fictive, public and private. Documentary theater in Latin America has evolved from its traditional European roots over the years into an exploration of the autobiographical, taken up by a new generation of theater makers in Latin America who present documents self-consciously and sometimes ironically to draw attention to how the legitimacy of testimony is constructed and questioned.

To document is to archive. Yet to perform the archive is to bring the document back to life. The use of autobiography onstage accompanied by personal objects, including letters, audio or video recordings, photographs, clothing, or the actual presence of a witness-as-actor, contribute to the archive, whose authenticity is constantly celebrated and questioned through performance. One effect of the autobiographical element has been to give agency to those other voices that are rarely heard or considered on the stage, such as undocumented migrants or refugees. It is at the intersection between self and others, between objects and documents, that the real onstage is exposed and interrogated. On the other hand, there seems to be a need to reconsider the archive not as something from the past but instead, as Derrida insists, as the "question of the future, the question of the future itself, the question of a response, of a promise and of responsibility for tomorrow."[39] This temporal projection of the archive with a future and its possibilities allows contemporary artists and theater practitioners who use documentary techniques to express their work not as a repository of the past but as a method to imagine possible futures. The autobiographical mode, in linking past lives to the present and future, is crucial for both narrating the past and envisioning the future.

The Autobiographical Stance

The role of the autobiographical onstage has a direct relationship to how lives are part of a document and how the reality of someone's life enhances the aura of the story. The autobiographical has been an important trend in a world where we are surrounded by reality shows, personal blogs, Instagram, Snapchat, Facebook, selfies, and a "culture of me or I" that obsesses with the personal.[40] Autobiographical stories help us understand the "other" in front of us and may even help us relate to or to empathize with their stories. They also hold the promise of truth-telling, of something simple and possible in a world of virtual realities. However, it is also clear that the need to stage autobiographical stories foments the interaction with a human face, an opening for marginalized voices to have a space, to be seen or heard. According to Jill Dolan, when staged, autobiographical plays "reveal performativity" and provide a subtle way to examine questions of identity, subjectivity, and memory.[41] In fact, autobiographical plays can be profoundly political by using the first-person narrative as part of a national identity as well as an affirmation of how their lives might or might not fit within the hegemonic parameters. By promoting the "I" as the central point of departure, works "use the facts of a personal story to make us rethink the concept of *self* and the relationship of *self* to other."[42] Among other things, they serve to make lives central, no matter how mundane the stories might be.

In the theater, the embodiment of the actor's own story, the physicality of his or her body combined with first-person narration serves as a powerful mechanism for truth-telling. The majority of the stories told in first-person meet the criteria for what Philippe Lejeune, in his writing about narrative, calls the "autobiographical pact," by which "the *author*, the *narrator*, and the *protagonist* must be identical."[43] He studies the notion of possible ambiguity in the way this genre creates room between how it is read (or performed) by creating an "illusion." He adds that "the autobiographer incites the reader to enter into the game and gives the impression that an agreement has been signed by the two parties."[44] Though Lejeune conceived of his pact specifically in relation to literature, I find it useful when applied to theater because of the fruitful space he creates by calling attention to the possibility of artistic simulation in autobiography. It is precisely his awareness of the "real" manifestations of this autobiographical pact that documentary theater provides. More concretely, he posits that "the paradox of the literary autobiography, its essential double game, is to pretend to be at the same time a truthful discourse and a work of art."[45] This "pact" or this "game at pretending" to be part of a truthful genre and simultaneously allowing for fiction to be part of this equation positions contemporary documentary practices in a rich and productive terrain. In other words, autobiographies "are *referential* texts. . . . Their aim is not simple verisimilitude, but resemblance to the truth. It is not 'the effect of the real,' but the image of the real."[46]

Yet the use of the autobiographical mode in the theater complicates how stories are performed and perceived. For instance, there is the constant duality between what the theater does as a fictional setting and what the autobiographical brings to the stage with its promise of authenticity. The reliance on the autobiographical mode for some of the playwrights tends to reinforce this ambiguity and expand the gray zone into a multisemiotic field of possibilities, what Susan Bennett defines as "a frenzy of signification."[47] When a documentary mode is utilized, either through photographs, videos, or letters, the mere fact that the objects are presented as "documentary" gives them authentic aura. And as Bennett states, no matter how much editing, cutting, adaptation, or selection of these objects is done, when we see the bodies onstage, we give them the agency of truth.[48]

In this book, artists use a variety of performers to retell their stories. Names and last names are frequently used in documentary theater as a technique for strengthening claims of authenticity and as a meaningful tribute to the individuals. Even if we have actors in front of us, many times, their names are an important part of the story, something that cannot be negated or changed. This also brings up an important point about many of the works that deal with documentary material that can only be staged with the same people or cast unless the play is modified accordingly. As Lola Arias states, "In documentary projects the actors are irreplaceable,"[49] therefore stories are ingrained in and within the personal. There is no denying the central role the body of a performer, or actor-witness can have when the autobiographical mode is implemented. Not only do their objects-turned-props onstage add agency to their stories, but it is within their own body-as-archive that produces other possibilities of understanding about how new documentary theater creates a sense of truth and agency.

Affect and the Audience

As bodies and objects take a central role in how stories are documented onstage, there is a tension or, in Nicholas Ridout's words, a "vibratorium," a kind of "radiation" by which the performance can transmit affect between actors and spectators.[50] I am indebted to Ridout's idea of a vibratorium as a way to explore and understand audience emotions and reception because he links how theater can be a central point of departure to experience an "energy exchange" that is part of a feeling, an aura that cannot be represented.[51] Influenced by Teresa Brennan's study of the transmission of affect, Ridout contends that the theater, as a sensory threshold, has the ability to bring the audience together in a "momentary communion."[52] In a similar vein, Jill Dolan describes what she terms "utopian performatives": "small but profound moments in which performance calls the attention of the audience in a way that lifts everyone slightly above the present, into a hopeful feeling of what the world might be like if every moment of our lives were as emotionally voluminous, generous, aesthetically striking, and intersubjectively intense."[53] Documentary theater practices offer the audience a unique opportunity to experience utopian performatives, where facts and fiction intermingle.

Modes of belonging and the exploration of the intimate worlds of ordinary people are key to how contemporary documentary practices have evolved. Thus, affect studies propelled by how emotions are felt in the theater, how the transmission of affect can detonate other feelings, and how new forms of intimacy and belonging can create new sites of performance that highlight conviviality and community are central. Throughout the chapters, there is a connecting thread that delineates how personal stories relate to the audience in a more direct fashion. I am especially interested in studying how the personal connections that documentary theater invigorates a closer, affective relationship to the audience's subjectivity. In this type of theater, a sense of connectedness to a witness or a survivor of a traumatic war, or even a biography of a peculiar person, can register a particular kind of empathy. For this reason, I am mindful of how ideas such as Dolan's utopian performances, Brennan's transmission of affect, and Jill Bennett's extraction of affective encounters from emotional identification question and highlight the relationship between art and affect. My intention here is to look at the processes of theatrical practices that allow for stories—some traumatic, some nostalgic, some humorous—to negotiate meaning through affective engagement.

New Documentary Theater

The concept of a new documentary theater derives from a genre that has its roots in political theater from the 1920s and after but takes new directions and develops new lines of interrogation, ones that tackle history, social issues, and politics from the end of the twentieth century into the twenty-first. This tendency toward searching for and utilizing documents or authentic materials, perceived as having historical, political, or personal value, remains part of new documentary theater, just as it characterized Piscator's historical model. However, although this new documentary theater demonstrates continuity with the idea that archival materials undergird the structure of a piece, it examines how fiction, editing processes, and the selection of materials showcase liminality and the blurry definitions of documentary versus fiction. This has resulted in a theater style that assures a certain level of legitimacy surrounding the events portrayed, while also showcasing the creative liberties that are part of generating theater. Even though the interest in social justice remains strong, some new documentary theater manifests itself in relation to political concerns with less urgency than the one of the 1960s and '70s. That is, this new documentary theater has created a space in which private and personal stories are welcome, the autobiographical tale, the "I" as the centerpiece, a connection forged between the person and their relation within and beyond the sociopolitical context.

More concretely, we can think of new documentary theater in the following ways:

> It works with advanced technology, via multimedia effects (video replay, superimposition of images, sonic stimuli, the computer-generated sound or image); this theater achieves an added layer of creative or fictional creation.
>
> It utilizes documents (interviews, letters, photographs, newspapers) as part of the archive to delve into not only political topics but also topics that are social and personal in nature. The importance of the documents resides in the way they are manipulated, how they

> become open to alternative meanings and possibilities to question their presumed inherent authenticity.
>
> It welcomes new forms of acting, often brought onto the stage from a perspective of a nontrained actor, who does not belong to the theater world. This blurs the line between person, performer, and witness, putting greater emphasis on the value of the autobiographical story line and less on actor methods or scripts.
>
> It blurs lines between commonplace reality and creative inspiration from the world of fiction, prompting uncertainty about the value of documentation as representative of "authenticity."
>
> It emphasizes an autobiographical mode, in (re)telling one's personal stories, in situating them within a broader political and historical chronology.
>
> It centralizes on self-referentiality as part of constructing a fictionalized version from documented sources.
>
> It distances itself from the seriousness of historical documents in a way that invites humor, doubt, and play and/or even chance as possible outcomes.
>
> It embraces the aesthetic value of creation. In many circumstances, documents and archival materials are transformed into props, in part, recodifying their value and signification.

This series of descriptions, which is definitely not exhaustive, illustrates to some extent what Latin American artists wrestle with when conceiving these plays. It also proposes the extent and prolific terrain that allows artists to create. The emphasis on the duality between fact and fiction evokes a new space for pondering and staging new possibilities and new theories about the past, the present, and the future. Thus, objects, bodies, and archives are animative in this new space; their codified value as evidence from the past plays with the many possible interpretations and manifestations in the present.

New documentary theater calls attention to the fact that there is no original object or event that one can go back to, since its authenticity can be questioned. The ephemeral nature of theater initiates a journey of twists and turns, an approximation to theater that is rooted in supposed originals or authentic elements, but consciously fuses the past with an imagined future. According to Martin, "Documentary theatre emphasizes certain kinds of memory and buries others," while, at the same time, re-creating documents onstage, the aspects that Diana Taylor considers part of the repertoire (gesture, movement, sensations, proximity), which need to be activated by other bodies, or different time periods.[54] The intended effect is to create a separate articulation that conjures the original source via the staged events of the present. In this sense, new documentary theater foresees ways of creating fiction from the ambiguity and friction that arise in bringing documents to the stage.

Under this configuration, Latin American artists have developed a variety of ways of imagining "theater of the real." Autobiographical theater, for example, has been a strong representative of how documentary modes inhabit stages, as well as a kind of theater that is deeply connected to re-creations. In the words of artist Lola Arias, this approach is what she first conceived of as "remakes," a form of re-creating the past in order to produce new perceptions by means of embodying the documented events from the present toward a future that she now calls "reenactments." Speaking specifically about *Mi vida después*, Arias affirms that the play "maneuvers at the edges of what is real and what is fiction, the meeting between two generations, a re-make as a way to revive the past and change the future, the crossroads between a country's history and personal experience."[55]

According to Allison Forsyth and Allison Megson, "Much documentary theatre has functioned to complicate notions of authenticity with a more nuanced and challenging evocation of the 'real.'"[56] Creative initiatives of twenty-first-century documentary theater draw attention to the search for the "original" and subsequently manipulate it onstage, emphasizing notions of recycling and/or copying a copy. Artists such as Vivi Tellas, Lola Arias, Federido León, Mariano Pensotti, Beatriz Catani (Argentina), Guillermo Calderón, Manuela Infante (Chile), Mariana de Althaus, Sebastián Rubio, Claudia Tangoa (Peru), and groups like Mapa Teatro (Colombia), Lagartijas tiradas al sol, Teatro Ojo, or Teatro Línea de Sombra (Mexico), are excellent examples of theater makers who manipulate original documents to offer a new take on events, or, at times, so that the audience learns about social issues that have an impact on people's lives, including their own.

The fluidity between what is artificial and what is real, what is documented and what is imagined, results in a gray area that many of the above-mentioned artists have chosen to mine as fertile terrain for their work. In this ambiguous zone, artists play with a theater that capitalizes on a document's authority while also imbuing it with sense of artifice. As I note in chapter 1, Vivi Tellas has called it the "Umbral Mínimo de Ficción" (UMF; Minimal Threshold of Fiction): a unity of poetic forms that she creates to signal these moments in which "reality itself seems to become theater" as a way of thinking about how this kind of theater works in a liminal space:[57]

> The UMF is a mechanism that allows Tellas to conceptualize her interest in *looking for theatricality beyond the theater*—expressions that she utilizes to describe the driving force behind this stage of her work—leaving the dichotomy of fiction-nonfiction and entering spaces of intersections and uncertainty to explore a new center of attention: people and their worlds.

> (El UMF es una herramienta que le permitió a Tellas conceptualizar su interés por *buscar la teatralidad fuera del teatro*—expresión que utiliza para describir el motor de esta etapa de su trabajo—saliendo de la dicotomía ficción—no ficción y adentrándose en espacios de cruce e indefinición para explorar lo que constituye el centro de su atención: las personas y sus mundos.)[58]

As previously noted, one of the most powerful aspects of new documentary theater has been the increase in autobiographical productions and the tendency to put the first-person experience at center stage. In some cases, in the work of Tellas, for example, people draw on their own autobiographical archives and generate "shared experiences" through the telling of their own life stories.[59] Her interest in documenting the lived experience of the everyday person reinforces the autobiographical nature of her work. Tellas interweaves theatrical practice and narrative in her presentation of their stories. Some recent documentary theater is motivated by the desire to create productions where the possibility of risk or failure exists. For Tellas, seeking theatricality in "the real" is a way to reveal fragility and a lack of guarantees; it is her own political position to expose this.[60] The probability of failure enters into staging from various sources: from the inclusion of people who are not formally trained actors, those whom Tellas calls "interpreters," to having animals or children onstage, or even the simple act of working with the "interpreter" to express emotion and expose personal stories.

Staging Lives is informed in part by personal interviews with playwrights and directors whose voices and perspectives are central to the analysis of the plays, as well as by my own interpretation of their work. At times, I depend on theater programs, videos of the plays or rough drafts of texts. However, I have been privileged to see live versions of almost all the plays included here. Specifically, I offer a new lens for reading documentary theater of the twenty-first century through the work of artists from Argentina, Chile, and Mexico. I study how artists generate a more nuanced approach to dealing with and manipulating the documentary mode in their practices. In many cases, their own theorization of the possibilities of this genre rejects, transforms, or expands on what their European counterparts have done in the past. But these artists ultimately forge their own paths in exploring the real onstage from a Latin American perspective.

✦

I have chosen to study specific artists who engage with the real and the new documentary theater techniques in order to tell a wide range of stories belonging to children of the disappeared, convicts, or migrants who cross the Mexico-U.S. border, everyday people and people whose voices are often not heard. The variety of my choices is a conscious selection to display the expansive panorama of new documentary theater. To this end, each chapter is organized as a case study and each requires a distinct analysis to understanding of the political, social, and contextual framework. There are also some conscious omissions, such as the Mexican collective Lagartijas tiradas al sol, which has recently been carefully studied by Julie Ann Ward in *A Shared Truth: The Theater of Lagartijas tiradas al sol* (2019), and the Colombian theater group Mapa Teatro, whose work has also been thoroughly analyzed by Diana Taylor and Ileana Diéguez, among others.[61] The case studies I have chosen traverse four specific manifestations of documentary theater: autobiographical stories of everyday life that are not explicitly political; first- and second-generation approaches to traumatic biographies; socially committed explorations of human rights; and the aftermath of the left-wing militia movement during and after Salvador Allende. Each chapter showcases the unique ways in which artists engage with their work—some use film or video installations as another approach to documentary, while others work with a more didactic and in-person event as a social and political commitment. But all chapters work with the idea of how actors and audiences relate their personal stories through intimate and affective relationships.

Chapter 1 studies the concept of "biodrama," coined by Argentine director Vivi Tellas, and its influential impact on Argentine and Latin American theater. As a trailblazing artist, curator, and director, in her work Tellas opens the possibility of understanding documentary theater through the personal lives of everyday people, claiming that every person is and has an archive. Her search for the Minimal Threshold of Fiction clearly defines a gray zone that is political by the mere fact that she provides her audience with stories of regular people through the theater, forcing the lives of everyday people onto the stage. In particular, I pay close attention to her work as a playwright and director in Proyecto Archivos (2003–2008), where her ideas about personal archives are central. I focus on three plays: *Mi mamá y mi tía* (*My Mother and My Aunt*, 2003); *Tres filósofos con bigotes* (*Three Philosophers with Moustaches*, 2004); and *Escuela de conducción* (*Driving School*, 2006). Each of these plays offers an intimate look at how family, friendship, and educational institutions are central in our lives. While each of them is distinct, *Mi mamá y mi tía* makes an important claim about the private versus the public lives of people as the director cast her own mother and aunt. With this intention, Tellas highlights the intricate lines between family, theater, public, and audience.

Similarly inspired by documenting personal stories, chapter 2 focuses on the work of renowned playwright, curator, visual artist, and director Lola Arias. Her own concept of "remakes" places a central role on reenactments and their powerful use on how people retell stories through their own perception and reception of facts. While every chapter in this book uses photographs as a main object of manipulation, it is in Lola Arias's works that photographs take an active role, one that offers a variety of interpretations. In particular,

I analyze two major projects: the trilogy that consists of *Mi vida después* (*My Life After*, 2009), *El año en que nací* (*The Year I Was Born*, 2012), and *Melancolía y manifestaciones* (*Melancholy and Demonstrations*, 2012); and a three-part project designed around stories of the Malvinas/Falkland Islands War (1982), referred to as "the Cycle of War" and comprising a video installation titled *Veterans* (2014), a play titled *Minefield / Campo minado* (2016), and a documentary film titled *Theatre of War* (2018). Through the different genres, Arias makes the Malvinas/Falkland Islands veterans' stories known. All of these performances deal with personal stories; how the autobiographical point of view can be doubtful; the first- and second-generation approach to memory and postmemory; and how humor can be a useful tool when speaking of political turmoil and traumatic stories.

Chapter 3 takes a pronounced political stand on immigration and human rights. The focus shifts toward Mexico and the work of theater collective Teatro Línea de Sombra (1993). I specifically study the impact of a socially committed group that brings difficult and timely topics to the stage by speaking directly about immigration issues, femicides, and human rights atrocities. Their productions are not only artistic but also work in conjunction with and in relation to their committed social and political agenda. Within Teatro Línea de Sombra's extensive repertoire of work, this chapter focuses on two key plays and one site-specific installation: *Amarillo* (2009), *Baños Roma* (*Roma Baths*, 2013), and *El puro lugar* (*Nothing but the Place*, 2016). *Amarillo* highlights distinct notions of migrants, the aftermath of crossing the U.S.-Mexico border, and the understanding of the (in)visible traces left behind by those who do not make the journey to the other side. On the other hand, *Baños Roma* grounds the story in Ciudad Juárez, a border town overcome by criminal gangs, drug trafficking, and *maquiladoras*. In this barren town, women disappear, houses are abandoned, and only those who are left behind tell the story of a weakened community that is no longer alive. *El puro lugar* takes audience members to revisit a site-specific place of violence in Xalapa, Veracruz. TLS works on building a memory intersectionality between previous acts of violence that interconnect Xalapa with specific atrocities that took place in 1924, 1981, and 2015.

The final chapter sheds light on the role of political discourse through two specific topics: ex-torture sites as memorial museums and the aftermath of left-wing militia groups formed during the Pinochet era (1973–1990). The focus is on three different plays by Chilean playwright Guillermo Calderón that deal directly with issues of memory politics and truth and reconciliation in the transitional years from Pinochet dictatorship to democracy and beyond. I contend that while Calderón's plays employ some factual information, the archive and history are irrelevant at times, forcing the audience to enter a liminal space where they are confronted with their own perception of historical truth. The site-specific aspect of *Villa+Discurso* (2011) triggers mediation of social spaces by encompassing places with a haunting history between what happened there, as a former torture site, and what it has turned into a new park of memory. The site becomes the object-turned-prop that haunts the play. This chapter also explores how two interconnected plays—*Escuela* (*School*, 2013) and *Mateluna* (2016)—inquire into the authenticity of legal documents, the justice system, and the theatrical modes of telling a story in order to make a political statement against a wrongly accused ex-militant. In the short conclusion, I quickly mention Federico León's *Las ideas* (2015), a play that upstages the real almost as an afterthought. By questioning the role of the real onstage through a humorous postulation of what is like to create a play, León pushes us to rethink the weight of the document and the actual role of the real onstage.

Together, the chapters in this book consider the extent and the limits of objects, archives and bodies through the process of theatrical interventions. They embrace new modes of utilizing archival documents as theatrical props that become a point of departure for considering the meaning of the past and the interpretation in the present. My aim is to make evident that new documentary theater techniques have been molded in order to give a sense of factuality. In this forged factuality, facts are central but bear the possibility of fiction when they are created, distorted, or imagined.

Chapter 1

Biodramas

Vivi Tellas and the Act of Documenting Lives

> Failure on stage is perfect theatre.
>
> —Stefan Kaegi

What is at stake when a theater director decides to welcome people with no formal acting training onstage? Or when everyday stories seen through an autobiographical mode become the pivotal focus of a play? How do the unpolished lines of acting become an artistic manifestation of what can fail in the theater? Within documentary theater practices of the twenty-first century, Argentine director Vivi Tellas sets a new and innovative course for exploring "the real" onstage. Tellas is considered by many to be a central figure in Argentine documentary practices that began at the end of the twentieth century and have continued for two decades into the twenty-first. As a visual artist, curator, and theater director, she explores ways to reexamine old documentary modes and create new possibilities for retelling a story. Not only is she a playwright and a director; more importantly, for the purposes of this book, she is a "documenter," someone who continually searches for how to fuse the real with the theatrical, how to tell an interesting story from the viewpoint of a particular personal life, or how to bring museums alive through the theatricality embedded in them as repository sites. Moreover, she has facilitated other artists' engagement with similar documentary forms and, thus, created important collaborative projects that invigorate new generations of artists. Engaging with Tellas's work means entering a world of creativity and vision that reshapes documentary technique in intriguing and novel ways, and it also means taking into account methods through which she encouraged other artists to shape documentary practices in their own ways. Her work as director or curator consists of researching, documenting, and editing archives to achieve a theatrical potential that can be shared with others while also exposing the fragility of her work and the possibility of failure and chance.[1]

Tellas, in addition to being a commanding figure in Buenos Aires's theatrical scene, is also recognized internationally. Today her name resonates in important theatrical venues because of her pioneering work to bring together the visual arts, curatorial practices, and theater. In the early 1980s, with Argentina still under a dictatorship, Tellas performed with the all-female ensemble Bay Biscuits, who developed a decadent imitation of a Broadway show that poked fun at the cabaret form.[2] The group also performed at the concerts of well-known rock star Charly García, whose audiences jeered and disapproved of their sarcastic style. Following the military dictatorship and the arrival of democracy, censorship loosened, allowing new forms of expression that blurred the lines between art, theater, politics, poetry, and music.[3] In this context of experimentation, Tellas transitioned from performer into the role of director with the creation of Teatro Malo (Bad Theater). With Teatro Malo, Tellas worked to renovate the cultural scene in Buenos Aires, which had suffered under the dictatorship, to try out a new approach to the theater by exploring unpolished work or work so badly written and conceived that she performed it as such, as "bad theater," in order to push the limits of representation.[4] This work made a point of emphasizing every error, every typo and grammatical mistake to clearly mark it as raw material and to underscore the possibility of failure. Tellas quickly became the muse of the underground theater scene, an association that would continue throughout her prolific career.

Later, as the coordinator of the Theatrical Experimental Center at the Centro Cultural Ricardo Rojas, she designed Proyecto Museos (1994–2000), where in five years and with fifteen works by fifteen young artists, she helped conceptualize museums as sites of theatricality. Specifically, her work explored rare museums in the city of Buenos Aires, such as the Museum of Odontology or the Museum of the Eye, among others, that few people even knew existed. She noted that her central focus in undertaking these projects was to see how the theater relates to other artistic practices, and to show how museums are infused with theatricality. This first step in using archival material to reinterpret the past guided Tellas into thinking about other documentary modes that instead of focusing on museums, sought to stage people's lives. At the turn of the twenty-first century and as the new director of Teatro Sarmiento, Tellas created the Biodrama cycle (2002–2008), as well as her own work, Proyecto Archivos (2003–2008). The latter responds to her desire to work with the real, with people not formally trained as actors; she calls these people "interpreters," and their everyday stories have become a central practice in her theater.

Unlike in other chapters in this book, here I primarily focus on Tellas as an influential artist who has not only embarked in one of the most prolific documentary practices in the theater but has also propelled other artists to follow. I am interested in exploring how different phases of Tellas's Biodrama mark a foundational and, I might add, transformational theatrical cycle to the already cutting-edge theater scene in Buenos Aires that began in 2002 and continues into the present. I intend to focus on why the role of documents and personal stories are central to theater's debate regarding what is real and what is manipulation of fact. In other words, how do personal archives and stories become a public matter? How can the archive make us understand the present and project toward a future? And why is the temporal projection so appealing and interesting to audiences? Whereas other chapters in this book focus on specific plays, my intention in this chapter is to explore Vivi Tellas's overall creative vision and innovative approach to theater, and thus I pay close attention to her process and development as an artist. I read Tellas's creation with an eye toward understanding the affective relationships between objects, people, their stories, and audiences. No matter how simple the stories are, they open up possibilities for failure onstage in the hands of performers, a possibility that thrills Tellas because she is a "fan of mistakes" and sees those moments as productive opportunities for capturing something different.[5] In particular, her work with Proyecto Archivos (2003–2008) conceived her pioneering documentary theater with the creation of six new plays that form the foundation of Biodramas. In her study of Tellas's biographical and documentary work, Pamela Brownell also points to Proyecto Archivos as the core of Biodrama, which she defines as a *macro-project* based on "a double movement: finding theatricality outside theater and filling up the stage with non-theatricality."[6]

Tellas's work, although unique and original, resembles projects undertaken by Stefan Kaegi, one of the founders of Rimini Protokoll, a theatrical group based in Germany, as well as those of Richard Maxwell, in the United States. She has also stated that she is attracted to the work of Argentine playwright, director, and screenwriter Federico León, and cinematographer Manuel Abramovich.[7] Her interest lies in excavating the liminality between the real and the theatrical, sharing a variety of biographies of individuals "just like us," and accentuating the everyday and extraordinary stories each person possesses. In Tellas's world, the stage parallels community building practices through artistic creation and curational events. In this way, Tellas introduces onstage communities of people brought together through a shared situation, event, or work environment. Their stories, according to Tellas, are "live archives" that allow spectators to enter and exit the theatrical fiction. The outcome of her project is a collection of autobiographies and biographies that explore the relationship between documents, archives, and lives.

Tellas's documentary theater consists of utilizing personal documents, letters, photographs, and clothes as a way to relate the theater to ordinary life. She casts people who are not formally trained in the theater and uses their stories onstage. These "interpreters" or "occasional actors," as she has called them become performers whose lives are part of a script that Tellas carefully edits. This way, she emphasizes ordinary life by looking at regular people through a theatrical lens. According to Tellas, her "premise is that every person has, and is, an archive" and the stage helps her develop a method, an interesting way to tell these stories.[8]

As I stated in the introduction, the foundational use of documentary modes can be traced back to Piscator, Brecht, and Weiss. New approaches to documentary theater, however, have begun to make audiences question what they are seeing and the extent to which it is truly documentarian. This new documentary theater, also known as "theater of the real," "docudrama," "verbatim theatre," "testimonial theater," and "theater of facts" is founded on previously established facts, but it approaches these "documentary facts" from an analytical perspective that is self-scrutinizing and even suspicious of its own truth as a document.[9] Flourishing in Latin America since the turn of the twenty-first century, this new form seeks to reassess the role of that which is documentary in theater by shifting attention away from a strictly political focus and, instead, turning toward an ironic questioning of the division between "reality" and narrative as well as representational forms. Documentary theater or theater of the real innovates as it strategically interrogates the objectivity of art, the idea that history is a network of relations, or that things happen for a reason, and it explores the idea that actors' realness cannot be contained only by their character.[10]

In documentary theater, performers tell their own stories, and for the most part, do not play any type of historical character. We revisit the past through the present, the real time of individual interpretation. In these works, the use of the autobiographical onstage, normally considered a peripheral form of theater, is placed at the center. According to Beatriz Trastoy, "Autobiography hopes to achieve, also in the sense of being a simulation, a literary humility capable of upending the categories of the aesthetic establishment." The autobiographical nature of postdictatorship theater "offers the possibility of narrating—in both a new and poetically illuminating way—what Argentine authoritarianism (and the authoritarianism of other Latin American countries) sought to silence."[11] Whereas some might argue that memory, like theater, exists in the realm of invention, others contend that fantasy is drawn from reality revealing that the real and the artifice of theater are mutually constitutive.

Tellas's work has always worked best at the crossroads of these paradoxes, on the margins of the performing arts where she felt the freedom to work with badly written stories and put them onstage, as what she did with Teatro Malo, or later in Proyecto Archivos. In a recent interview, she notes that her work exposes the inefficiencies of the stage to explore the aesthetic value in the bewilderment, for instance, the unknown factor or the uncertainty that an untrained actor brings to the stage.[12] As Marcela A. Fuentes notes, "Tellas's documentary theatre is rooted in the exaltation of the ordinary and the marginal, and in the fascination with working with the clumsiness of non-actors."[13]

In Tellas's own words, there is a fine line between someone's everyday life and the theatricality of one's own actions, which she has dubbed the Umbral Mínimo de Ficción (UMF; Minimal Threshold of Fiction). The UMF is a poetic way to measure those moments where "reality seems to start doing theater."[14] In this way, the UMF allows her to find theatricality outside the theater and to fuse fiction and the real in an intimate fashion. Through her documentary practices, she uncovered ways to work with a variety of spaces and people. Specifically, she discovered how to transform a mundane someone or something into a theatrical figure or event.

Her central and most important project since 2002 has been the creation of the Biodrama, which can be divided into different stages: Biodrama cycle (2002–2008); Proyecto Archivos (2003–2008); and Biodramas (2009–present). As the director of the Teatro Sarmiento (2001–2008; 2016–present), Tellas designed the Biodramas cycle, an innovative theatrical work that called on other playwrights and directors to design plays about people living in Argentina. The concept produced distinctly different plays; some more fictional; others more documentary, but all forged a sense of ambiguity on how to best stage someone's life.[15] The variety of plays, authors, and directors represented show that the Biodrama cycle was an open invitation to understand how to stage the concept of recounting a person's life onstage. Each playwright had the freedom to take his or her work in different directions.

During the same period, Tellas also designed her own work that she named Proyecto Archivos (2003–2008). In it, she exposed the intimate world of people with six different plays: *Mi mamá y mi tía* (*My Mother and My Aunt*, 2003); *Tres filósofos con bigotes* (*Three Philosophers with Moustaches*, 2004); *Cozarinsky y su médico* (*Cozarinsky and His Doctor*, 2005); *Escuela de conducción* (*Driving School*, 2006); *Mujeres guía* (*Women Tour Guides*, 2008); and *Disc Jockey* (2008).[16] This work pushed boundaries of ordinary people's theatricality, as will be explored in detail later.

Beginning in 2009, her work transitioned as she started to travel abroad and lead workshops about family albums, pieces she eventually called Biodramas.[17] At that point she began to label all her autobiographical work as a Biodrama. Her later Biodramas, such as *Rabbi Rabino* (2011), *La bruja y su hija* (*The Witch and Her Daughter*, 2012), *Maruja enamorada* (*Maruja in Love*, 2013), *Las personas* (*People*, 2014), *El niño Rieznik* (*Rieznik, the Kid*, 2016), and *Los amigos, un biodrama afro* (*Friends, an Afro Biodrama*, 2018) resemble the casting done in Proyecto Archivos, by staging people's lives without formal training as actors, to tell their stories and personal struggles in front of an audience.

Biodrama

The Biodrama cycle (2002–2008) expanded opportunities for directors, actors, and performers to explore these areas of failure, of error, of mistakes to further the instability that theater creates between facts and fiction, spectators and actors. The search for the process and what these mistakes can bring to the table can probably best be exemplified by one of Vivi Tellas's choices as a director in the fourth Biodrama staged in 2003: Stefan Kaegi, a Swiss director and member of the prestigious Rimini Protokoll, based in Berlin, Germany. Kaegi understood the project as a place to find the limits between representation, the real, the ready-made as well as a way to visualize zones of insecurity or instability. His work fuses art and life very closely, by switching our perception of what we are watching and who is watching us. Kaegi, as well as other members of Rimini Protokoll, believe that people not formally trained as actors, what they call "experts of the everyday" bring particular knowledge and skills to the stage, something opposed to amateur theater, and "those on stage should not be judged on what they couldn't do (i.e. act), but rather on the reason for their presence on stage."[18] Kaegi's work as one of the Biodrama directors enhances relations created between local and international theater while Rimini Protokoll's work with "experts of the everyday," invigorates documentary technique. Their research explores the "small things that become important" and how "the actual material—like a readymade—becomes a prop, on the one hand underpinning the documentary character of the work, [and] on the other destabilizing it, since its authenticity is always uncertain."[19] For all the members of Rimini Protokoll, "reality has to be scripted," and "authenticity is fictionalized just as fiction is often dragged into reality."[20] Their understanding of theatrical practices fits well with the concept of working with the real in Biodramas.

When Kaegi arrived in Buenos Aires in 2003, he was quickly fascinated with the zoo next to the Teatro Sarmiento, where the Biodrama cycle was being staged.[21] Paying attention to the urban setting of Buenos Aires and the relational experience this entailed (the zoo, the theater, and the state fairgrounds [La Rural] are all in close proximity to each other), Kaegi decided to explore how these sites interact with each other via geographical proximity. *¡Sentate! Un zoostituto* (2003), the play he describes as a zoostitute, a play on words that references the word "substitute" to indicate, here, where animals stand or "act" for people. This work explored "the promiscuous proximity" between the theater, the state fairgrounds, and the zoo and how, when they combine, they "create another type of art."[22] Casting for this play was publicized through a newspaper ad in which Kaegi called for pet owners to come to the theater with their pets. The end result was a cast of two turtles, one iguana, one dog, fourteen rabbits, four pet owners, and one dog-walker, who brought along the dogs he walks every day.[23] The play highlights the interactions not only between pets and owners but also between the spectator and the unexpected. Kaegi emphasizes the intimacy that people build with their pets and how theatrical those relationships can be (i.e., who gives the orders, who actually walks whom, and who decides when to go out for a walk). The ability to work with animals onstage, with the element of unpredictability this created, is what attracted Kaegi to this incarnation of Biodrama. He has noted before that it is not the artificiality of the theater that interests him but, rather, the ways in which that artificiality is made and constructed.[24] Working with animals brings to the fore the difficulty of engaging with a script and challenges with staging: the "real" suddenly becomes very real with pets scurrying across the stage and even having to clean after them while still performing.

I point out this play of the Biodrama cycle because it successfully emphasizes an ambiguity between the real and any artifice through the unpolished work of people not formally trained as actors, and, in this case, animals that push the theater spectacle into possible chaos and an undeterminable end. With Tellas's overall work with Biodramas, Kaegi's piece is an example of how the project has expanded to explore the borders of the unexpected, and what this Biodrama highlights is how the real and the fictive are sometimes difficult to discern.

As Pamela Brownell and I have previously explored, Tellas's work does not fit into a set category. Her work lies in between those roles in the visual arts, and that of a curator who is in constant search of the theatricality in all of us. She is also a theater director who creates spaces for creation to take place.[25] But what is most striking, and most relevant to this study, is how Tellas's work brings together the return of the real as well as the return of the document to the stage. Alan Pauls offers a good description of this aspect of the Biodrama cycle:

> The biodrama cycle at Teatro Sarmiento demonstrated that there are multiple ways to approach the staging of a life. These ways are at least hybrid and almost always as unclassifiable as the experience for which they attempt to account. The documentary, the biographic theater, the invocation, the re-creation in terms of genre, the display and the reenactment method are some of the strategies through which Biodrama tries to make present the irreducibility of human life. The final "form" of each Biodrama always depends on the exchange between the director and the specific life that they take as their object.
>
> (El ciclo biodrama del Teatro Sarmiento demostró que las formas de abordar el traslado de una vida a la escena son múltiples, a menudo híbridas, casi siempre tan inclasificables como la experiencia misma de la que intentan dar cuenta. El documental, el teatro biográfico, la evocación, la recreación en clave de género, el display y el método del *re-enactment* son algunas de las estrategias mediante las cuales el biodrama procura hacer presente la irreductibilidad de la vida humana. La "forma" final de cada biodrama depende siempre del intercambio entre el director y la vida específica que toma por objeto.)[26]

Through documentary methods—especially through objects-turned-props—a powerful recodification onstage and the reenactments of people's past, this project explores the irreducibleness of human life by altering the power relations that define whose lives count as valuable. In other words, in choosing to explore the ordinary as a central focus, Tellas generates a political message about power dynamics in cultural contexts.

While the Biodrama cycle had a clear beginning and an end (2002–2008), what is unclear is how the borders of Biodrama function as an umbrella project. In part this is because of the basic premise of the project itself: it is an open forum for artists to stage their biographies as they see fit and use documents while they simultaneously create fictional narratives. But also, as Beatriz Trastoy suggests, the Biodrama is a collection and as such it cannot be determined to be finished if the creator is still alive.[27] Giving Biodramas a life is part of what Vivi Tellas accomplished through her constant revisions about what this work meant to her, to her artists, and to the spectators. Tellas's explanation of Biodramas is key:

> Biodrama revolves around what one could call "the return of the real" in the field of representation. After almost two decades of simulations and simulacra, what returns—in part as opposition, in part as a reverse—is the idea that there is still experience and that art should invent some new way of entering into relationship with it. The tendency, which is global, is comprised of everything from mass-culture phenomena, like reality shows, to the most advanced expressions of contemporary art, passing through a resurrection of genres considered until this point as "minor," like the documentary, the testimonial or the autobiography. The return of experience—what Biodrama calls "life"—is also a return to the Personal. The "I" returns, yes, but it is an "I" that is immediately cultural, social and even political.
>
> (Biodrama se inscribe en torno a lo que se podría llamar el "retorno de lo real" en el campo de la representación. Después de casi dos décadas de simulaciones y simulacros, lo que vuelve—en parte como oposición, en parte como reverso—es la idea de que todavía hay experiencia, y de que el arte debe inventar alguna forma nueva de entrar en relación con ella. La tendencia, que es mundial, comprende desde fenómenos de cultura de masas, como los *reality shows*, hasta las expresiones más avanzadas del arte contemporáneo, pasando por la resurrección de géneros hasta ahora "menores," como el documental, el testimonio o la autobiografía. El retorno de la experiencia—lo que en Biodrama se llama "vida"—es también el retorno de lo Personal. Vuelve el Yo, sí, pero es y un Yo inmediatamente cultural, social, incluso político.)[28]

Biodrama as a concept is clearly defined by the friction between the real and the document and by questioning how this friction affects the autobiographical mode of narrating our own lives. As Tellas, states, the "I" becomes the central being, but it carries with it the political, social, and cultural weight that makes each individual unique and valuable. In the handbills that accompany the performances, she notes the difficult definitions of a Biodrama and the tension between the real and the fictive that is magnified:

> In a disposable world, what value do our lives, our experiences, our time have? Biodrama proposes to reflect on this question. It is about investigating how the facts of life for each person—individual, singular, private facts—construct the story. Is a documentary or testimonial theater possible? Or does everything that appears on the stage inevitably transform into fiction? Fiction and truth propose a tension with this experience.
>
> (En un mundo descartable, ¿qué valor tienen nuestras vidas, nuestras experiencias, nuestro tiempo? Biodrama se propone reflexionar sobre esta cuestión. Se trata de investigar cómo los hechos de la vida de cada persona—hechos individuales, singulares, privados—construyen la Historia. ¿Es posible un teatro documental, testimonial? ¿O todo lo que aparece en el escenario se transforma irremediablemente en ficción? Ficción y verdad se proponen en tension en esta experiencia.)[29]

The Biodrama cycle reveals the life of a real person who lived in Argentina to create dramatic material to push the limits of what is real in the theater. Using documentary techniques in the mutual exploration of what constitutes life and theater gave Biodramas a unique methodology, moving it from theater project to a movement filled with possibilities.[30]

The Biodrama cycle utilized an innovative way of doing and seeing theater: each play had its own director with his or her own aesthetic choices, the variety of the works conceived created a wide range of opportunities for exploring the idea of the document onstage, the role of the autobiographical, the borders of self-reflexive theater, and the limits between the real and fiction. For instance, some plays began with only the concept of a person's life as a premise for creating a fictional setting, with real actors and with no testimony or breaking of the fourth wall. *El aire alrededor* (*The Air Around*, 2003) by Mariana Obersztern and *Budín inglés* (*Poundcake*, 2006) by Mariana Chaud offer examples of this technique. Other plays, however, such as *Los 8 de Julio: Experiencia de registro sobre el paso del tiempo* (*8 of July: Experience through Time*, 2002) by Beatriz Catani and Mariano Pensotti and *¡Sentate! Un Zoostituto* (*Sit Down! A Zoostitute*, 2003) by Stefan Kaegi featured actors as well as people not formally trained in the theater and animals to push the limits of the real in a productive, postdramatic staging.[31]

Biodrama and Its Historical Context

The beginning of the Biodrama cycle correlates with the sociopolitical upheaval that Argentina underwent as a result of the 2001 economic crisis. After a decade of neoliberal policies propagated by President Carlos Saúl Menem (1989–1999), the economy collapsed, and Argentina's social fabric quickly unraveled. The turmoil seen at the end of the decade known as *menemismo* (1989–1999), and the social, political, and economic crisis of 2001 signaled to many artists a need to return to less artificial ways of conceiving art.[32] According to Philippa Page, "The Menem years can be likened to a simulacrum of First World affluence under the banner of modernization and neoliberalism."[33] To other theater scholars, this period can be categorized as a time when society was blinded by "simulacra and fictions" of possibilities that ended up in an economic explosion. In response to these events, "both art and the media have tried to create a reality effect beyond what is fictional, what is a deception, and what is theatrical."[34] The search for ways to work with the "real" required new tools for working with documentary modes.

And while the sociopolitical context had an impact on how theater began to explore these issues, for Tellas it was also a personal choice to work with the real and documentary perspectives. The impetus to change her theatrical practices had more to do with her own weariness from producing traditional plays. After a successful four-year production of *La casa de Bernarda Alba* (*The House of Bernarda Alba*, 2002), where she collaborated with visual artist Guillermo Kuitca, Tellas felt the need to work with purer and rawer materials. She sought a stage devoid of artificiality. To do this she turned to her own mother and aunt as a way to find intimate channels for creating theater.[35] By 2000, though, her work *El precio de un brazo derecho* (*The Price of a Right Arm*), where a brick layer constructs a wall in real time on the stage was considered a pivotal moment in her move into the exploration of the fluid space between the real and the fictive.[36] It is evident that Tellas's work with Biodramas and later with Proyecto Archivos pays close attention to how our lives have been inundated by artificiality, and how the intimate space of theater could be seen as a small space to explore people's lives. Biodramas and Proyecto Archivos welcome testimonies and first-person narratives to elicit a personal, more real event in the theater.

Staged biographies are not new to the theater nor are testimonial narratives to literature. The autobiographical onstage intensifies the "affirmation of the individual self in a collective mode."[37] In other words, the stage provides a live audience to the individual who is willing to come forward. Historically in Latin America, the idea of truth-telling became a central point of debate during the 1980s when testimonial writing, especially that of Rigoberta Menchú, first came to fame. And although my aim is to show how autobiographical modes are quite distinct from testimonial writing of that time, there are some connections. Just as *testimonio* literature seeks a "powerful textual affirmation of the speaking subject [where] the voice that speaks to the reader in the form of an 'I' demands to be recognized," the autobiographical in the theater does the same. Both *testimonio* literature and the new autobiographical used onstage in Latin America demand a dynamic relationship between the actor/narrator and the audience/reader. As Ana Elena Puga has cleverly argued, "Testimonial subjects . . . give the reader (or spectator) the sensation of experiencing the real."[38] The bond that testimony activates onstage creates a special connection with the narrator, the story, and the spectator. Even with the demand of truth-telling in *testimonio* writing, and the controversy surrounding how truthful or constructed Rigoberta Menchú's accounts were, there is still room for what John Beverley has framed as "textual simulacrum of direct address."[39] In addition, Beverley contends that *testimonio* is about truth-telling, but the order in which the story is narrated might not follow the exact chronology in which the events unfolded in the past.[40]

In contrast, autobiographical theater relies precisely on exploring the borders between fact and fiction, of defying chronological order of events. It demands entering that gray zone between truth telling and interpretation; it does not portray stories as truthful, nor does it gain its legitimacy from an assertion of truth. And whereas *testimonio* writing gives voice to the "voiceless," eliciting an ethical and political response from the reader, the autobiographical in Tellas seeks to elaborate stories of everydayness that makes us also part of theatrical event. If the power of *testimonio* writing relies on the political ramifications of the stories of those we do not see or hear, then Tellas's theater creates space to speak of the ordinary in our lives, not the subaltern, as Beverley—using Gayatri Spivak's term—famously expressed, but of regular people with regular lives, whose archives can bring light to details not thought of before.

The Return of the Real

If, for Jacques Derrida, influenced by Freudian thought, the archive "is only a notion, an impression associated with a word . . . an impression, an insistent impression through the unstable feeling of a shifting figure, of a schema, or of an in-finite or indefinite process," it reinforces the ephemeral, or, as he calls it, "the unknowable weight" that the archive carries.[41] What is helpful to my own analysis of how the new documentary theater emerges as an exponent of this "notion" is that the archive is not fixed but, rather, "is a question of the future, the question of the future itself, the question of a response, of a promise and of a responsibility for tomorrow."[42] In a similar vein, Hal Foster pushes the idea of the archive as an "impulse" that makes artists alike consider the past, the document as their point of departure. He calls archival artists those who "seek to make historical information, often lost or displaced, physically present."[43] Broadly speaking, the impact of the archive lies in its treatment of "materials as found, yet constructed, factual yet fictive, public yet private."[44] There exists a fine line between what is produced and perceived for what Nicolas Bourriaud sees as a manipulation through postproduction; one which underscores the impact of choosing, editing, and in the theater scene, directing. In other words, there is a relational platform with which to begin and perceive the work. Because the archive that Tellas brings to the foreground exposes material objects, as fragmentary, they require human interaction and interpretation for fuller understanding.[45] But Foster suggests that "archival art is as much preproduction as it is postproduction: concerned less with absolute origins than with obscure traces."[46] He also notes that archival art is more "institutive" and "legislative," thus proclaiming this type of artistic venue as less "transgressive" than others. However, the impulse reflected not only by the archive but of the object itself, as fragile and undetermined bestows Tellas's Biodramas and Archivos with an aura of possible failure, as it exposes the rough edges of the mise-en-scène through the lives of regular people who become interpreters of their own lives. The work that Tellas created starting with Proyecto Museos and continuing with both the Biodrama cycle and Proyecto Archivos transgresses any set definition of theater originating from a textual play. The archival impulse, the fragile contours of fact and fiction, and the web of relations that her work engages all point toward transgressive and antiestablishment models and practices.

Proyecto Museos (1994–2000) convened a group of directors to research types of museums in the city that remain in the periphery of people's minds in Buenos Aires. They sought to uncover those museums forgotten by society or barely ever mentioned. Fifteen different museums were chosen, and some of the most intriguing ones consisted of Museums of Dentistry, Money, Penitentiary, Eye, and Medicinal Herb. The project asked each director to work with one of these museums and explore the theatricality buried within it. The goal was to transform the museum into an object of investigation and future theatrical product while taking into consideration the political and socioeconomics decisions that made these museum spaces what they are today.[47] Her work with directors on researching new spaces of theatrical reconfiguration, as well as changes in the gaze (who is watching and who is being watched), establish a fine line between what is documentation and what can be revived through the theater. This line is what catalyzes her interrogation of the real onstage.

In a similar sense to what Richard Schechner suggested as "the twice behaved behavior" when referring to the essence of performance, Tellas explores "the natural tendency toward repetition that is found in human behavior."[48] In order for her to make someone's life theatrical, she adopts the idea of "kidnapping reality" or distilling what she sees as the fine line between someone's life and the theater (what is staged and what is not).

In order to kidnap the real, she begins her casting with a simple workshop where people without acting training bring their stories to the forefront.[49] The work of Tellas with Proyecto Museos (1994–2000), the earlier Biodrama cycle (2002–2008), Proyecto Archivos (2003–2008), and Biodramas (2009–present) provide evidence of biographical and documentary techniques that have been in play for years.

Proyecto Archivos

The work with documentary material became a central method in Tellas's productions. While in previous interviews she stated that the Biodramas cycle belonged to the plays staged at the Teatro Sarmiento by other directors, and the Proyecto Archivos was her own self-directed documentary work, both iterations of her work with explorations of the real become fused and sometimes difficult to separate. In a sense, the concepts she worked with Biodramas made Tellas more acutely aware of the impact of documentary practices, and with Proyecto Archivos found a more personal and direct expression to explore. Thus, in Tellas's own approach to her work with Proyecto Archivos the autobiographical, the sense of the "body as document," is highlighted more directly. Using the idea that "every person is an archive," in Proyecto Archivos she searched for a different dimension in the theater: a space and a way for how to stage the private realm of a person's life when the same person tells his or her story.

Proyecto Archivos, with its six different plays between 2003 and 2008, strives to find the liminal state between what is real, what is autobiographical, and what is fictional by staging the simple life stories of ordinary people. For her, this forging of the real and the staged is what brings new approaches to understanding where theater begins and ends. According to Tellas, with Proyecto Archivos she returns to work with an aesthetic that explores the fragility of human beings: having people share their personal stories, working with mundane topics, and using small and intimate spaces. Her UMF method of theater explores fiction in the most peculiar and unique renditions of the stories. There is an intimate connection between museums and theater: how, for instance, art gets staged, what lighting and spatial design is used, and the proximity objects can have with the spectator. The liminality that Tellas always seeks responds to her constant examining of the barriers between categories and set definitions in theater.

The personal and the private that Proyecto Archivos underscores pushes the limits of representation through the familial setting. Tellas's first Archivo, *Mi mamá y mi tía* (2003), was conceived in her own studio with her mother and her aunt and serves as the first of many private collections of archives that combines theater, curatorial practices, and repetitions with fiction. For Tellas, then, the family circle, the stories we hear as children, the rituals we witness, and the festivities share encompass theatrical, spectatorial, and participatory modes. The process of her work begins when the process of selection, editing, and production gets underway. In interviews, Tellas states that she is attracted to situations where there is instability, a doubt, an innocence, or even a fragility in how a story gets told.[50]

As academics we like to have more definite lines about when a project begins and ends. However, this is nearly impossible to delineate in Tellas's work.[51] While the Biodrama cycle existed from 2002 to 2008, and the Proyecto Archivos became better known in 2008 with four of those plays staged at Teatro Sarmiento, her way of conceiving theater is woven between Biodramas, Archivos, documentary theater, and installations. As Beatriz Trastoy concurs, the concept of Biodrama belongs to a live collection, and as such it cannot be considered finished. In subsequent plays, such as *Maruja enamorada* (2013), *Las personas* (2014), *El niño Rieznik* (2016), and *Los amigos, un biodrama afro* (2018), there is a clear fusion between her methodology to Proyecto Archivos and her work with Biodramas as the overall concept of documenting a person's life.[52] While the chronological and methodological borders are not well defined, the two collections clearly expose brilliant possibilities on the stage as she defines an urge to go back to personal archives and private lives. She seeks to displace staid theater practices and political hierarchies.

As with the Biodramas, in this type of documentary theater the possibility of failure is central to the notion of authenticity. Failure reinforces the idea that the document is an object that can be questioned, manipulated, and revealed in myriad ways. For Sara Jane Bailes, "failure *works*," and "in its status as 'wrongdoing,' a failed objective establishes an aperture, an opening onto several (and often many) other ways of doing that counter the authority of a singular or 'correct' outcome."[53] Basing her analysis on J. L. Austin's discussion of the unhappy performative in speech act theory as "things that can be and go wrong," Bailes points to the productivity of reading these "misfires" as "social and political implications that the condition of accident and failure evidences."[54] Looking at failure in the theater, many times populated by interpreters, animals, babies, or children in Tellas's work, represents a space for potential allowing the play itself to become more real, more tangible, and "it makes failure occur just as failure enables its occurrence."[55] The poetics of failure help us consider how the work of Tellas opens a space where we can see the everyday, the mundane, the real more intensely, where the UMF she developed becomes more evident, more raw on the stage.[56] While the poetics of failure underscores the production and the aesthetics of the work as a way to see the unpolished of the "real," it also serves as a site of resistance, through the performance's promise and through the unpredictability of interpreters. The welcoming of failure in the theater is also "a socially transformative mode of production intrinsically linked to ideology, politics, and to the production of value through meaning."[57] The power of

Tellas's work lies in reconfiguring the hierarchies of power and confronting possible failure in her own work.

The Affective Side of Theater

Theater scholar Jill Dolan suggests that theater can create utopic moments by bringing people together not only to share "experiences of meaning making and imagination" but also to consider notions of community building and the possibility that a better future can be "captured and claimed in performance."[58] Thinking or "feeling" theater through the invisible affective relationship that the moment of the performance exposes allows possibilities for understanding theater as a sensory experience. More precisely, in the theater, an affective connection to the moment resonates through the presence of live bodies onstage that make us aware of the passage of time through long pauses, or of something unique and unrepeatable that happens before our eyes. We feel the other person sitting next to us, breathing, laughing, or crying. As Jill Bennett suggests, "Affect, properly conjured up, produces a real-time somatic experience, no longer framed as representation."[59] And she goes on to explain that an "engagement with affect and immediate experience [are] fundamental components of a dynamic between the artwork and the spectator."[60] It is evident that the work Tellas designed first with the Biodrama cycle, later with Proyecto Archivos, and then as Biodramas has clear and direct relational links to how affects make us, in a sense, more in touch with our humanity through the theater. Intimate, personal autobiographical stories may have the potential to create spheres of sharing more acute than those in other types of theater.

As Dolan's assertion that the theater builds a close relationship with the hopeful sense of the utopic, it becomes evident in how Tellas approaches her work, by creating plays that connect in an intimate way. With Proyecto Archivos she not only brings to the forefront everyday stories; she also reveals clearly that "each person has an archive within themselves—a reserve of experiences, knowledge, texts, images."[61] One of her goals is to make her audience experience the world of these lives, while promoting the theatrical side of their stories. She asks the "interpreters" to have "some manner of spontaneous acting . . . a threatened kind of acting, marked by chance, error, a lack of reliability."[62] As with Dolan's utopian ideal of what the theater can build, Tellas gives value to the stories we all carry within us by generating an intimate portrayal of the past and by bringing in the audience to listen carefully and to share a moment where a life becomes worthy as a subject for portrayal on the stage. Proyecto Archivos is to Tellas a "process of deconstruction" that unveils "a sensibility, a way of life" about the past that together "create a very strong theatricality." And through this process the affective relationship to what the audience experiences is part of the construction of the spontaneous ephemeral community.[63]

The Intimate Space

With Proyecto Archivos, family members, doctors, philosophers, tour guides, disc jockeys, and instructors inhabit the Minimal Threshold of Fiction, where through their autobiographies, stories, and objects-turned-documents, they compose nuances in their personal lives. In this way, *Mi mamá y mi tía* (2003), *Tres filósofos con bigotes* (2004), *Cozarinsky y su médico* (2005), *Escuela de conducción* (2006), *Mujeres guía* (2008), and *Disc Jockey* (2008), utilize personal belongings such as photographs, videos, letters, to help create an intimate space, almost semiprivate experience that allows the audience to presence something that is not fully polished, or fully scripted; something that shows that these plays are under construction. With her most personal play, *Mi mamá y mi tía*, Tellas experiments with the most organic element of her life: her own family. She creates affective spaces where the family makes the audience aware of their own standing as spectators, and they feel as if they were watching something they might not supposed to be.

Tellas's own mother and aunt (Graciela and Luisa Ninio), two women with no theatrical training, help us observe the limits of the theater (see fig. 1). Through this pair, the audience shares a moment of vulnerability onstage that is magnified by the emotional relationship they hold with their objects-turned-props (dresses, photographs, love letters). At the same time, they also build a space where family secrets are shared. According to Tellas, "The work is very fragile, somewhere between violent and exciting while also being raw. It makes me a bit embarrassed. . . . You never know what is going to happen during the performances."[64] Instability, vulnerability, and the looming sense of failure is staged in a raw and direct manner. We hear about the women's lost loves, their childhood dreams, their teenage dances; we also hear and see Tellas on the sidelines, helping them remember what comes next. We laugh when they show us their old photographs with the face of an ex-partner erased. In this way, Tellas became an added member of the cast, working as a subtle director and sometimes as a scripter who kept the interpreters on task, who was often visible to the audience. This overlap also reveals a close relationship not only between family members, but also within the confines of theater, as the action onstage unfolds right in front of the audience's eyes. The unpolished lines are there for all of us to see.

In other words, Tellas explains how the search for the private moment becomes a catalyst in her work. She states:

> In Proyecto Archivos, intimacy is at the center of my work. In these documentary works where I am searching for theatricality outside of the theater, intimacy becomes an unstable zone and, in this movement, innocence appears.
>
> The position of the work is very fragile, and I hope to find the minimal threshold of fiction, to recognize that moment and it is the

Fig. 1. Graciela and Luisa Ninio, mother and aunt of the author. From Vivi Tellas, *Mi mamá y mi tía.* Publicity still. Buenos Aires, 2003. Photograph by Nicolás Goldberg.

key that runs through everything. Intimacy is continuously present without opinion and without skill—an awkward zone capable of generating unknown moments that we do not control at all. I like being in that soup.

(En el Proyecto Archivos, la intimidad es el centro de mi trabajo. En estos trabajos documentales donde busco la teatralidad fuera del teatro, la intimidad se vuelve una zona inestable y en ese movimiento aparece la inocencia.

La situación de trabajo es muy frágil, y espero encontrar el umbral mínimo de ficción, reconocer ese momento y que esa clave destiña sobre todas las cosas. La intimidad es un presente continuo sin opinión y sin ninguna destreza, una zona torpe capaz de generar momentos desconocidos que no controlamos para nada, y en esa sopa me gusta estar.)[65]

The reference to uncontrollable moments we generate drives Tellas's thinking about the tension between the carefully crafted stage and the production of emotions beyond our control. It is an "awkward zone" that generates the possibility for creative moments where control is lost. And in this space, not everything will succeed. As she did earlier with Teatro Malo, Tellas exploits the ambiguity between what one can expect of a work and what might actually come out of it.

In *Touching Feeling*, Eve Kosofsky Sedgwick also uses the word "intimate" to describe the relationship that exists between textures and emotions.[66] By exploring the emotional realm of humanity, she contends that "affects can be, and are, attached to things, people, ideas, sensations, relations, activities, including other affects."[67] In Proyecto Archivos, tension builds through the affective connections the interpreters have with their objects. Their presence as interpreters with no formal acting training create an atmosphere of possible failure. Similarly, the audience is already in a private space (the director's own studio, with her family members), and they have been invited either through tickets they received or email invitation. In this way, a closeness is invoked even before the play even begins.[68] Lauren Berlant suggests that "intimacy builds worlds; it creates spaces and usurps places meant for other kind of relation. Its potential failure to stabilize closeness always haunts its persistent activity, making the very attachments deemed to buttress 'a life' seem in a state of constant if latent vulnerability."[69] What Proyecto Archivos proposes is not only the affective relationship to the building of these intimate worlds. There is also an emphasis on the role of the autobiographical in our lives. Biographies become intriguing, interesting, and attractive when staged in the enclosed space of theater; they become part of a convivial event generated from proximity as well as a vulnerability that is visible and palpable.

Tellas's methodology is crucial to achieving a close relationship with the audience as well as with the interpreters. When she first begins her work with possible "interpreters," she explains that she is "always telling them that failure is a possibility. That it is possible that we get together, and nothing happens, that nothing is interesting, that no good idea occurs to me. It's like a scientific experiment: failure is always on the horizon. 'It can go wrong.'"[70] Speaking about failure and being honest about this real possibility from the start accomplishes two things: it creates a sense of togetherness and honesty; and it also allows everybody involved to be more daring as they dig a little bit deeper into their pasts to find possible stories that might make good theater pieces. Tellas's frank approach to working with people's documents and their stories as archives allows interpreters to think about their worlds, their bodies, and their objects as possible theatrical archives. For the stories to succeed, Tellas has to forge a bond and confidence between the members of the cast so that no matter how private their stories may be, there is a willingness to allow them to be part of the theatricalized play. In other words, "what the archives bring to the stage is an attempt to act; because of that, because it is essentially innocent, the interpreter's acting produces uncertainty: there are no guarantees, the spectator never knows what is going to happen—if the work will turn out well, if it will make it to the end, if there won't be an accident."[71] The unscripted flair that characterizes Tellas's work is brought in through the interpreter's stories and also explored through the uncertainty of the objects and their meaning onstage.

Intimacy becomes the basis for Tellas's method. She chooses small places to stage these plays, where in some cases they hold only twenty-five people.[72] When the audience enters, the action is already underway, so they feel as if they are dropping on a conversation. Proyecto Archivos, like all of her plays, features a visible live clock that keeps time onstage. All props and objects rest atop a couple of tables in plain sight. The small space converges with the action, creating an interesting private-versus-public tension for the audience, but also a very basic and bare stage that showcases the simplicity of Tellas's theater.

At the end of each play, Tellas or someone from her team invites the audience to a *buffet froid* that has a thematic connection to the play.[73] This is yet another way to foster intimacy through a genuine convivial experience between the audience, the interpreters, and the production team. As Jorge Dubatti has stated, the convivial setting of the theater is not only found in the relationship between the audience members and what happens onstage; rather, it also emphasizes that "in the theatrical gathering, the bonds of socialization are multiple and affect the poetic and expectational sphere of the event."[74] The spectator's potentiality is pushed to the extremes, where the actors (or interpreter, in this case), director, producer, and audience members belong to the same process: they share a convivial moment by watching, listening, and finally mixing and mingling over a snack that references to the stories onstage.

Relational Spaces

Designing small spaces and inviting the audience to share a meal after the play is only one aspect of Tellas's methodology in Proyecto Archivos to cultivate relational experiences. According to Leonor Arfuch, biographic space "allows for the consideration of respective specificities without losing sight of its relational dimension, its thematic and pragmatic interactivity, its uses in the distinct spheres of communication and action."[75] The affective connection between the interpreters' autobiographies and the audience resonates fully on the stage, because live action makes us aware of how we may or may not be relating to their stories in real time. To this end, "thematic and pragmatic interactivity" accentuates relational potential for the audience to connect with what they see and hear onstage. Spaces like the director's own studio emphasize the centrality of intimacy in allowing the relational activities to take place.

In *Relational Aesthetics*, Nicolas Bourriaud suggests that what all artists share is an interhuman relationship. He explains that art produces conviviality, but the purpose of relational art is "the product of conviviality," what he defines as "a complex form that combines a formal structure, objects made available to visitors, and the fleeting image issuing from collective behavior."[76] While Bourriaud's background is anchored in visual culture, especially art, there is a sense that the live aspect of sharing a moment is a connecting thread between what art (or, in Tellas's case, the theater) is and what it can do. Tellas's own background in visual arts helps us to understand the connections that Bourriaud points out in relation to the arts and how these influences make Tellas's works differ in unique ways from more traditional theater.

Proyecto Archivos places an aura of togetherness among audiences and interpreters that goes beyond the mere spatial relations of the theater. Through the gray zone, the Minimal Threshold of Fiction, Tellas offers audiences the peculiar and unique experience of witnessing interpreters onstage embodying personal stories of the ordinary. By introducing stories by "people just like us," Tellas emphasizes the ephemeral nature not just of the everyday experiences that make up our lives but of theater itself. As Peggy Phelan suggests, what remains in the theater is the moment itself, since "the particular cultural moment [which] exerts an urgent pressure to account for what cannot be reproduced" has already disappeared.[77] Phelan adds, "It becomes increasingly imperative to find a way to remember the undocumentable, irreproducible art [performers] make."[78] This pressure to capture that which is often undocumentable in theater becomes a central element in Tellas's conception of how to produce and reproduce the lives of others onstage. Reclaiming that which is undocumentable through lives that have been mostly left out of historical records highlights just how (un)documentable these lives can be. The contrast between what is fleeting in performance (when no two performances can never be the same), and the personal belongings, their anecdotes, photographs, and letters that become part of a documentation provided onstage, asks us to reconsider the meaning of what Tellas has called "evidence." For her, this evidence is not just the objects-turned-props but, rather, the archival weight that each of her interpreters brings with them.[79]

In other words, Proyecto Archivos' fulcrum is the idea of "being together" in theater's aura in order to capture an ephemeral moment. Conviviality is actualized through theater; more precisely, conviviality allows Tellas to put into tension ephemerality and repeatability through shared liminal moments. She constantly makes the audience aware that it is witnessing everyday aspects of life. On the stage, these individual and discrete lives are made repeatable through performance night after night, endowing them with theatrical weight. They are also rendered weightless through each unique performance. Proyecto Archivos, then, is remarkable in taking the audience on a different type of journey: looking closely at something that otherwise would never have been documented, seeing the theatrical through the real and the real through the theatricalization of belongings, telling anecdotes about people's lives, and exploring the affective connections between people, their objects, and their present contexts. Much like other female playwrights who work with autobiography onstage, Tellas makes us aware of how these unpolitical spaces become, in a very distinct way, part of a political message.[80] The construction of theatrical space to tell stories that normally would be of no interest to mainstream culture is a political stance and a tool for creating opposition within institutional forces. It is, as Bourriaud would suggest, a way of "experiencing art's capacities of resistance within the overall social arena."[81]

Authorship

Because Tellas's methodology is unorthodox and none of the plays she works with are presented as autobiographical dramas in conventionally realist ways that characterize other stories we have seen about famous or important figures, they are an ensemble of voices and interpretations.[82] In this respect, the authorial design becomes a shared event by virtue of the fact that each interpreter is the premise of the story. As a result, claims of authorship become vexed even as we hear stories that belong to others. Yet it is clear from the beginning that Tellas is the one who intervenes, who brings out the Minimal Threshold of Fiction, and who can add or delete scenes that are not theatrical. She has also claimed that she adds fiction to the stories when necessary so that, interestingly, the story becomes more "real" and compelling. In the stories she decides to stage, she tries to avoid binaries such as "dramatic/nondramatic" and "fiction/nonfiction," seeing her role as that of a biographical editor who can edit someone's life for the stage.[83] Thus, the stories the interpreters bring are their own, but the theatrical bent is created by Tellas through her use of the UMF—something she achieves by altering, splicing, cutting, and adding to the stories.

Tellas's work becomes participatory in the mere act of bringing stories to life. In her book *Artificial Hells*, Claire Bishop distinguishes between those who create political art and those who witness it in order to understand the audience's role. She argues that the "artist is conceived less as an individual producer of discrete objects than a collaborator and producer of *situations*," and in this way emphasizes the importance of the speech as participatory.[84] Tellas's work seems to fit the category of making the audience "a participant" or involved, at least, in the experience of sharing an intimate, unique "situation." Her interpreters are the collaborators who participate in the active role of examining their stories and collaborating on their witness reports of their own pasts, and Tellas makes their stories the main objects of this participation. Her efforts to reactivate the role of the spectator recalls Jacques Rancière's work on the emancipation of the spectator, in which he states the "spectator also acts" when "she observes, selects, compares, interprets . . . she participates in the performance by refashioning it in her own way."[85] I would even argue that working with interpreters who decide to bring their lives to the stage explores how emancipation not only takes place on the spectator's side but is also part of the entire process for constructing this project.

The Plays

Beatriz Trastoy has described Tellas's work as a collection "*in fieri*," or "open," that "becomes installation,"[86] while Marcela A. Fuentes affirms that Tellas's "work focuses on 'eventhood' as a particular 'charging of attention' into the present of meaning making."[87] Both Trastoy and Fuentes see events, installations, and temporalities as central to Proyecto Archivos. Experiencing the event in real time, through both form and theme, reinforces the idea of conviviality. Moreover, the need to study the specific work of Proyecto Archivos where self-referential narration "literally brings to the stage the publicized and recognized institutional traits that the theater and the museum have in common" exacerbates the personal as a way to exhibit life and preservation of the past.[88] It is, at the same time, an entrance to autofiction, a space of interplay between humor, playfulness, and the fiction of the self. It proposes a key role for the gray zone of the UMF—a liminal space between fictional and documentary. These intersections arrive at what Jordana Blejmar refers to as "*a new cultural formation of memory*."[89] The construction of intimate memories passes through the collective stage where Tellas proposes a possible theatrical way of seeing the past through an ever-present process of reenactment. Although Proyecto Archivos comprises six plays, I will focus on only three—*Mi mamá y mi tía*, *Tres filósofos con bigotes*, and *Escuela de conducción*—because of the connections they establish between family, friendship, and work.

Mi mamá y mi tía

Tellas's first Archivo, *Mi mamá y mi tía*, brings together the project's main attributes: two women with no formal theater training who create stories using their belonging as props. This is the most personal of these six plays, however, because here Tellas works alongside her mother and aunt. The play explains: "Graciela and Luisa Ninio—the real mother and aunt of Vivi Tellas, two Sephardic women who are in their 70s—unfold a family autobiography based on their most 'theatrical' moments: recurring stories, deceptions, journeys, traumatic episodes, betrayals, loves, deaths."[90] Also different from other plays is the fact that the audience sees Tellas directing them on the spot. We experience being in her own workshop, as if it were a work in progress, a rehearsal. The stories they narrate begin with a familiar plot: The interpreters explain who they are and how, as Sephardic Jews, they still speak in Ladino, with its ancient bits of Spanish incorporated.

What is unusual, perhaps, about bringing her mother and aunt to the stage is that, for Tellas, "what made me decide to do something with my mom and my aunt was that my aunt, at 71 years old, fell in love and completely changed her personality. She began to develop sensuality, pleasure—after having been married with three children and having been left a widow. She became a different person. My mom would talk to me about that change."[91] The sisters tell us the story of their lives, their loves, and their journeys through life while Tellas helps them, by guiding them from the margins, by adding stories or asking them questions. What is crude and what is fragile is found there as the sisters swing back and forth between what constitutes personal history and what is constructed through acting, the theatrical script, and the instructions of the director, their daughter and niece. In this way, this work creates tension between autobiographical and biographical components that these women expose through acting and the theatrical spectacle. According to Brenda Werth, "By oscillating between an autobiographical and biographical space, the performance also questions the notion of authorship and complicates the relationship between the real and the fictional on the stage."[92]

Because Tellas edits the different versions of her interpreters' stories and intersperses her own way of formulating dialogues, this collective effort stimulates a fusion between memory and fiction that allows for a world where the emancipation of the interpreters can take place. Not everything is about their life stories. Sometimes other plays or books intersect in humorous ways. For instance, both women reenact a short fragment of *En familia* (*In the Family, 1905*), by well-known early twentieth-century playwright Florencio Sánchez. They chose the scene where two female characters question the traditional patriarchal society embedded in the play. Graciela and Luisa come in and out of character to speak about their own interpretation of the play and the problems they had with mispronouncing words when they staged it in their childhood. However, it is also a subtle way to illustrate the role women had in society then, since the short dialogue centers on their looks, what they wear, and how to fix their hair.

The feminine world, surrounded by bolts of fabric and sewing onstage, results in the sharing of secrets, singing tangos, dancing, and inviting the audience to get to know their personal world. Humor acts as a portal into the past, as the audience sees how they play cards or listens to a linguistic discussion on Ladino and Sephardic Jewish origins:

GRACIELA: "*Niurlía*."

LUISA: *Niurlía*.

GRACIELA: *Niurlía* is a very industrious person. I'll say it again: their house, for example. They invite you to a house and everything is extremely meticulous, everything is marvelous. The woman of the house is a *niurlía* woman. In general, it is something that is said about a woman.

What else?

VIVI: "*Ainaráh que no te caiga.*"

LUISA: *Ainaráh que no te caiga*: I hope that no curse falls upon you . . . that you are . . . that you are well.

GRACIELA: That they don't cast a spell on you.

GRACIELA: "*Niurlía.*"

LUISA: *Niurlía.*

GRACIELA: *Niurlía* es una persona muy hacendosa. Vuelvo a repetir: la casa, por ejemplo. Te invitan a una casa y están todos prolijitos, todo maravilloso. La mujer de la casa es una mujer *niurlía*. Se le dice a la mujer, por lo general.

¿Qué más?

VIVI. "*Ainaráh que no te caiga.*"

LUISA: *Ainaráh que no te caiga*: que no te caiga ninguna maldición . . . que estés . . . que estés bien.

GRACIELA: Que no te echen mal de ojo.[93]

With Tellas's intervention, the Ladino language adds a humorous tone to traditional games, and sayings linked to black magic or curses. Thus, the world of the family, presented through photos and made up of stories full of histories of love or quarrels, is staged before our eyes, fusing documentary and fiction in such a way that they are difficult to disentangle. We see two older women come forward with their stories, with shared secrets of betrayal and love. And while this play can be seen as a theatrical exercise or having a work-in-progress aura, the power of emancipation lies in the two women who come forward to tell their own side of their stories.

Tres filósofos con bigotes

In the same way that Tellas explored her family's world as a source for theatricality both inside and outside the theater, *Tres filósofos con bigotes* investigates how the logical and cerebral work of philosophers can serve as material for the theater (see fig. 2). After taking a philosophy class at the University of Buenos Aires, she saw an opportunity to create another "archive" of how they think and how theater can engage with their thinking. Because philosophers often inhabit a cerebral realm, expanding their world into a theatrical space requires even more emphasis on body and stage presence, so Tellas based scenes and movement on the tenets of Zen philosophy.[94] As an example, in one scene interpreters practice archery while debating whether "the body thinks" or "movement does not exist." A work that decidedly

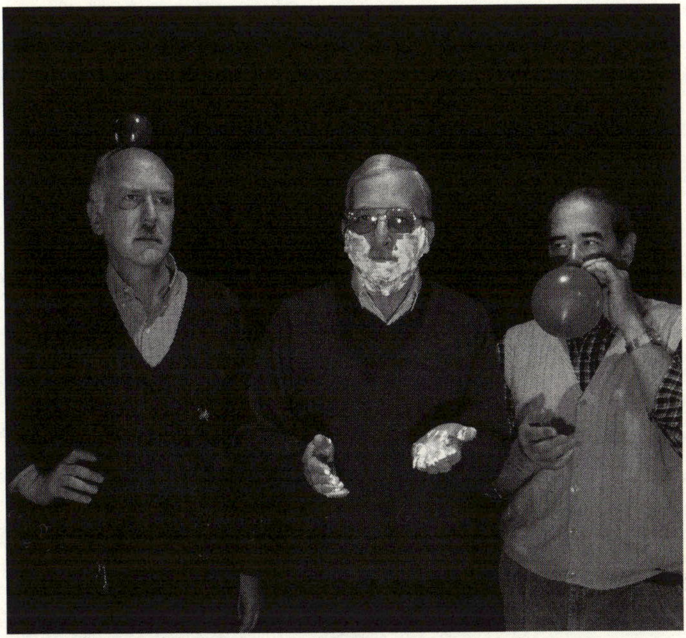

Fig. 2. Left to right, Alfredo Tzveibel, Jaime Plager and Eduardo Osswald. From Vivi Tellas, *Tres filósofos con bigotes*. Publicity still. Buenos Aires, 2004. Photograph by Nicolás Goldberg.

confronts themes of thought, truth, memory, and the human condition investigates the most unexplored aspects of a human being through a dependence on the corporeal. From the re-creation of the light and shadows of Plato's cave to the constant questions about which of the three of them is a professor of philosophy—and also as actors representing themselves—the work underscores concepts of relativity:

JAIME: Stop, look. (*He moves from one end to the other of the lantern.*) If it had occurred to Plato to move the campfire, he would have discovered relativity.

EDUARDO: The prisoner is chained up, looking into the depths of the cavern. Help me, Alfredo. And there is a wall in the cavern. He can only see the shadows.

JAIME: Pará, mirá. (*Mueve de un extremo a otro el farol.*) Si a Platón se le ocurría mover la hoguera, descubría la relatividad.

EDUARDO: El prisionero está encadenado, mirando al fondo de la caverna. Ayudáme, Alfredo. Y hay una tapia en la caverna. Sólo puede ver las sombras. (102)

Framed within the well-worn theories of philosophy, the three professors narrate personal stories, youthful memories, and love stories. Their letters and photographs reveal personal moments. These three real philosophy professors from the University of Buenos Aires (Eduardo Osswald, Jaime Plager, and Alfredo Tzveibel) take the stage to share anecdotes and thus integrate the corporeal into the world of thought. Throughout the performance, the philosophers question philosophical foundations, recite fragments in Greek, and, as we have seen, re-create the lights and shadows of Plato's cave. They question the permanence and reliability of a mask made of warm wax that takes on different forms depending on the face onto which it is placed. At the same time, they investigate the theme of acting and self-referentiality—a theme that is central to Proyecto Archivos:

> EDUARDO: One is acting out oneself, but it is more like a spontaneous action.
> JAIME: This suggests to you that we may or may not be truly representing ourselves. That is to say: authenticity and falseness.
> EDUARDO: Kant says that if you ask reason if I can superimpose two objects, reason says yes.

> EDUARDO: Uno se está interpretando, pero es más una acción espontánea.
> JAIME: Esto te plantea si no estamos siendo representados. Es decir: autenticidad y falsedad.
> EDUARDO: Kant dice que si vos le preguntás a la razón si puedo superponer dos objetos, la razón dice que sí.[95]

The world of theater approaches philosophy through the question of whether acting is an isolated action or a way of being. The ironic and self-referential gaze toward what they appear to do in the moment and what they are actually doing complicates notions of acting versus simply being oneself that Tellas exploits theatrically.

Escuela de conducción

Viewership and gaze are equally important in Tellas's *Escuela de conducción*. In one of the interviews with Tellas about Proyecto Archivos and Biodrama, she comments that "the intention of the Biodrama cycle was always to offer people something from the perspective of 'the theater of the city'; and provoke a reflection about how a city sees these people."[96] Perhaps one of the most theatrical ways of understanding how urban "gazes" are exposed and questioned through theater is with *Escuela de conducción*. A driving school is in itself a fictional world, one of re-created streets used for practical instruction. The Argentine Automobile Club (ACA), which Tellas experienced firsthand by taking a class, provided the basis for her theatrical research: Tellas never took the final exam or passed the driving course, and still takes taxis everywhere around town, but she was able to use the experience for theatrical purposes. In contrast to other works that make up Proyecto Archivos, this project begins with the premise of theatricality from the first moment because, in order to learn how to drive, one must enter an artificial world—a mini–driving course. The work straddles the relationship that exists between a play about a driving class and the theatricality inherent in the driving class itself.

In *Escuela de conducción* we face three interpreters—Lili Segismondi, Carlos Toledo, and Guido Valentinis—who work in the ACA's driving school. Although both men are driving teachers, Lili becomes an interesting figure because she is the only person at the school who does not know how to drive. In a fictitious world where the streets, houses, and city are artificial, the three occupy the stage as living archives that distance us from the space's artifice. Thus, the director investigates: "How does someone spend seven years of their life in their car? What relationship is there between a driver's education instructor and a castle in the Friuli region of Italy? Can you learn to drive on a stage? Who has the right-of-way in a roundabout? And on a single-lane hilly road? Does doing theater make you sexier?"[97] With a humorous touch to learning about the world of driving, Tellas opens up the stage to play with these questions.

Even though all of Proyecto Archivos' works tend to show the vulnerability of actors, with personal stories often only partially told, it is perhaps this work that highlights human dimension of lives often overwhelmed by artifice. Staged as a school, the play begins as a lesson. We hear the main teacher, Guido, give us instructions about how to drive, when and where to stop if pedestrians are present, and who has the right-of-way in a roundabout. Given that Argentina is one of the countries with the highest number of traffic deaths, the topic of driving quickly becomes serious. On the back wall, a video of a televised interview with Guido, the safety engineer of ACA, shows us some of the facts about car accidents and fatality rates. However, when the actual recording ends, Guido comments on the artificiality of the show:

> GUIDO: . . . When the recording ends, the person that had interviewed me was in a hurry, he says goodbye and leaves. The rest of the personnel busy themselves and I stay there seated. There, alone. Time passed and I said: What do I do? Well, I decided to get up. I say: I'll leave slowly . . . I exit into the immense hallway we had entered through and there was the girl that had done my makeup (*Guido touches his face*) talking with someone else. She didn't even look at me. But I remembered that I had this on (*he touches his face*

> *again*). I say to her: "Tell me something, what do I do with this?" And she, without saying anything to me, signals me to go there (*Guido signals with his arm outstretched to the left*). Where? The bathroom. In less than an hour I had passed from being really important to being practically nothing. The truth is that I felt used. TV is like that, you see? It uses you and throws you away.

> GUIDO: . . . Cuando termina la grabación, la persona que me había entrevistado Estaba apurada, hace un saludo rápido y se va. El resto del personal se pone a hacer sus cosas y yo quedo sentado. Ahí, solo. El tiempo pasaba y yo dije: ¿qué hago? Bueno, decidí levantarme. Digo: me voy despacito . . . Salgo al inmenso pasillo por el que habíamos entrado y estaba la chica que me había maquillado (*Guido se toca la cara*) hablando con otra persona. Ni me miró. Pero yo me acordé que tenía eso (*vuelve a tocarse la cara*). Le digo: "Decíme una cosa, ¿qué hago con esto?," y ella, sin decirme palabra, me señala ahí (*Guido señala con el brazo extendido hacia la izquierda*). ¿Dónde? El baño. En menos de una hora había pasado de ser lo más a ser prácticamente nada. La verdad es que me sentí usado. La tele es así, ¿vieron? Te usa y te tira.[98]

I call attention to this scene because it plays with the idea of spectacle, artifice, and learning. As the safety engineer, Guido teaches the public about how to avoid accidents and how to follow the rules. However, he is confronted with how easily he is discarded. As part of a televised show, the artifice, the quick change of set makes him feel like yet another statistic. And even though the play constantly uses humor to speak about cars, to explain how they even become like pets to people, it is evident that the theatricality embedded in the driving school can fail, that statistics can be easily forgotten or that, as here, driving school can be a mere theater exercise.

Tellas's affective work demonstrates an ability to manifest itself through new forms of relating to and in the theater. Her gaze in and of itself toward something new, something that can fail, something that is not totally polished contains the UMF—that gray zone that expands documentary forms of creation and revision. The affective, intimate, and relational aspects of these works are foregrounded as the interpreters take the stage in order to narrate their most private personal and autobiographical stories. But one also encounters Tellas's use of fiction to retouch the stories and enhance their theatrical aspects to compel her public to experience the play as it is partially constructed during the live event. The interpreters already carry with them some measure of theatricality, in the roles they play as professors, instructors, mothers, or aunts. Theatricality here refers to the acting present during everyday life, free of the artifice of professional modes of acting. It is here that one finds Tellas's theatrical eye, which searches for the UMF that hides inside people. Tellas seeks to find that space between listening to a personal story and understanding how fiction enters into the stories of each individual. It is about another way of creating documentary theater to allow personal archives to come to life via the staging of personal stories. Thus, Tellas constructs intimate and affective worlds by investigating the limits of how much fiction exists in our lives and how much realness can be presented in a staged biography.

Chapter 2

✦

Reenactments

The Autobiographical at Play in Lola Arias

> Photography is a kind of primitive theatre, a kind of Tableau Vivant, a figuration of the motionless and made-up face, beneath which we see the dead.
>
> —Roland Barthes, *Camera Lucida*

Clothes fall from the ceiling; an actor tumbles down with the clothes. The actor tells us that the jeans she is putting on used to be her mother's when she was her same age. The proximity between past and present is quickly conveyed through the suggestion that there is a material specter. This specter comes to life as clothes from the past become "costumes" of the present, and a filial cord allows the actor to unite with the audience in this opening of *Mi vida después* (*My Life After*). Through personal objects, six actors begin an autobiographical search in which they speak about their parents' political lives during the last Argentine dictatorship (1976–1983), what their lives were like, and how the children, now young adults, reinterpret the stories about their parents from their own recollections, imagination and fact-checking.

Lola Arias, Argentine writer, performer, visual artist, musician, playwright, and director, became an international theater sensation who found success with documentary theater techniques. For critic Jorge Dubatti, Arias is part of a new collective of playwrights and directors renovating the Argentine national scene, calling them "amphibious" or multitalented.[1] With her play *Mi vida después* (2009), which, as we saw in the previous chapter, was conceived as the last Biodrama but not staged as such,[2] Arias expanded the theater scene in Buenos Aires and abroad. *Mi vida después* has since become a fundamental work in her repertoire.[3] Her work is defined by what Brownell calls a "theater-that-works-with-documents," the constant liminal presence of chance, as when using animals or children onstage, and the blurring of the boundaries between the real and fiction on the stage. Some have even dubbed her technique the "Arias method."[4] She is known for her "remakes," where she fuses the creation of the real in the theater as a "way to revive the past and modify the future," what she now calls "reenactments."[5] Interested in the constant friction between authentic objects, such as photographs, clothing, tapes, and the construction of fiction through them, Arias searches for new possible connections to understanding the past. As someone who likes to explore other possibilities in the theater, she welcomes the intrusion of elements that are out of her control as a raw connection of the real on the fictional stage. Even a quick look at the interest this play garnered in Argentina and abroad is sufficient to gauge the impact that the Arias method has had since the play's premiere in 2009 until its last show in 2014.[6]

In this chapter I study how Arias's work has become key to understanding and promoting documentary practices in Latin American theater through their alternative way of speaking about the traumatic effects of the last and most oppressive military dictatorship in Argentina. I play close attention to the active role of photography onstage, an exploration of the "reenactment," and the manipulation of how memories are created, both within and outside family circles. Through these lenses, I consider how the autobiographical mode is framed by constant doubt and the playful way Arias tackles traumatic memories. My aim is to reflect on the technique of autoreferentiality—that is, witnessing and telling, and how they get used in a humorous, doubtful, and playful manner. My focus will be on two major compositions: what Lola Arias has called her trilogy, composed of three separate plays (*Mi vida después*, *El año en que nací*, and *Melancolía y manifestaciones*), published as *Mi vida después and Other Texts*; and what could be considered her Cycle of War, comprising a video, *Veterans*, a play, *Campo minado / Minefield*, and a film, *Theatre of War*. These are central examples of how documentary practices have made an impact on how theater is conceived.[7]

Published in 2016, *Mi vida después y otros textos* encompasses three foundational documentary works: *Mi vida después* (*My Life After*, 2009), *El año en que nací* (*The Year I Was Born*, 2012), and *Melancolía y manifestaciones* (*Melancholy and Demonstrations*, 2012). This trilogy, according to Arias, "stems from the same concept: children that reconstruct their parents' lives through photographs, films, texts, memories."[8] For Arias, these three plays can be seen as "sisters" or as "a play within another play," each play nurturing ideas and possibilities that feed the others' existence.[9]

Due to its success and its importance as the first in the series, the one that sets up some of the basic methodology and techniques to documentary theater, scholars in the field have paid close attention to how *Mi vida después* became a major play that showcases the use of the autobiographical onstage, as well as the need to witness through the creation of the stories of six children who lived through the dictatorship and recall the events through very young eyes. They now re-member and reembody the past with the help of photographs, videos, letters, and tapes. The sequel that features the Chilean dictatorship, *El año en que nací*, takes the same approach; in this work, however, eleven actors belonging to different generations with different cultural, economic, and political identities tell their parents' stories during the Pinochet regime (1973–1989). While I will not closely analyze the last work in this trilogy, *Melancolía y manifestaciones*, it marks a departure from the other two by taking a more personal stand, as Arias herself tells the story of her mother, who suffers from chronic depression. With the addition of this last play, Arias sought to tell her own story as a response to questions some have raised about the legitimacy of her work because she had not personally lost a parent to the dictatorship. By adding this last play, Arias explains that it is an example of why everyone touched by that era should have a place to speak. She states: "The story of my mother—a literature professor who in 1976, the year the dictatorship begins and I am born, her second daughter, she falls into deep depression—that too could be a generational story."[10]

Whereas family secrets, misunderstandings, and perceptions are the focus of Arias's *Mi vida después* trilogy, her second project is quite different. In *Campo minado / Minefield*, the value of testimony from real-life veterans of the Malvinas/Falklands War (1982) becomes the principal thread. Published in 2017 as a bilingual, visually evocative book, *Campo minado / Minefield* has become an important focus of study in the field of Latin American theater. Through a playful and inviting manner and in documentary mode, six soldiers (three from Argentina and three from Great Britain, one of them a Nepali citizen who fought for the British) recount episodes from their participation in the short-lived war. With *Campo minado*, Arias created a new and intriguing way to capture the acts of witnessing and telling about a war that is still very central in the Argentine imaginary.[11] Thus, the technique of having six real veterans of war onstage, divided by their language, the country they fought for, and their patriotism to their respective nation, exposes the fuzzy corners of memory and perception of a traumatic war. Through her clear use of reenactments, Arias pushes forward the idea of building a story through collective memory, and in this way the exploration of witnessing and telling becomes a central aspect of the play.

All of the projects discussed in this chapter rely on the use of multimedia that emphasize the role of theatrical and fictional elements when relating to the real. As was seen with Piscator and Weiss in their early versions of documentary theater, Arias makes clear that to bring the real to the stage, a multimedia approach is a productive method, one that can unveil the different manifestations of documentary theater. Thus, she relies on multimedia to play and reformulate how stories are retold. As Brenda Werth has succinctly stated, "Multimedia in documentary theater serves to introduce evidence of past events, multiply spatial and temporal registers, and manipulate the tensions between embodied testimony and mediated narratives juxtaposed onstage."[12]

It is noteworthy that in these two larger projects (the trilogy and the Cycle of War), while theater is the main domain, Arias makes use of a combination of methods, techniques, and genres, especially video installations and film. In particular, the Cycle of War was first conceived as a video installation called *Veterans* in 2014 with five Argentine veterans.[13] It was later shown in *Doble de riesgo* (*Stunt Double*) in 2016, an installation with multiple participatory booths, video testimonies, and a wide array of historical information to contextualize the personal stories and featured the original version of *Veterans* from 2014. *Doble de riesgo* was strategically staged in Buenos Aires at the Parque de la Memoria, a park dedicated to honoring those disappeared in the last dictatorship.[14] And, as Arias suggests, this installation's primary goal was to grapple with the ways in which veterans remember, what they remember, and how "to film a flashback."[15] This material was later modified and became the basis for the play *Campo minado*. The play text was later published as a bilingual edition in 2016. The third and last element of the cycle is a documentary film titled *Theatre of War / Teatro de guerra* (2018). The film was created in part from hours of film that were taken during rehearsals of the play, but there is also a combination of clips from *Veterans*, casting for the *Campo minado*, and new scenes that were done for the film.

The common denominator to all elements of the cycle is, of course, the documentary mode, the need to tell a story, the search to destabilize the authority of the archive using a playful approach that questions the implications of what photographs, images, letters, and stories have ingrained in people's memories from a devastating war that involved Argentine and British nationals, as well as the addition of the Nepali Sukrim Rai. *Campo minado* is a collaborative project that, for the most part, relies on the same six veterans: Lou Armour, David Jackson, Rubén Otero, Sukrim Rai, Gabriel Sagastume, and Marcelo Vallejo.[16] The multinational approach to telling their story on the stage through their own recollections and highly mediated by a multi-angle use of technology becomes an attractive new way of constructing yet also morphing a story, creating in the meantime an intriguing visual buffet for exploring the same testimonies through an array of genres that rely on documentary research. However, it is my intention to pay closer attention to the play as a live product, in which the use of the autobiographical provides nuanced testimony to the soldiers' intimate memories. Because of its liveness, the play is able to generate conviviality and affective relationships more compellingly than documentary film could.

Foundational Work

As a director, author, curator, poet, and performer herself, Arias is a prolific, transnational, and creative artist who breaks boundaries when telling stories and is mainly attracted by real stories, testimonies, and documents. Her work has had an important trajectory before and during the two trilogies that will be analyzed here. Since her debut with *La escuálida familia* (*A Kingdom, a Country or a Wasteland in the Snow*, 2001), Arias has expanded how we think about and view theatrical events as she approaches dramaturgy in postapocalyptic ways. In her trilogy *Sueño con revolver* (*Dream with Revolver*, 2007), *Striptease* and *El amor es un francotirador* (*Love Is a Sniper*, 2007), she was already working against the grain of traditional heuristics. With *El amor es un francotirador*, chance plays a central role, since a different character dies in every performance, in a game of Russian roulette. In *Striptease* a real mother/actor enacts a scripted phone conversation while at the same time her one-year-old baby also occupied the stage and disrupted any previously rehearsed version of the conversation. The baby's impromptu behavior meant that actors had to improvise and react in time to what was happening onstage—even when it conflicted with stage directions.[17] This is where Arias first began to explore the tension between unpredictable life and fiction on the stage through performance. Over time, for Arias, these concepts became distilled into what she sees as "the real" and "fiction" and where she began to stage something that goes against fiction.[18]

Her trajectory quickly changed from producing traditional theatrical plays to thinking about theatrical interventions, urban installations, and documentary modes as the focus of her work. In 2007, with *Chácara paraíso* (*Small Farm Paradise*), she joined forces with her then partner, Stefan Kaegi, cofounder of the cutting-edge German-Swiss group Rimini Protokoll, to work with military police in training in São Paulo. They later developed *Airport Kids* (2008), another documentary work about twelve-year-old children who live in an international community in Lausanne, Switzerland, where they become nomads, with two or three passports, many languages but no nation. Arias's work with Stefan Kaegi, became even more participatory when she and Kaegi cocreated *Parallel Cities* (2010–2011), an urban intervention performance piece that called for a participatory experience by people not formally trained in the theater, people they call "experts of the everyday."[19] With *Parallel Cities*, Kaegi and Arias invited international artists from England, Germany, Switzerland, and Argentina to explore their perception of the city (Berlin, Buenos Aires, Zurich, Warsaw, Singapore, and Kolkata) and its relationship to people. Eight different installations offer the inhabitants a way to experience their own city, a city they might be familiar with, but they might not have really thought about certain aspects of its presence in their everyday life.[20] The main idea behind this ten-day project was to experience places that are usually unseen or unthought-of. As online information about *Parallel Cities* states: "Hotel rooms, shopping centres, factories . . . these are functional places, not usually thought of as interesting to the outside eye. But without them life in the city would be uninhabitable. Their ubiquitous, parallel existences the world over mean these places are instantly recognizable, each modelled on similar rules but displaying a local face."[21] The program proposes multiple interventions: audiences can occupy five hotel rooms and learn about the lives of the maids who clean them (Lola Arias), listen and sing with a Renaissance choir that takes over the courthouse singing about the judicial cases of the day

(Christian García), follow directions via a headphone while at a library (Ant Hampton and Tim Etchells), walk through a factory line and learn about the person who is behind the machine (Gerardo Naumann), peek into someone's life through an apartment window (Dominic Huber), listen to a blind's man tale of the city on a rooftop (Stefan Kaegi), follow directions while walking in a mall and trying new poses (Ligna), or read mundane live comments typed live by fellow artists on a subway or a train station and project onto a screen so that passengers can read them (Mariano Pensotti).[22] Some are more "theatrical" than others, meaning there is more of a staged presence, as in the case of the hotel rooms designed by Arias in *Hotel/Maids*, or the example of Ant Hampton and Tim Etchell's *The Quiet Volume*, in which library visitors are the actors who listen to instructions via headphones on what and how to read certain pages. Others, such as the subway station's live writing projected onto screens, makes people aware of how they see and are seen by others, often with humorous remarks on how people react to these comments.

While this work exemplifies how the boundaries of actor and audience are blurred, *Parallel Cities* underscores the real behind the staged by giving audience members an opportunity to take part in the event while unveiling the forces behind the machine, the legal system, or, in this case, the hotel room. In a sense, *Hotel/Maids* utilizes some of the techniques from documentary theater by providing the visitor with a collage of pictures, video fragments, or actual sex toys found in hotel rooms, all contextualized by the biographies of real people, in this case the maids who clean up after us. It also employs this documentary technique in order to make the visitor aware of the real behind the staged, making a political commentary on immigration situations, labor inequalities, lack of education, or bleak future possibilities. Once again, the blurring of the boundaries can be seen through the mixing of documentary techniques in a site-specific place, but it simultaneously performs the space in order to bring the real story to life. While Peter Weiss used documentary theater as a truthful tool to stage something real, *Parallel Cities*' use of documentary techniques pushes the boundaries on what documents can tell us and what we can understand or interpret from them. Similarly, Kaegi and Arias make use of documentary techniques in a way to blur the distinction between the real and the fictional so that the audience member remains active in questioning what he or she is experiencing. Specifically, the projects make theater out of everyday, mundane public spaces and seduce the viewers into staying long enough for their perception to change.

Within Arias's vast work with documents and documentation, *Parallel Cities* clearly marked an important step in her creative process, allowing her to relate more urban and nomadic spaces. It is certain, then, that her work, as evidenced by *Parallel Cities*, more than a decade ago began to extend beyond national boundaries while simultaenously transgressing the limits of theater and the theatrical experience by engaging with conviviality, community, documentation, and participation in unconventional ways.

Arias's documentary work can also be seen in subsequent projects, such as *My Documents*, a lecture performance cycle that lasted from 2012 to 2017, and then another lecture given in February 2020 in Lisbon, where a variety of artists share their life, their personal stories, in a very intimate and personal way. As the title suggests, documents are the primary element of this work, and artists employed that word freely and productively.[23] During the COVID-19 pandemic, when theaters shut down and stay-at-home orders significantly limited social interactions, Arias returned to *My Documents*, except that this time she took advantage of the Internet and Zoom to invite artists from dance, visual arts, documentary film and from different parts of the world (China, Portugal, Lebanon, Germany, Mexico), to share their screens and present a lecture performance. As she states, "The programme seeks to delve into the genre in search of a contagion among conceptual art, research, and theatre. A space where speeches, formats and audiences from different disciplines can come together."[24] Arias's ongoing work with documents and archives makes her one of the most visionary artists today.

Mi vida después

As I have written previously, Arias's *Mi vida después* stems from issues surrounding how a second generation speaks about the dictatorship in personal and intimate ways (not always governed by matters of authenticity regarding the story) through the close relationship these children of postdictatorship Argentina hold to familial objects as they formulate questions about their parents' absence.[25] However, different from previous work on how to represent trauma and victimhood on the stage, *Mi vida después* evokes laughter while confronting painful memories. As Jordana Blejmar suggests, this play is an example of the "return of the (auto) fictionalized real . . . but as a way to playfully point to the narrative nature of life."[26] In *Mi vida después*, six actors (Vanina Falco, Pablo Lugones, Blas Arrese Igor, Carla Crespo, Liza Casullo, Mariano Speratti) born between 1972 and 1983 present their versions of personal stories that they either vaguely remember or have heard from relatives about their parents' disappearances or involvement during the last Argentine military dictatorship (1976–1983) (see fig. 3).

For Arias, this play is "a remake to re-create those stories heard, known, imagined of the parents."[27] These remakes or reenactments relay a spectral connection between past and present, because some actors are the children who remain, and they are also the ones who embody their absent parents. Although not all of the parents in this play have disappeared, the spectral connection is close and personal, exploring other ways to connect to the past. For example, as Liza Casullo falls onto a pile of clothes onstage, she states: "When I was seven, I used to get dressed up in my mum's clothes and parade around the house, tromping on her dress like a miniature queen. Twenty

Fig. 3. Left to right, Vanina Falco, Pablo Lugones, Blas Arrese Igor, Moreno Speratti de Cunha, Liza Casullo, Mariano Speratti, Carla Crespo. From Lola Arias's *Mi vida después*. Publicity still. Buenos Aires, 2009. Photograph by Lorena Fernández.

years later I find a pair of my mum's Lees from the seventies, and they fit me just right. I put the jeans on and start to walk towards the past."[28] The spectral connection between past and present becomes a central point in this play as well as the others discussed in this chapter.

Objects, memory, photographs, and family secrets reveal a traumatic historical moment of the last dictatorship in Argentina, when families were broken up, tens of thousands of people disappeared under the military regime, and hundreds of newborn children of "subversive" parents were appropriated and "adopted" by families connected to power. For instance, *Mi vida después* incorporates into its story the first time the daughter of a military repressor and appropriator, Vanina Falco, attempted to testify against her own father, and it would later become the gateway for allowing her to testify against her father in court—something not allowed until then.[29] Vanina's father, Luis Falco, was subsequently sentenced to eighteen years of imprisonment after being found guilty of appropriating Juan Cabandié as his own son. Vanina Falco's presence in this play highlights painful dichotomies in her life: how she adored her father while growing up; and how she sees him now—a monster who committed crimes against humanity. Others, such as Carla Crespo, reenact different versions of what they have heard about their parents' deaths. Crespo's father was a militant in the Ejército Revolucionario del Pueblo (ERP [People's Revolutionary Army]). Mariano Speratti shares a spectral audio recording of his disappeared father with his four-year-old son, who has run to meet him onstage. He and others explore their own lives looking for clues about the stories they have heard. Blas Arrese Igor and Pablo Lugones share the stories of their fathers who were not part of any militant group but who worked, respectively, as a priest and a banker under the dictatorship. A turtle, a family heirloom, is brought onto the stage so that by walking it can choose "yes" or "no" when asked if there will be a revolution in the future of Argentina. And finally, musician Liza Casullo delves into the world of books written by her once-exiled philosopher father, Nicolás Casullo.

The Effect of Postmemory

Actors rely on the use of photographs from their childhoods that they carry with them onstage. The family photo album becomes a central prop onstage that allows them to dig deeper into the differences between image and memory. We see the image shown on the photograph as well as how the children reinterpret their memories over time. Documents, photographs, recordings all become malleable props that bridge the gap between fiction and fact, where personal stories come to light as vague recollections from adults who were once young. Thus, actors become their own doubles, their own detectives of the stories they want to re-create and reveal in a public setting.[30] Within this framework Arias creates a play about the second generation and the doubts, questions, and secrets that this generation molds into what Marianne Hirsch calls the "family frame." Scholars in the field, such as Cecilia Sosa, Mariana Eva Pérez, Brenda Werth, Jean Graham-Jones and myself, have studied the different formulations of Marianne Hirsch's "postmemory" in regard to *Mi vida después* and *El año en que nací*.[31]

For some, as in the case of Mariana Eva Pérez, the concept of postmemory does not answer her personal questions resulting from the trauma of being the daughter of two disappeared parents. In fact, she proposes that many of the children of disappeared parents in Argentina do not belong to the second generation; rather, they are part of the first, as victims of kidnappings and their own memories of what they suffered during the dictatorship. Pérez explains that "as children, they experienced—in their own bodies—traumatic events for which they had no language or memory."[32] To her, the label "transgenerational transmission of trauma" is more accurate for understanding the true situation experienced by these children, whom she sees as both firsthand witnesses and receptors of inherited memories.[33] Although I agree with Pérez that a "second-generation" approach to trauma is not the only method that can unveil memories, Arias's work does put onstage the general notion of how memories evolve and get constructed. In other words, what is salient in this documentary mode to telling stories is not so much the concept of second-generation versus first-generation. Rather, stories are activated through the second generation's affective relationship to their own memories and to those given to them by previous generations.

Thus, the concept of postmemory helps us to think beyond generations and beyond the idea of what constitutes authentic memories while simultaneously opening up the possibilities to generate affective meaning through other sensorial modes. As someone from the same generation as these children who are telling their stories onstage, but without any direct familial connection to the disappeared, I believe Hirsch's concept of postmemory is productive in the sense that it projects the idea of remembering, imagination, and creation into the gaps of childhood memories. In her study, Hirsch defines the term as follows:

> Postmemory describes the relationship that the generation after those who witnessed cultural or collective trauma bears to the experiences of those who came before, experiences that they "remember" only by means of the stories, images and behaviors among which they grew up. . . . Postmemory's connection to the past is thus not actually mediated by recall but by imaginative investment, projection, and creation.[34]

As other studies have also suggested, Hirsch's postmemory concept is very productive when analyzing Lola Arias's work, where family stories of war and memory are reimagined and reenacted.

My main interest in Hirsch's concept lies with the idea of openness, vulnerability, and doubt that imagination and creation bring to bear on the construction of stories. It is also a validation of this generation as members speak from their own perceptions, allowing them to "remember" from their own perspectives as well as those they inherited, while at the same time they incorporate their own sense of embodied experience of traumatic events. In fact, Hirsch, a daughter of Holocaust survivors, argues that second-generation witnesses have such a deep connection to the memories of the generation before them that they "seem to constitute memories in their own right."[35] In her own definition of this term, Hirsch brings forth the idea that postmemory might also be useful to those who were not actual victims of trauma but learn through it.[36] I concur with Cecilia Sosa when she claims that postmemory is productive in the reformulation and rethinking of trauma, given that it is not just a second-generation territory but that it also opens the field to other witnesses and spectators alike.[37] This is an important point because Arias, herself—not a survivor of disappeared parents, nor someone who had close family members who participated in either side of the dictatorship—makes clear that this has been a point of contention for some of her critics. As I stated earlier, she created *Melancolía y manifestaciones*, in part, as a way of responding to those constant questions she received from the media about her own lineage and personal experience with disappeared family members. But it is also a way for Arias herself to do what she has asked others of the same generation to do: to look back at the generational gaps, the childhood memories, and figure out how to recompose them onstage. As she states: "*Melancholy and Demonstrations* breaks off from *My Life After*. It's the missing story: mine."[38]

Arias's work brings together concepts of testimony, autobiography, and a second-generation approach to a postdictatorship era where children, now in their forties, can claim their own perception of the stories they have heard since childhood. For Arias, it was paramount to create plays in which the first-person narrative was never lost, where affective and emotional sentiments took a central role, in which humor was cultivated, and in which the work could be thought of as a continuation, as a "time machine."[39] This oscillation between time periods reinforces the possibility of reading this work as part of "a structure of inter- and transgenerational return of traumatic knowledge and embodied experience."[40] In this regard, concepts of testimonial theater, autobiography, and second-generation memories are useful terms when analyzing the last two trilogies of Arias's work.

Family frames and familial links are a central connection to her work, especially in the first trilogy, where the three plays deal directly with afflicted children of dictatorships. And, as Arias clearly states, not just family members of the disappeared were victims, because everybody involved during this time has some connection to these issues. As Cecilia Sosa argues, "*Mi vida después* displays an uneasy machine of affects that helps to explore the resonances of grief beyond those usually considered as victims."[41] Exploring the affective connection to loss from a childhood perspective is clearly conceived in the trilogy *Mi vida después y otros textos*. In *Mi vida después*, for example, one of the six actors' fathers was an apolitical banker and had no direct link to the government or political movement, yet the son provides his testimony of what he remembers about his father from that time. Similarly, Arias's own life is on display in *Melancolía y manifestaciones*, where she clearly states that her only connection to the dictatorship is through the fact that her mother falls into a deep depression in 1976, the same year the military regime takes power. Therefore, even though the family is the center of all these stories, the connecting thread is the perception and reception of how such a gruesome change in power modified or changed all citizens lives.

Stories and Family Secrets

Secrets and different stories of someone's past habitate the theater, as when Carla directly expresses doubt about her own father's death.

CARLA: During my life I've heard so many versions of how my dad died that it's as if he died several times, or as if he never died. If my dad's life were a film, I'd like to play his stunt double.[42]

This testimony by Carla Crespo in *Mi vida después* emphasizes the core idea of this play: stories are unreliable. Fiction—or, as Arias calls it, re-creation through a "reenactment" or through the use of a stunt double—in a sense highlights the play's centrality: bodies reenact other absent bodies. Congruently, family secrets and stories bring with them unauthentic and unreliable forms of expressions, amplifying the different possible stories one can remember from childhood. Dressed as a leader of a guerrilla group, Crespo reenacts different possibilities of her father's death and, with the help of the other actors, explores issues of unreliability:

CARLA: Death number 1. When I'm six, my mum tells me my dad died in a car crash. (*The actors make a car using chairs, turn on a fan and the radio. While the radio plays, they act as is they are travelling in the car. Then, their heads drop.*)

Death number 2. When I'm 14, during a family gathering, my grandma says right in front of me that my dad died in 75 at the Battle of Monte Chingolo, in a clash between the People's Revolutionary Army and the military . . . my dad gets shot in the stomach and his mate in the leg. They fall to the ground. The rest of the comrades try to help them, but from the ground he gives the order to retreat. They bleed to death shortly after. (*The actors move the car made from the chairs, stand up, point their fingers like guns, fall to the ground.*)

Death number 3. When I'm 20, I read a letter that the party sent to my mum, saying that all those wounded at Chingolo had been taken prisoners and shot three days later. (*The actors go upstage and fall onto the pile of clothes.*)[43]

The search for a possible truth within these theatrical reenactments plays a central function. On the one hand, reenactments bring out the constant anguish a child feels growing up (and still does), while on the other, there is a sense of distance, of playfulness that renders Crespo's testimony a theatrical piece, where "reenactments" become scenarios of what could have happened. However, even though there is constant tension between the humorous and the traumatic side of her story, at times words are not enough, as when Crespo later realizes that she is now older than her father was when he was killed. She cannot speak, and instead plays the drums as a cathartic scene in which speech is not necessary. As the play matured and years went by, Crespo's DNA testing confirmed that, indeed, her dad had been buried in a common grave. This new information is added to subsequent performances in a somber and acknowledging way.

Touching Photographs

In *Camera Lucida*, Roland Barthes studies the "affective intentionality" of photography, when we, the audience become spectators by looking at images in front of us.[44] This affective relationship is nascent in the binary between the *studium* (field) and the *punctum*, what pricks or pierces the viewer; in other words, "punctum is what I add to the photograph and *what is nonetheless already there*."[45] Relating photographs to and through the image of an "umbilical cord," Barthes explores family ties constructed through photography.[46] Influenced by Barthes's reading of family photographs, Marianne Hirsch studies photography through the "familial gaze [that] situates human subjects in the ideology, the mythology, of the family as institution and projects a screen of familial myths between camera and subject."[47] Relating to Hirsch's work, Margaret Olin suggests that "photographs are visible, but photography is not only a 'visual' practice."[48] Indeed, photography lends itself to other possible connections that go beyond what the eye can see, engaging "the tactile sense." For Olin, the "slippage" between both senses is what gives photography its "power as a relational art."[49] Thus, for Olin, there is a sense of power or "authority" that makes the viewer a central piece in the perception of photographs, whether "real or illusionary."[50] Her approach is closely related to the indexicality of photography, where the understanding of photography stems from it being a product we can indeed touch. In dialogue with Barthes, where he calls the "'photographic referent' the necessarily real thing which has been placed before the lens, without which there would be no photograph," Olin connects the umbilical cord through tactility to what she refers to as "navel" and sees the materiality of the photograph.[51] Even if photographs allure us with their indexicality appeal—that moment when we stand in front of the camera to capture that instance—it is not just the image that is most interesting. Rather, "its material and presentational forms and the uses to which they are put are central to the function of a photograph as a socially salient object."[52] Consequently, photographs are more than objects; they have physicality and volume that relate to subjective and affective interactions.

Photographs become a malleable, questionable prop that bring with it the object-turned-prop stance. Even when photographs are personal objects that connect the past to the present, there is a certain insubordination as actors contest the photograph's possible and various meanings. In a recent study on the role of documentary photography during the Chilean dictatorship, Ángeles Donoso Macaya argues that "photography became a paramount documentary tool to denounce, protest, and challenge dictatorship."[53] Indeed,

Fig. 4. Liza Casullo. From Lola Arias's *Mi vida después*. Buenos Aires, 2009. Photograph by Lorena Fernández.

she contends that the use of photography as documentary practice opened up a space for resistance, creation, and humor, and as such, she explores the "expanding field of photographic practices" that engages all involved in the creation of the photograph—from the person behind the camera, to the subject being photographed, to the viewer.[54] And while Donoso's focus is not family photographs as Arias's is, the photograph is able to perform, to redocument, through its interpretation onstage. In other words, photographs can bring the archive to life (see fig. 4).

The weight of the image's materiality, the intervention between image and indexicality, has proven to be a strong filial and political cord. It is, perhaps, in the understanding of the materiality of the photograph that "extends the indexicality of the image through both bodily interaction with the photo-object, especially the tactile, and through interventions with the indexical image."[55] In a country where the Madres de Plaza de Mayo have carried photographs of their disappeared children since the dictatorship began in 1976, photographs have intervened in the filial and political arena. In Arias's work, however, there seems to be a distinct distance between the indexicality of the disappeared and how they are utilized today by the younger generation. The children question the photograph, cut it, draw on it, manipulate it in order to think of other ways to relate to this object that has created different stories in their lives.

As with every play in both trilogies, photographs become a questionable and unreliable prop that helps maneuver and manipulate the stories actors and performers want to tell. In *Mi vida después*, actors find a constant link between the stories they heard, the images they see, and the construction of the story they want to tell. Past, present, and future are all linked and exposed in Arias's work. Photographs from childhood are introduced to reveal the past but also to explore the possible interpretations that take place in the present. While an actor describes the photographs, others help manipulate, cut, draw, or superimpose photographs reflected on the big screen. Indeed, the relationship between "happy" childhood pictures from birthday parties, swimming lessons, and family times become a haunting and spectral understanding of what actually happened in and within families. In similar fashion, Barthes contends that while the old mechanism of developing the photograph was a chemical process, what becomes "undevelopable [is] an essence (of a wound), what cannot be transformed but only repeated under the instances of insistence (of the insistent gaze)."[56] Thus, the essence of the image is born through the human gaze, and developed in the theater, through the stories that lend themselves to reenactments of the past.

A variety of family photographs become props that make us pry into someone's private life. A documentary method to understanding the past through constant manipulation of the perception of a photograph and perception of it in present time conveys one of the essential tenets of this play. A case in point is Vanina Falco's stories, where her father, who was a policeman, is defined by his "police attitude" in pictures.

> VANINA: This is my childhood photo album. 1976. My uncle, my grandfather and my father. All policemen. They have police faces, police moustaches, police attitude. My father never wore a uniform, because he was in the secret police and worked undercover. That's me at the bottom, sitting behind my birthday cake, with some strange line slicing through my head. 1978. This is me at three, watching my mum bathe my brother. In the photo you can see I'm happy but confused. I don't quite understand where my brother came from, because I don't remember ever seeing my mum pregnant. 1983. My father and me on a diving board. Whenever I look at this photo, I wonder why he's sitting at the safe end, leaving me on the edge. It looks as if I'm about to fall.[57]

While she confronts her own childhood memories of a father figure who loved her, who took care of her when she was ill, photographs are manipulated by another actor to question how he could have been such a good father while appropriating her brother from a young couple who was disappeared. Projected onto a large screen, we see the marking of the moustaches, the circling of people, the emphasis on their funny macho poses, and we laugh at how they too become props of a humorous moment. Falco's ironic descriptions of her uncles and father also add to what the pictures show and how she reinterprets them through humor. Memory gaps between what an adult remembers of that childhood moment become ambiguous spaces. Photographs, then, are the perfect questionable prop: they carry authenticity through visual weight, yet incongruent proclamations of the attached memories, all constructed before our eyes in a playful and inviting manner, making the audience aware of the intricate connections between what we see and what we hear.

In this regard, photographs house ambiguous images. In some cases, memory helps construct a narrative. At other times, it is only an image surrounded by other people's narratives that create some sort of connection between the story and the photograph and between the actor and the audience. As Annette Kuhn states, "Family photographs are supposed to show not so much that we were once there, as how we once were: to evoke memories that might have little or nothing to do with what is actually in the picture."[58] Hence, Arias's work proposes through the interpretation and reinterpretation of family photographs, the idea of what might lie behind each of them and what memory (or memories of memories) create about the image itself onstage. In this play, there is an intimate connection conjured between what the photograph shows and what the reenactment of the image proposes. In a sense, Arias's emphasis on crafting her plays as more like time machines with no specific chronology helps us understand how the manipulation of photographs in the present explores other possible options for remembering. Along the same lines, Kuhn explains that family photographs "may affect to show us our past, but what we do with them—how we use them—is really about today, not yesterday. These traces of our former lives are pressed into service in a never-ending process of making, re-making, making sense of, our selves—now."[59] For Arias, the temporality of how to deal with family photographs defies time and chronology. Instead of giving the audience an authentic, reliable tale of the past, Arias suggests a way for this new generation to think about themselves in the present moment and "after" in the projected future. The truncated stories of the past do not seem to be an obstacle in their perception of their own place in relation to the parents' past. Instead, the search to explore a possible present and future through the gaps of memory, through the multiple possible stories, allows the actors to move on.

The autobiographical storytelling by each of the actors in *Mi vida después* creates an ambivalent link to authenticity. It is less how "true" the story is than how believable the story may seem through its retelling. Kuhn proposes that we think of autobiographical photography as revisionist autobiography, through which she explores the gap between the "I" that writes and the "I" or "me" who is the subject of the writing. In this space, she states that "revisionist autobiography is not purely, nor arguably at all, about the lives and times of particular individuals: rather, it is about the relationship between the personal or the individual on the one hand and the social or the historical on the other—or, to put it another way, between experience and history."[60] I rely on Kuhn's reading because in Arias's work there is a constant revisionist position in the approach to what documents may or may not show vis-à-vis individuals and the times and spaces they inhabit.

As Arias explains, this play centers on a generation and its stories, at times of epic strength and at others filled with secrets.[61] These stories changed and transformed over time, as did the play that premiered in 2009 and its iterations over the subsequent five years after that. As long as the actors probe their own memories and their own legal battles with the past, the play keeps on morphing and growing in organic ways. Stories like Vanina Falco's, which began as a theater exercise and later became a legal case against her own father, prove the impact that documentary theater can have as part of a legal action. Other stories also evolved. Carla Crespo finally found out that her father lies buried in a common grave in a cemetery in Avellaneda. Actors Carla Crespo and Pablo Lugones fell in love and had their own child. As a live documentary play, the available space for stories to grow conveys the immediacy that this type of work offers, and, it proclaims documentary theater as a live genre that draws on the present to keep scrutinizing the past. By placing a child and a turtle onstage during this play Arias conveys the possibility of failure or chance that she is willing to risk. Moreover, adding a turtle that is set to decide if there will be a revolution or not in the future of Argentina (an old turtle that belongs to one of the actor's childhood and had to be replaced when it died) helps bring laughter and relief to stories that delineate a traumatic past. Similarly, the idea of chance is also complemented by Mariano's four-year-old son, who rushes onto the stage to sit on his father's lap while listening to the voice recording of his dead grandfather. As Marvin Carlson attests when speaking about the real in the theater, animals "bring to the stage an uncompromised reality that can never been completely under the control of either the actors' or the audience's imaginary world."[62] The same could be said about having a baby or a toddler onstage. Taking a chance with animals and children shows the ambiguous liminal position that Arias wants this play to occupy.

While *Mi vida después* has been the lead play within the trilogy, it is also evident how Arias's documentary modes of expression have led her to consider other ways of telling similar stories. As we will see, in the case of *El año en que nací*, she employs comparable documentary techniques, incorporating childhood photographs and videos to explore the weight of the past these adult children carry as they consider the images vis-à-vis their own recollections of the time. Through a combination of testimonies, manipulation of images, and live music, Arias explores the labyrinths of memory.

El año en que nací

As with the Argentine-focused *Mi vida después*, *El año en que nací* brings together eleven actors and nonactors who grew up during the Chilean dictatorship (1973–1990) to reconstruct and remold their own childhood memories through an array of letters, photographs, and revised or incomplete stories of their parents from this time.[63] Born in a workshop that Arias conducted while *Mi vida después* was part of the Santiago a Mil International Festival in 2011, this play premiered later that same year and was part of the same festival in 2012 and 2013, which coincided with a series dedicated to "Memory 1973–2013."[64] With the commemoration of the fortieth anniversary of the coup led by General Augusto Pinochet—where 3,200 people were killed, 38,000 tortured and hundreds of thousands exiled—the year 2013 marked a significant change in the relationship between the public and politics, "heralding an era of greater social progress, transparency, and justice."[65] Unlike in Argentina, where trials of the military began immediately after democracy was regained in 1983, in Chile President Patricio Aylwin, who took office in 1990, maintained Pinochet's neoliberal economic priorities. As the new democratic government was created under the *Concertación*, a center-left coalition, leaders of the party sought to reconcile and find peaceful ways to move forward instead of proclaiming social justice. Thus, "a consensus-driven series of pacts and negotiations ultimately prohibited Chileans from interrogating their past and confronting their conflicting memories."[66] In 2011, massive student demonstrations mobilized the country to regain the streets and to voice their dissent for the deregulation of education and to reform the education system established by Pinochet and the "Chicago Boys" neoliberal economy that had dismantled public institutions, converting students into high-paying customers.[67] This student movement is considered the strongest confrontation against a government that enforced laws from the dictatorship era, which also propelled a young generation of students to become politicians and take on important roles in the House of Representatives.[68]

The emergence of the questioning of social issues coincided with the inauguration of the Museum of Memory and Human Rights in 2010. When Arias brought *Mi vida después* to Santiago de Chile in 2011, the time was ripe for social upheavals and public demonstrations. As a result, it is no surprise that performers asked the director to create a workshop that would later become the play.[69] The call to future participants makes this clear: "When and where were you born? How was the world at that time? What was your father's occupation at the time? What are your memories of historical facts from your childhood? What newspaper, images or political slogans can you remember today? Do you have any memories from your parent's youth like photographs, letters, tapes, objects?"[70] The call resulted in eleven people from different walks of life; some actors, some musicians and dancers, and—in contrast to *Mi vida después*—all from very different political affiliations and inclinations. They employed a similar method to Arias's previous work by retelling traumatic memories through documentary modes. Through a multimedia, intergenerational play—utilizing their family photographs, video recordings, live music, letters, and an array of documents—each performer seeks to situate his or her life in and around the time period of the Pinochet regime.

It is not my intention here to provide an analysis of how similar or different these plays are.[71] Instead, my argument explores how a similar methodology of documentary theater, propagated by autobiographical stories, is a successful paradigm for presenting childhood memories. Unlike Carol Martin, who argues that performers in this play "attempt to set the record straight about what happened during those years [1973–1990],"[72] I see this play—and every other work that Arias has created within her latest projects—as the construction of an ambiguous space, that gray zone of memory that we cannot completely grasp. There is no clear "straight" story; the manipulation of their archival objects provides them with possible manifestations of what the lives of their parents might have been like during this time.

Arias makes the central focus of this historical documentary play from Chile clear in her program notes: "*El año en que nací* is a piece in which the performers are telling their own family stories: they are reconstructing and imagining the past. The piece is like a big reenactment in which the performers take the role of their parents to reconstruct historic events. . . . The performers are like stunt doubles of their parents, willing to enact the most dangerous scenes in their life."[73] The reconstruction of historical events prompts performers to act, reenact, and experiment. As their political associations (or those of their parents) differ from one another, there is a constant tension between those who are more on the left or on the right of history. Social class and race come up as actors line up according to whose parents made more money or whose complexion is fairer.

Performers frame their stories within Chilean history that begins in 1970, when Salvador Allende came to power through 1989, the year of the plebiscite that gave way to a democratic government and to the present day. Performers bring up their parents' political affiliations in a way to highlight who was more left- or right-leaning, or whose parents were truly heroic. Similar to Vanina Falco's story, where she was able to use her testimony against her own father in court, Viviana Hernández Polanco utilizes theater in order to learn the story of her absent father. Holding up an old photograph of her father, she asked the audience if they had any information about him. Eventually she was able to

Fig. 5. Left to right, Ana Laura Racz, Fernanda González, Alexandra Benado, Ítalo Gallardo, and Pablo Díaz. From Lola Arias's *El año en que nací.* Santiago de Chile, 2012. Photograph by Fundación Teatro a Mil.

find out that her father—who had been a policeman during the repression—was serving a ten-year prison sentence. As a result of Viviana's search for her father, her mother stopped talking to her.[74] The traumatic events still have serious repercussions. It is, perhaps, through Ana Laura Racz's testimony that this documentary play makes another effort to understand the trauma of the past. Ana explains that her mother, who had belonged to the Movimiento de Izquierda Revolucionaria (MIR; Leftist Revolutionary Movement), is still undergoing trauma and is in need of constant psychological help.[75]

Staged in a school-like production full of lockers, school desks, and maps, *El año en que nací* reproduces the setting of a history lesson. With the massive student demonstrations that were taking place in 2011, the backdrop of a school adds to the complexity of this play. Some performers make direct references to how much money they owe on their student loans and how debt is one of their major concerns. The performance portrays the distance between those whose families were exiled and those who were not; it conveys notions of how generations of this era dealt with family breakups and deceptions; it plays with the idea of chance that the future holds by tossing a coin to know if the presidential elections will go to the left or to the right. (see fig. 5). Thus, Arias's documentary theater creates an ambiguous relationship between the past, the present, and the future where different voices of a generation who were silent speak up in their own way and their own terms.

While *Mi vida después y otros textos* is a key example of how documentary modes help to tell a story of traumatic times during the dictatorship, it is also evident that Arias's historical approach to Argentina's recent past is central in her work. The Malvinas/Falklands War was another traumatic moment catalyzed by just how far the dictators were willing to go.

Malvinas/Falklands War

On April 2, 1982, I wasn't feeling well and stayed home from school in Buenos Aires. As I was sitting at the dining room table and watching TV, a sudden wave of breaking news interrupted regular programming: Argentina had invaded the Malvinas Islands and was thereby contesting Great Britain's claim to the Falkland Islands, which had been in effect since 1833.[76] In a televised event, the de facto president under the military junta, General Leopoldo Galtieri, came out of the Casa Rosada and walked among the thousands of euphoric people who gathered at the historic Plaza de Mayo square, as if to portray himself as a common, heroic man. With many congratulatory slaps on this back, he ascended to the balcony to speak and proclaimed that the Malvinas were back in Argentina's hands, where they belonged.

I was only twelve years old then, but the nationalistic fervor that this invasion generated could be seen and felt everywhere during the seventy-four-day-long war. Later, when more Argentine troops were sent to the islands to combat the British retaliation, schools, churches, and community centers asked all of us to knit, sew and send candy, clothes, jewels, letters—whatever we could do to help our soldiers in need. I still remember getting together with friends, sewing scarves, wrapping short letters around chocolates, and getting others to contribute as well. As far as I knew, we were going to win the war, or at least the idea of what we imagined the Malvinas war was. As Rosana Guber explains, this war had "the capacity to embody 'Argentinianness' much more than any other symbol," and it thus served as a strong metaphor of national unity and as a community of belonging, where citizens felt part of the equation.[77] It was, after all, a great way for the military junta to create national fervor, when they had not much more to pander. The Malvinas Islands became a strong political symbol that united everyone and every political party: it was a just cause to recapture what Argentines felt was their own, and an emblematic fight against an imperialist force.[78] Many of us, myself included, fell for the farce. We believed we were winning the war in the South Atlantic, as it was heralded in state-controlled media.[79] We believed our soldiers were receiving good care as well as the supplies being sent to them. Only later did we find out that most of the food and other supplies were stationed at Puerto Argentino and never reached the troops. Essentially, we believed in the show the junta staged.

It was a performance, a mise-en-scène choreographed when Galtieri summoned thousands of people to the square, when he walked among them stoking the nationalist fervor and inciting public imagination of victory. With the help of state-controlled media, the military junta orchestrated the illusion that they were winning the war.[80] In reality, Argentine soldiers were sent with little to no training; the majority of them averaged eighteen years of age, were conscripts, not professionals (military service was mandatory then), and barely had any previous formal understanding of military equipment or battles. Most certainly had never fought in a full-fledged war. Some soldiers did not even know they were being sent to war until they were on a plane to the islands. So while imagination brewed new waves of patriotism over the regained idea of sovereignty, the Malvinas/Falklands became a real, violent, and destructive short-lived war that took many lives on both sides.[81] The war ended on June 14, 1982. The military junta dissolved after this devastating loss, and democracy was finally back in October 1983.

For the British, the story of success strengthened the conservative government of Prime Minister Margaret Thatcher, who had garnered public support for the war and gained confidence in the new nationalistic stage. The post-Falklands mood, or the "Falklands Factor," gave her and her party an edge, and Thatcherism gained momentum.[82] Thus, both governments used this war as a way to gain popularity. It worked for Thatcher, and she was reelected.

Cultural Production of Malvinas

Today, almost forty years after the war, cultural production about Malvinas is a strong reminder of these events and their impact. Novels, films, plays, and short stories relate fragments of the war, some more gruesome, some with real testimonies, and some resort to fictional settings. As Julieta Vitullo states, due to its political ambiguities little scholarly research focused on the Malvinas/Falklands conflict; instead, fiction delved more deeply into questions about the violence and its social impact on soldiers and civilians.[83] Public fascination with the islands persists as well on the streets, at schools, and on murals, where slogans *Las Malvinas son argentinas* (The Falklands are Argentine) are easily found. The nationalist fervor that this war created, during the most violent and cruel dictatorship in Argentina's history, was a way for society to come together in what many were led to believe was a "just cause." Retaliation against Britain, a longtime occupier of the islands that most Argentines see as part of the national territory, was seen as a real reason to go to war.

However, after the war, and during the postdictatorship period from 1983 to 2003, a public political stand on the Malvinas was hardly seen, and according to historian Federico Lorenz a "demalvinization" began. Only the veterans' associations seemed interested in keeping the Malvinas conflict in the public's eye, in part to help veterans collect benefits owed to them. This "demalvinization" started once the war was lost and resulted from the fact that when veterans came back from the islands, they were kept out of the public eye by the armed forces to be fed and cleaned up so that the public would think they were well taken care of during combat. Veterans were also forced to sign a kind of nondisclosure agreement. The idea of "demalvinaizing" the war was also a strategy meant to align this conflict with the dictatorship and legitimize the military junta and the armed forces actions as needed.[84] Veterans, in a sense, were also "demalvinaized" and left with little to no support, as society at large preferred to forget the conflict.[85]

It wasn't until 2003 that Malvinas became part of the national discourse as an antiimperialist symbol of retaliation. Together with different human rights associations, such as the Interamerican Commission of Human Rights, the Community of Latin American and Caribbean States, and the Union of South American Nations, the Malvinas became the new political bastion for Argentine sovereignty under Néstor Kirchner's government (2003–2007) and continued with Cristina Fernández de Kirchner (2007–2015). In 2014, for instance, a new museum, the Museo de Malvinas, was inaugurated inside the former Mechanical School of the Navy, the biggest torture center during the last dictatorship, and in 2004 was converted into a "Space for Memory." After many years of silencing and forgetting, the Malvinas veterans were finally recognized by important institutions and organizations who made them legitimate historical actors. Nevertheless, Malvinas is still a difficult topic for Argentina. As Lorenz states, because this war was triggered by a dictatorship, the military junta and all of the democratic governments thereafter have been forced to mesh the reality of violent dictators' legacy with the just cause of fighting British occupation since 1833.[86] The legacy of regaining the Malvinas as a just cause overshadowed by an inhumane military government has been a tricky obstacle to overcome. Thus, the topic of Malvinas remains contentious and politically charged even today; the utopic ideal of recuperating the archipelago that has been in the hands of the British for 180 years also persists.

As stated before, fictional representations are probably the best vehicle for speaking and writing about this war. Since the first picaresque novel by Rodolfo Fogwill, *Los Pichiciegos* (*Malvinas Requiem*, 1983), a large number of subsequent novels, films, plays, and short stories have come forward with testimonies, autobiographies, and fictional stories about this war. Important films that provide both a historical overview and a powerful understanding of the psychological effects the veterans suffered include Bebe Kamin's film *Los chicos de la guerra* (*The Kids of the War*, 1984), based on Daniel Kon's novel of the same title; Carlos Gamerros's *Las islas* (*The Islands*, 1998); José Luis Marqués's *Fuckland* (2000); Tristan Bauer's *Iluminados por el fuego* (*Blessed by Fire*, 2005); Patricio Pron's *Una puta mierda* (*A Fucking Shit*, 2007); Julio Cardoso's *Locos de la bandera* (*Crazy about the Flag*,

2012); and Edgardo Dieleke and Daniel Casabé's *La forma exacta de las islas* (*The Exact Shape of the Islands*, 2012).[87] While some writers and directors sought to explore a historical or testimonial angle to representing the war, others contributed a more nuanced and even humorous approach. Marin Launfenberg's study on the Malvinas conflict investigates how humor in theater pieces such as Julio Cardoso's *Islas de la memoria: Historias de guerra en la posguerra* (*Memory Islands: History of War in the Postwar*, 2011) or *Continente viril* (*Manly Continent*, 2000) by the group Los Macocos work through laughter and humor to connect to the audience in a different way.[88] More recently, theater scholar, Ricardo Dubatti has edited three volumes that compile plays focusing on the Malvinas War.[89] Literary production from Argentina has not only been more abundant than in Britain; it is also part of Argentine national discourse and memory politics. As Jordana Blejmar states: "The growing interest in both the war and the postwar in Argentine theater is also not surprising if we remember that even though this was a relatively short military confrontation, it is one that has not really ended."[90] Perhaps a better example of how cultural production about the islands has permeated many different spaces of Argentine culture can be seen in the words of British veteran and performer in *Campo minado*, Lou Armour, in these lines from the play: "When I arrived in Buenos Aires for the rehearsals, I was shocked: The Malvinas was everywhere: T-shirts, car bumper stickers, wall murals, photographs down the corridor of a children's hospital. We don't really talk much about the Falklands in the UK. And British schoolchildren don't learn about the Falklands War."[91]

After the War

In 2014, with an invitation by the British festival LIFT (London International Festival of Theatre) to produce an original work in a series titled *After a War*, Arias, one among twenty-five other international artists, began collecting testimonies for a video installation about the Malvinas/Falklands War, titled *Veterans*, that would later become part of a Cycle of War, which also includes *Campo minado* (2016) and the subsequent film, *Theatre of War* (2018).[92] This project has undergone a noteworthy evolution: it began as a video installation, transformed into an extremely successful transnational play, and ended as a film. The director sees her shows as "living creatures that evolve," which explains why she seems to prefer to work in threes, as we have seen with the different trilogies she created.[93] Despite the vast number of films, plays, and novels that the Malvinas war has inspired, none has explored the human side of the war so sharply as this one. In this work, six veterans on opposing sides, who tried to kill each other during war, now come together to narrate and reenact each other's stories onstage.[94] Indeed, each veteran speaks and commemorates his own traumatic past and present through testimonies, facts,

Fig. 6. Kneeling, left to right, Marcelo Vallejo, Lou Armour; standing, left to right, Gabriel Sagastume, David Jackson, Sukrim Rai, Rubén Otero. In Lola Arias's *Campo minado / Minefield*. Publicity still. Buenos Aires, 2016. Photograph by Manuel Abramovich.

documents, and anecdotes. With the help of playful masks, authentic letters, photographs, magazines of the time, and live band music, these six veterans assist each other through reenactments to explore their story about this war in an honest approach that combines humor with sordid stories about their time on the islands.

The cast of *Campo minado* includes Marcelo Vallejo, a triathlon champion and the only Argentine soldier in this play who volunteered to go fight in the Malvinas; Gabriel Sagastume, a retired criminal lawyer; and Rubén Otero, the only *Belgrano* cruiser survivor onstage, who has a printing press and is also a drummer in his own Beatles tribute band. On the British side, there is Lou Armour, who is now a special needs teacher; David Jackson, a psychologist who specializes in treating veterans of war; and Sukrim Rai, a Gurkha soldier born in Nepal who fought for the British and later traveled the world as a professional private security person (see fig. 6). As Arias states, the six of them "ended up becoming a group of performers sharing their memories and helping each other in the scenes," thus creating a stronger bond between them than the war. As one of them later pointed out, the rehearsals lasted longer than the short-lived war.[95]

In her opening installation, *Veterans*, Arias begins with simple questions that are the foundational parts of exploring the aftermath of war: "What does it mean to be a veteran of a war: having fought, having killed, having seen death and having survived? What does the experience of war turn into over time?"[96] Five Argentine veterans respond through testimony and reenactments directed toward the camera that films them. They each choose their strongest memory of the war to reenact them in his current environment: the past reenacted in the present. Because "theatre is an experience and not a spectacle," Arias's Cycle of War is created through the weight of affect, memory, and trauma these stories bring to life.[97] Through reenactment, she explores a way to re-create, re-member, and reconsider how these veterans' bodies acted, and how their actions (and probably good luck) made them survivors and not casualties. And as Arias claims, "I like theatre that has the power to make you believe that you didn't go see a show but, rather, that you lived an experience. That means that you *were* there, in a place where something *actually* happened."[98] For the play, and after auditioning around sixty other veterans from each side, Arias maintained the same idea of having veterans tell their own stories through reenactments, but this time it would be a live event instead of a film. During casting and interviews she asked veterans to think of the one image that had been fossilized in their memory, thus pushing her work beyond a historical or military representation, and instead remaking what veterans remember and what the war did to them.[99] Only one performer, Marcelo Vallejo, remained from the video *Veterans* and became one of the six final men chosen for the stage production. With this three-part product (video installation, play, and film), Arias has explored different modes of production relating to autobiographical stories made through the re-creation of testimonies from the Malvinas/Falklands War. And while my analysis will focus primarily on the play, I will also take into consideration a holistic approach to Arias's Cycle of War by referring, when appropriate, to *Veterans* and *Theatre of War*.

Campo minado / Minefield

In November 2016, Lola Arias premiered *Campo minado / Minefield* in an empty warehouse that belongs to the Center of Experimental Arts from the Universidad Nacional de San Martín (UNSAM) in Buenos Aires.[100] After a very successful run at the Brighton Festival and the Royal Court Theatre in London, expectations were high in theatergoing circles of Buenos Aires.[101] Because tickets were free (although reservations were needed and were very difficult to get), the nontheatrical venue of the Center of Experimental Arts instantly became a place for "underground" performance, where artists and scholars alike lined up for this highly anticipated production that ran for only one month (a short time by Argentine standards). The large empty warehouse was quickly adapted for the theater: bleachers for about four hundred people were added, lights were mounted, and all theatrical props were brought in: a white triangular mobile base became part of the stage where performers could step in and out of to speak or play musical instruments, depending on their roles. As a spectator myself, I found the open space a welcome addition to this story. All the theatrical props were visible (film cameras, screens, masks, military jackets, music instruments), and the absence of static theater seating made it less polished and provided a sense of a work-in-progress performance where errors, vulnerability, and the impossibility of hiding meant constant exposure of the performers. As spectators, the idea of proximity, of being close to each other (there was no room left on the bleachers or floors or in the aisles) gave us a sense of a temporary community. Our community as audience grew out of both geographic as well as political proximity, because, as the director correctly claims, "in Argentina everyone [still] talks about the Falklands/Malvinas."[102] But beyond a physical proximity, this play helped us to understand feelings and emotions of closeness, what Jill Dolan refers to as utopian performatives, where strangers are receptive to emotion.[103] In this play, spectators are confronted with the rawness of seeing and hearing real-life veterans from both sides, where tensions, disagreements, and misunderstandings are part of the play.

Having the UNSAM support this performance for free was a way for the institution to make a stand in a national political climate that had dramatically reduced funding for public institutions. It was also the only institution that was willing to sponsor this performance, due to its incendiary political content. In an interview, Arias recounted that when she approached theatrical spaces in Argentina to cofinance *Campo minado*, she found herself explaining that the play did not focus on the topic of sovereignty; it was mainly about the effects of war in soldiers and its aftermath. Resistance also came from veterans who could not fathom the idea of seeing British veterans next to Argentines.[104]

The dual title possibly affected the way the Argentine institutions understood the content of the play and thus financial support was denied at the time.[105] A noteworthy detail is the slash between Spanish and English. The double Malvinas/Falklands reinforces the division as a representation of what the islands mean to each nation. The same dichotomy is mirrored by Arias's Spanish/English divide, *Campo minado / Minefield*, to highlight the nature of the ongoing linguistic division of the islands' names. I call attention to this slash, to this gap, because it is exactly where Arias wanted to work: in the space fraught with misunderstanding. She explores both languages, both stories, and both sides of the political spectrum. Language, translation, and the undecipherable also become key concepts in a project about misunderstandings. She reveals these spaces through songs that pertain to each culture and asks her audience to think about how stories are formed through language. Even how one refers to the islands reveals one of the many tensions:

> LOU: We call these the Falkland Islands.
> GABRIEL: We call them Islas Malvinas.[106]

Language is also the focus of the play from the beginning, when Marcelo Vallejo explains, "The Brits don't speak Spanish, we Argentines don't speak English. But somehow we understood each other."[107] Both languages are spoken at all times. Translation, via supertitles, becomes an important factor in this play, as Jean Graham-Jones explores the effect that the access to language (or lack thereof) may have, and how it causes challenges to spectatorship, creating a gap. It is precisely the gap, the in-between, that Arias seeks to create. Not everything is translated. For instance, when music is played in English or when Sukrim Rai sings a Nepali song or closes the play with a poem in his own language without supertitles. Here Arias highlights what Graham-Jones refers to as a "testament to cultural untranslatability" that "disturb[s] the Malvinas/Falklands binational archive."[108] Translation is necessary to fully understand both sides of the story, and the testimonies, but I would also add that for Arias the stage reveals the limits of translatability; it becomes an unstable shared space that welcomes vulnerability, fragility, misunderstandings, as well as compassion and empathy that can be sensed beyond language. Sometimes language is not primary; documents, photographs, clothing, music make a stronger connection without the need to translate.

With her documentary approach to telling a story, Arias begins the play by staging a casting-like scene, where cameras and a large screen are present. Onscreen, vets metatheatrically audition for their roles, answering basic questions about name, age, title, and rank during the war, as well as current profession. Each of them plays the roles of the interviewer as well as the interviewee, creating a constant theatrical need among them and a sense of comradery that will take place in various reenactments throughout the play. They ask and answer questions about why and how they joined the military and about whether they ever had to kill or witness a killing on the battlefield, and they describe what their lives were like after returning from the war and what their lives are like today. It is clear from the start that facts and fiction commingle. As María Delgado states, "*Minefield* is in many ways about modes of narrating history. It eschews an 'edited highlights' approach in favour of retelling of lived experience[s]."[109] The large screen and the obvious mechanical apparatus of filming prompt the audience to question not only how to distinguish what is artificial from what is real, but also how to promote the modes of narrating their own stories.

The human factor in representing veterans' memories can also be gauged by the sense of surprise or lack of preparation of the Argentine soldiers who were sent to war. From the beginning, it is also obvious that the British veterans were trained soldiers who volunteered to join forces to fight in this war, emphasizing, too, the role of Sukrim Rai as a professional Gurkha fighter. By contrast, the Argentine soldiers for the most part were eighteen-year-old conscripts who had been sent with little to no training and without the right equipment for war.[110] As Gabriel states, "I didn't want to be a soldier. But in Argentina military service was mandatory until 1995."[111] The discrepancy between trained, enlisted soldiers and conscripts with no knowledge of military action becomes one of the major angles of this work, where Arias relies on how testimonies are constructed and how memories, documents, and authentic material become part but *not all* of the story to tell where post-traumatic stress lingers and gets reconstructed through the stage.

According to Deirdre Heddon, performance becomes a "tempting (and dangerous) medium through which to make claims for the 'real' or 'truthful' self" because it never loses its ground "*as performance*," thus making the point that indeed "performance is *not* the real world."[112] In this regard, this cycle of war is an example of how documentary practices help us relate to these veterans' stories while also fomenting from the beginning (through the "casting scene") that what we are seeing is theater, film, or an installation, and thus fictional. As fiction and documentary practice, this hybrid manipulates and makes us aware of the tension between the two, of the "contamination" that exists between facts and fiction.[113] However, within the array of fictional products that the Malvinas War has spawned, Arias's piece represents the first time an artist has explored the two opposing sides of the story on the *same* stage, where the idea of constructing this story is based on facts, memories, testimonies, and documentation, but it is also part of a communal and understanding relationship between six veterans who would or could have killed each other but are now friends. As Arias makes clear, this type of work is "more like a social experiment" that invites a "new community that will produce specific accounts about a historical moment."[114] I would also underscore the fact that this group works as a team. They physically assist each other onstage (moving props, helping each other dress or undress, and playing as a band), and this in turn contributes to memory building. Veterans, whether they are Nepali, English, or Argentine, help each other act and reenact scenes, all of them performing other soldiers, and other memories, an embodiment through reenactment that is central to Arias's success in documenting and staging their stories. As Elizabeth Jelin succinctly states, "One does not remember alone but with the help of the memories of others and of shared cultural codes, even when personal memories are unique and distinct. . . . All memories are more reconstructions than recollections."[115] Having two opposing sides onstage, speaking and listening now as enemies-cum-friends, helps the vets reconstruct their memories within a different context. The spatiotemporal distance from the war, as Jordana Blejmar states, allows for a postwar narrative in which these veterans are able to explore each other's memories in a collective and productive way that was not possible before.[116]

As with other plays and productions previously discussed, *Campo minado* relies on autobiographical performance. This genre expands the notion of just storytelling and adds weight to biographical stories as it brings together six veterans in real time to reenact their own stories. They put on their old uniforms and work through traumatic times with the help of their "enemies" onstage. In this play autobiographical performance expands mere biographical exploration, because "the veteran is both witness and survivor, subverting any realistic representation."[117] Fact and fiction are in constant tension, while historical documents as well as playful manipulation of photographs, video, and toys urge a destabilization of personal and collective memories. This play, then, deals with the aftermath of the war through a collective examination of accounts offered by perspectives of six witnesses, thus "avoiding a Manichean reading" of the war and "fostering instead a more productive relationship between past, present, and future."[118] Through autobiographical performance, this play exposes private stories of oppression and silencing to the public; it creates a productive and engaging atmosphere among the veterans and the spectator; it prompts scrutiny of what constitutes historical fact; and it uses performance as a medium to explore how veterans (and spectators) might process their own past and present.

Testimonial Stages

After the Malvinas/Falklands War, the Argentine conscript soldiers were told not to speak of the war. As I noted earlier, the transitional government in place after the military junta preferred not to speak of the war either, and society at large turned toward a more hopeful future. Through this larger project and thirty-five years later, Arias opened up the door for testimonials to take center stage. First, with her video installation *Veterans*, where five Argentine veterans speak and reenact some of their memories in front of a camera; next with an installation, *Doble de riesgo*, at the Parque de la Memoria; then through the play *Campo minado*; and finally in a film version, *Theatre of War / Teatro de guerra*, she shows how these performers become actors in their own stories. However, it is in *Campo minado* that testimony is performed live. In their testimonial roles veterans have a chance to be affected by the ephemeral theatrical community that each of their performances creates and to relate to their fellow actor-veterans now, after many years have passed. As Heddon suggests, autobiographical performance is a collective affair that will "have an impact on the representation of that autobiography or the re-presentation of self."[119] She goes even further, in fact, contending that by its own nature autobiographical performance is unstable because it tries to retain "the real as a reference point" while also engaging in an ambivalence that subverts the form and still relies on its "rhetorical function for political effect."[120] This ambivalence between self and other, between the real story and the possible manipulation of its political effect, create the tension that Arias's documentary theater thrives on. A clear point of reference in Lola Arias's work is casting real veterans who have not been trained as professional actors to collectively build their testimonies. The function of autobiographical performance, then, takes a step forward, and as a result, all testimony is also helped by others and other stories. The threading of stories and the need to physically reenact some of the unspeakable give authentic materials their own context and story. Photographs, letters, and videos become tools to build a story through the unveiling of traumatic events that are shared with the spectators, and once again, documentary objects become their own protagonists.

At the end of the twentieth century and the beginning of the twenty-first, an age of testimony of bearing witness proliferated.[121] In Latin America, testimony is arguably one of the most notable forms for narrating traumatic times and a wide range of human rights abuses.[122] Indeed, as scholars frequently point out, testimony and trauma seem to be linked and inseparable from one another.[123] In her insights about the act of writing, Susan Henke asserts that "it is through the very process of rehearsing and reenacting drama of mental survival that the trauma narrative effects psychological catharsis."[124] When testimony and theater are combined, there is a more affective and close connection that can have adversarial effects on the veterans/performers. The double-edged sword of exploring autobiographies through performance "encourages the practitioner to use the pretexts of memory; the traces of the past that remain in the present, as raw material in the production of *new* stories about the past. They may also transform the ways individuals and communities live in and relate to the present and the future."[125] In the aftermath of this war, veterans construct their own stories about the past; they also, through the shared space of theater, "transform" not just their own perceptions of their memories but the spectators' as well. Empathy and affect surround the stage, the veterans, and the spectators alike. Not only is testimony one of the main mechanisms that exposes each ex-combatant's vulnerability onstage; all of them are also on the same platform and share some of the same fears. This forces a bond of comradery, or, as Cecilia Sosa puts it, suggests a "more emphatic form of citizenship."[126] Live testimony emphasizes the vulnerability of spectators as well. Some brought their own memories of war, and watching these soldiers onstage brought them to tears. On a personal note, I had not heard the Malvinas song, nor had I seen the magazines with the captions that said we were winning the war, since the 1980s. All of a sudden, after seeing and hearing these pieces of propaganda again, I was back in 1982, watching it all unfold before me, and I had tears in my eyes. I was moved by the spectacle of what the war had meant to all of us.

Behind the Scenes

During rehearsals in Buenos Aires, five months before the premiere of the play in London, veterans underwent a strenuous and cathartic regimen of remembering, sharing, and speaking about the war. This became a safe space where testimonies were accompanied by documentary material that they each shared while also keeping personal diaries to be read and reworked by the veterans with the director. The many hours of rehearsals were also filmed, and some would later become part of *Theatre of War / Teatro de guerra*. Under these regimented and long rehearsals, one of the British veterans, Lou Armour, needed psychological therapy to overcome the post-traumatic stress that the unveiling and sharing of stories was causing him. This fact is later incorporated into the play, first with Lou confirming that in Buenos Aires, therapy is a welcome addition to everyday life.

> LOU: During rehearsals some questions brought back memories of something in my past that I never told anybody about. I began to have sleepless nights, flashbacks. My mind would just go wandering off. I'd never had therapy before, never even considered it. But in Argentina visiting a shrink is more common than dancing tango. So I thought I'd give it a go.[127]

Even though Arias succeeds in telling their stories, in projecting a new space for the autobiographical to be staged, it is also a slippery slope. As Lou acknowledges, speaking out made his traumatic memories return and led him to seek therapy.

In her seminal work *The Limits of Autobiography*, Leigh Gilmore examines what she calls "limit cases" of autobiographies, where she poses that through "first-person writing about trauma . . . we are able to discern the limit testing about form and subjectivity that the self-representation of trauma entails."[128] In her analysis, she asserts that "language fails in the face of trauma and that trauma mocks language and confronts it with its insufficiency."[129] However, she also points to the assertiveness of conscious language and the role it has when a witness relates a traumatic event. Thus, "the unconscious language of repetition through which trauma initially speaks (flashbacks, nightmare, emotional flooding) is replaced by a conscious language that can be repeated in structured settings."[130] There is certainly a risk when casting real war survivors, and there is also a need for the veterans to talk, to be heard, to make a connection with the audience. While Gilmore's attention is given to written autobiographies, it is useful to think about the limits of self-representation onstage. When dealing with first-person autobiographical performances done by interpreters, who are not professional actors but ex-combatants, how high are the stakes?

Staging the Real

As with some autobiographical narratives, like *I, Rigoberta Menchú* (where testimony is perceived as less than faithful, and which caused controversy regarding authenticity in testimonial writing), much documentary theater of the twenty-first century seems to rejoice in ambiguous spaces. Arias's work, an ambivalent space that mixes humor, conviviality, and fiction with somber testimony from the war, might be one of the few ways for audiences to hear difficult stories from the past. For instance, in the scene appropriately titled "Therapy," Marcelo, the champion triathlete, and David, the psychologist, sit facing one another onstage to simulate a therapy session, where both performers take time to ask the other about their states of mind. It is here that the audience learns about Marcelo's attempt to commit suicide and about David's detachment and depression when he returned from the war. Both veterans open up about their need to return to the islands, to walk on that rocky land, and to pay their respects to their fallen friends. David states after finding a photograph of his friend who died in the Falklands: "I didn't realise what a great friend he was when I was younger. So I returned to say goodbye. He was killed in a helicopter crash, there's no grave. So I stood on the edge of San Carlos water and said goodbye."[131] Even with this solemn scene, an ambiguous approach can be seen through humor when Marcelo jokingly asks David how much this "session" will cost. David responds in kind: "Well, I charge fifty pounds for civilians. I charge twenty-five pounds for veterans and their families. For you, Marcelo, it's free."[132] Here the spectator does not fact-check the content; rather, the authenticity of the moment, of the affect, makes her sit on the edge of her seat.[133]

For different vets in the production, performing in front of a live audience had both benefits and drawbacks. Lou Armour has confessed that while he loves acting, which he views as an extension of his work as a teacher, he is not so sure about performing in front of veterans. Others, like Sukrim Rai, found rehearsals very difficult, even more grueling than the war, as he acknowledges in an interview: "The Falklands war was not hard for me. I know what the army is. I know my job, my duty. But when I went to Buenos Aires, I didn't know. I lost it. I couldn't sleep for three days. What is my job?"[134] Onstage, Sukrim often seems to be an observer instead of a protagonist, someone who is always on the outskirts of the play, of the English/Spanish communication binary. As a professional Gurkha soldier, he knew what his role was when it was about combat.[135] As a performer, however, he found it difficult to understand. A clear communication struggle is emphasized in the film version, *Theatre of War*, where during rehearsals for the play, Sukrim Skypes with his mother to explain that he feels that he can't perform, that "sometimes it is difficult because of the language, because of Argentinian language and English makes it difficult. I get lost."[136] This candid moment—which works as a reality TV scene—not only exposes the doubts that Sukrim had about his work as a performer but also portrays what has been "staged" before our eyes.

How real is this moment? Are his doubts about going on with theater authentic? Or is this part of the whole process of documenting a scene that seems truthful and personal (while cameras are rolling)? While the staged versus the real as a concept can be endlessly analyzed, the focus here is the sense of vulnerability and fragility. Perhaps it is through the film *Theatre of War / Teatro de guerra* that Arias more thoroughly examines these questions. As an Argentine director, she is not an objective observer when it comes to the topic of Malvinas. In the film, one scene is especially poignant in this regard: over beers in a bar, the two British veterans talk about how they feel like pawns, since the project is after all Argentine. Again, the reality TV type of scene is staged and designed by Arias to relay a conversation the British vets often had with each other. For Arias, this scene demonstrates the overlap of what is real and what becomes staged in *Theatre of War / Teatro de guerra*, because the whole team "intervenes in the real, they decide and choose which situations to tell" relying on how real conflicts can actually be staged as such.[137] The result is a staged documentary film that explores real issues and concerns that took place during rehearsals, promoting the ambiguous relationship between fiction and reality, theater and film. For the director, the play borrows from a cinematographic documentary mode (using technology, screens, video, speaking directly to the audience), while the film version takes from the theater, employing ideas about staging concepts and methods of acting. But it also enhances the notions and abilities the theater can show by adding nontheater locations and casting younger doubles for an outdoor reenactment, as I will explore later.

For Sukrim, the soldier who does not fit the binary of the two nations, the possibility of making mistakes, of getting it wrong, of being out of sync, is where the rawness of the theater may become more tangible, more real. What are the possibilities of getting something wrong and seeing it onstage? As he states, he fears forgetting what to say or how to say it. Here, what is unpolished might engage the audience in a direct way. Sukrim positions himself outside the binary, as someone who does not entirely fit within either of the two nations. His language fails him at times, but his careful and quick movements do not. In fact, he communicates best through his kukri, a Gurkha knife that gives him the flexibility to move around and demonstrate the role he played during the war.

The Limits of Language

Campo minado also exposes moments when speech is fragile. One example is when Rubén speaks of his experience as one of the survivors of the *Belgrano* cruiser bombing. The ship was hit by an illegal attack that killed 323 Argentine soldiers, half of the total numbers of Argentine casualties for the entire war. Through reenactments onstage, we get a sense of the ocean as one of the veterans splashes water in a bucket. We even see smoke and hear shouts to abandon the ship. However, after the veterans work in unison to recreate the scene, Lou, the English vet, adds, "We were relieved to hear that the

Belgrano had been hit, because she was a well-armed threat. We didn't care if it was turning away, because she could have turned back and attacked us."[138] Although the *Belgrano* cruiser was outside the two hundred nautical miles of the exclusion zone and thus should not have been bombed, we hear vets stand their ground as they defend their army's decision to sink the ship. We also see Rubén's desperation and inability to communicate through speech. Instead he shouts out abuses and punctuates them with his drum rolls while he acknowledges the lives of the 323 dead soldiers. Music is the only possible means of communication in that moment. Even though Rubén can shout out the abuses committed against soldiers, the scene is emotionally overwhelming, and similar to the scene in *Mi vida después*, when Carla Crespo's drum solo conveys the pain of the knowledge that she is now older than her father when he was killed.

The impossibility of speech triggers a bodily reaction, and in these two cases music is the medium through which to cope with this inability. Walter Benjamin writes:

> Language has unmistakably made plain that memory is not an instrument for exploring the past, but rather a medium. It is the medium of that which is experienced, just as the earth is the medium in which ancient cities lie buried. He who seeks to approach his own buried past must conduct himself like a man digging. Above all, he must not be afraid to return again and again to the same matter; to scatter it as one scatters earth, to turn it over as one turns over soil.[139]

The metaphor of digging through the past becomes even stronger in a play titled *Minefield*, where soldiers unearth battle stories in front of each other using memory as a medium for representation. While language at times fails, as we witnessed with Rubén, veterans still find entertaining ways to relate gruesome events and sift through their own recollections.

We experience this when Gabriel tells us a story about hunger and devastation. With a model of a toy house projected on the backdrop, toy soldiers and sounds of wind and water made by other veterans onstage, Gabriel shows us how soldiers were blown up in a minefield when they went to steal food from a nearby house: "When they come out, they see a wooden boat on the river. They decide to load the things into the boat. . . . They lift the boat on to their heads and start to walk. And suddenly, an explosion."[140] Later, only body parts were found, and Gabriel claims that he recognized the leg of his friend by the football socks he was wearing. Gabriel adds: "Much later we found out that the field had been mined by the Argentine army at the beginning of the war. But no one ever told us."[141] The whimsical model and the toy soldiers, along with the made-up sounds of nature, help alleviate the heavy burden of just using words. Furthermore, the idea of reenacting the scene through toys, filmed and projected onto the larger screen, showcases Arias's tendency to rely on documentary theater techniques to tell a true story while she also deviates from the grisly nature of what is being retold.

Reenactments

In a play, war veterans as performers and reenactors (both in the theatrical sense of reembodying a person onstage as well as the basic fact of reenacting a war) become the essence and the foundation for understanding how archival memory is and can be reperformed in repetition. Arias relies on the use of reenactments in her work as a way to infuse theatrical practices with multifaceted notions of temporality that the reenactment harbors. As Rebecca Schneider suggests in her studies about the U.S. Civil War, "The experience of reenactment is an intense, embodied inquiry into temporal repetition, temporal recurrence."[142] The focus on temporality, on the question of "What if time (re)turns?," is a cornerstone in much of Arias's work.[143] In other words, what is central in *Campo minado* and in much of her other work is what Schneider sees as "a constant (re)turn of, to, from, and between states in animation."[144] For instance, the six vets in *Campo minado* position themselves in a crossed temporality—an axis for memory, testimony, trauma, place, and acting—to excavate forgotten or obscure moments of war. Unlike in other reenactments, where actors embody historical soldiers from wars (as with the U.S. Civil War reenactments, for instance), here, we are faced with what I would call *present reenactments* via the same bodies that experienced the war they are presenting. Thus, as spectators, we witness the veterans' own reenactments "in the leak of another time, or in a syncopated temporal relationship to the event," but without the fake representation of other bodies that did not experience the original event.[145] Still, the positioning and repositioning of these six veterans pushes the limits of the authenticity question, of the fact that a performance is never as authentic as the event on which it is based. This is true even for the vets who re-perform the original event they experienced. While Schneider's focus is on Civil War renactments, she contends that reenactment "not only engages the uncanny (and theatrical properties of the double, the clone, the second, or even simply 'other' people), but also challenges the given *placedness* of an original through re-placedness, challenging the singular attributes of the auratic and 'timelessness' of 'master' through the mimetic problem-magic of the *live*."[146] It is precisely the re-placing of the present into the past through vivid expositions of memory that each of the soldiers remembers, thus their bodies record and re-record the past. The live version of their own memories onstage, the present placedness, positions their own bodies to retake and to refashion movements and events so that the audience, as well as the other veterans onstage, see, feel, understand, and are affected by their stories. Thus, they all help each other reenact their memories; they all become stagehands and assistants to relay stories.

Throughout the play, memories are collectively shared while they are also informed by digital and media visuals. Understanding the complexity of private memories, vis-à-vis the recorded fragments of film, magazine covers, or even original speeches by government officials, exposes the complexity of how we remember but also how corporality, those bodies onstage—can help record and refashion memory. Thus, reenactments of war, and of politicians also, demonstrate how bodies can re-create the past on a live stage. With grotesquely real masks, two vets reenact General Galtieri's and Prime Minister Thatcher's actual speeches right after Argentina's occupation of the islands. While we hear a recording of the original speeches given by Thatcher at the House of Commons and by Galtieri from the balcony of the Casa Rosada, two vets don the Galtieri and Thatcher masks and mimic their respective speeches. The masks, as British reviewers have noted, recall the popular TV show *Spitting Images*, a political and satirical show that mocked Thatcher.[147] A screen on the background enlarges their images and their own national flags behind them:

> DAVID AS THATCHER: (*miming*) Mr. Speaker, Sir . . . we are here because, for the first time for many years, British sovereign territory has been invaded by a foreign power . . . Mr. Speaker, I'm sure that the whole House will join me in condemning totally this unprovoked aggression by the Government of Argentina against the British territory . . . the people [of the Falklands] were in tears. They do not want to be Argentine.
>
> GABRIEL AS GALTIERI: (*miming*) . . . The Argentine government and the Argentine people in this open council have reason to be outraged and pile offence on offence. If they want to come, let them come. We will give them battle.[148]

Their reenactments, different from other interventions, do not belong to their own bodies and their own stories. Now David and Gabriel interact with prerecorded material to stage their own stand, by mimicking the politicians' speeches and using humorously realistic masks. In this way they explore how bodies onstage can reshape archives and, in Richard Schechner's words, perform a "twice behaved behavior"—in other words, behavior in performance "is always subject to revision" because it can never happen the exact same way, therefore behavior such as the one Arias suggests with this scene needs to be rethought, redone for a second or "the nth time."[149] Within the theatrical realm these speeches come alive through the same bodies of the soldiers that went to the islands where they now act on the stage as soldiers from the war. In the performances, as each of the leaders state their national claims to the islands, a sense of discord and danger permeates the theater. This feeling is augmented when Argentine vet Gabriel states that after watching this speech at a bar in 1982, he "knew this was going to end badly."[150] He then adds that two days later he boarded a plane knowing only that he was being taken to the Islas Malvinas.

Joseph Roach in *Cities of the Dead* uses the word "surrogation" to argue that performative acts of substitution help us to rethink or renegotiate collective memory within a community. And due to the selectiveness of memory, "surrogation rarely if ever succeeds."[151] The process of surrogation, then, requires many attempts and failures, because there can never be an exact copy. In the theater, where an actor stands for someone else, or in this case, the vets stand for themselves at a temporal distance, questions about authenticity, and whose stories we hear are brought to bear. As Roach suggests, "The surrogated double so often appears as alien to the culture that reproduces it and that it reproduces. That is why the relentless search for the purity of origins is a voyage not of discovery but of erasure."[152] As doubles of their own experiences, these vets stand in front of a live audience to reenact their memories and to collectively create in the present a connection to the timelessness of the past.

The effect of doubling or the idea of surrogation is central to the play's film version, *Theatre of War*, where in the closing scene, the six veterans pass on the baton to a younger generation of "stand-in" actors. Each vet tells them what they lived through and helps them with makeup or poses as they take on their roles. In a true-to-form war reenactment, the young actors watch how the original vets re-create a battle scene. Slowly, one by one, each of them takes a spot, reinforcing the notion of how their stories can now be reenacted by others, by a younger generation who was not alive when this war took place. At the same time, the vets become spectators of their own stories, watching their surrogates close the film. As Schneider suggests, "Performance challenges loss" as well as "any neat antimony between appearance and disappearance, or presence and absence through the basic repetitions that mark performance as indiscreet, non-original, relentlessly citational, and remaining," and it "plays the 'sedimented acts' and spectral meanings that haunt material in constant collective interaction, in constellation, in transmutation."[153] The archival knowledge transferred through bodies, through the reenactments is in itself what remains. While the reenactments of the six veterans are key to the idea of authenticity onstage, the film version pushes the possibility of repetition, of losing the "true" version to copies and stand-ins that will replicate and retell the stories as their own. As Peggy Phelan affirms, "Performance becomes itself through disappearance," and it is here, with the passing of the baton in the last part of the cycle, that the vets cease to exist as performers and, as such, can rediscover themselves through the repetition and reenactments through others.[154] Performance, like memory, repeats a previous original, but never in quite the same way.

When interviewed about the possibilities this work can have on the performers, Arias responded that it creates a new perspective and a new encounter, and she states that both the play and the film created "a utopic community, something that did not exist before."[155] By emphasizing the vulnerability, the possible unpolished reactions of vets onstage, the failure of the war, for Arias the dichotomy of the winners and losers disappears. As a result, what remains are the human aspect of emotions, memory, and friendship. To the live audience who watches the play, the connection between the vets is clear, and it conveys a camaraderie that is shared onstage. Their affinity is also strikingly evident when the vets join forces playing their instruments as a live hard rock band in a last song that speaks directly to us, the audience:

> LOU: Would you vote to go to war? Would you send your sons and daughters to war? Would you? Would you? Have you ever been to war? Have you ever watched a friend commit suicide? And have you ever visited a dead friend's grave with his mother? Have you? Have you ever been to a war?[156]

This gut-wrenching song, while still a performance onstage, has the effect of removing the artificial elements we associate with theatricality. There are no reenactments, no masks, no voice-overs, no mimicking. We see the vets playing their instruments, singing to us, watching us, and asking us about our own choices in life. Their song played in unison as a plea makes the audience aware of the long-lived implications and aftermath of war. And they raise the question of whether we can truly understand their story, their reenactments, if we have not taken part in a war.

Lola Arias has distinguished herself as an artist who utilizes the documentary modes to tell, show, and re-form stories. To delve into how people may remember and how the stage can serve as a platform for working through intertwined stories, Arias relies on the autobiographical, on the objects as actants, and on the bodies as reenactors. It is within the idea of "filming a flashback," as she stated when she first began her work with *Veterans*, that the past becomes the material for a possible story to be retold and replayed. She is constantly drawn to division, confrontation, trauma, and speculation while she explores through the dramatic a possible revisiting of the past. It is in this ambivalent zone between telling, showing, and remembering that Arias forges a new path, a way to rethink and reenact stories that may have a different outcome onstage.

Chapter 3

✦

Shadows of the Real

Teatro Línea de Sombra

> There are no hard distinctions between what is real and what is unreal, nor between what is true and what is false. A thing is not necessarily either true or false; it can be both true and false.
>
> —Harold Pinter

Many theater groups use documentary methods to create significant and impactful work onstage, but few of these groups explore intersections between art and political action as deeply as the Mexican theater collective Teatro Línea de Sombra (TLS). Founded in 1993, TLS consistently works in liminal zones, between "the real" and the fictional, always mindful of its commitment to social and political causes. Composed of a diverse group of visual and digital artists, musicians, actors, sociologists, and anthropologists (Jorge Vargas, Alicia Laguna, Eduardo Bernal, Zuadd Atala, and Raúl Mendoza), they explore theater and theatricality through research, political activism and artistic creation. As artists based in Mexico City, they have traveled to a variety of international festivals, and more recently they have been invited to work as artists in residence at the Museum of Contemporary Art Chicago (MCA)—the first artists in residence the MCA has hosted with the goal of creating a brand-new work.

Their work and international reception stem from participatory research. In other words, they create work through their own experiences, studying—relying on their anthropologist members—the nuances of the city or place they inhabit, and exploring how art can intercede in these spaces. In this respect, their work usually combines research in carefully chosen locations, where TLS members explore the connections between place, history, and the possible reinterpretations of space that acting bodies can provide. While they strive to be a politically and socially committed group, their attention to aesthetic beauty and the creation of an artistically attractive work becomes an important aspect of how they operate, something that I will analyze at length later on.

During their residency in Chicago, it was clear that their creative work coalesced as they read, researched, added and discarded possible paths. At the time of my various visits of about two weeks each to the MCA in 2016 and 2017, they were developing their play now titled *Filo de caballo(s)* (*Poppy Trail*).[1] Their point of departure was a journey that had been undertaken by director Jorge Vargas in order to experience the long forty-eight hours on a bus linking the cities of Iguala, Mexico, and Chicago via the *camino de amapola*, or the Poppy Trail. The inherent danger of this trip was clearly the experience they wanted to underscore, but only as a generator of ideas and possibilities. It was certain that the haunting story of the forty-three young students from a rural teachers' college in Ayotzinapa who had disappeared in the southwestern city of Iguala, Mexico, on the nights of September 26–27, 2014, was a real-life referent for Vargas's own travel.[2] This story of disappearance, heard and seen all over the world, had revealed once again the unbridled violence plaguing Mexico. On the nights of their gruesome and still unresolved disappearances, about a hundred students decided to steal buses to travel to Mexico City. They planned to hold a march to commemorate the 1968 student massacre that took place in Tlatelolco, where hundreds of students were murdered by the police because they were demanding freedom of political prisoners and more transparency about other government repression.[3] The tradition of stealing buses had been tolerated by the bus companies for many years, as they allowed students from a college known for its activism to perform this ritual. On the nights of September 26–27, however, different buses were intercepted by police; shots were fired; six people died, three of them students; and forty-three student teachers disappeared. There are different narratives and testimonies regarding why these buses were targeted, but according to ongoing studies by the Forensic Architecture Team (commissioned by Argentine Forensic Anthropology Team and Pro Human Rights Group), which examined thousands of testimonies, videos, and phone records compiled by the Inter-American Commission on Human Rights (IACHR), there was a coverup between state agents and organized crime, and the final official account diverges from the one presented by the IACHR.[4] With digital graphs and data points, Forensic Architecture builds an interactive platform with possible outcomes to investigate crimes committed against the forty-three students, as well as to confront the failures of Mexican law enforcement. Their investigation is now part of the permanent collection at the University Museum of Contemporary Arts, at Mexico's National Autonomous University in Mexico City. Relying on Forensic Architecture's digital platform, TLS has explored theories positing that the intercepted buses may have been used in the drug route from Iguala to Chicago and thus that the students were in the wrong place at the wrong time.[5] In this way TLS had to consider and acknowledge that some of their own research might have to take place on a bus that could be carrying drugs across the border into the United States.

During their residency in Chicago, the group was deciding whether to use the well-known Chicago stockyard as part of their story, to explore the testimony of a longtime Mexican museum worker, or to go in search of other stories of women working in factories around the area. Their creative process to think about a play that deals with a highly charged contemporary issue, such as re-creating particular drug trafficking routes, pushed the group to attempt to also understand the lives of those migrants already living in Chicago, as well as the immigrants' struggles and dreams. This process of witnessing attests to TLS as a collective of artists, who not only investigate, document, and explore the many literary intertexts in their own work, but also dig into and collect the layers of possible stories to tell, layers that sometimes depart from their own concept of documentation.

In this chapter, I turn to the impact of a socially committed group that brings contemporary and difficult topics to the stage by speaking directly about immigration, femicide, and human rights atrocities. Thus, I study their work not just as artistic production but in conjunction with and in relation to their committed social and political work. In doing so, I privilege a performance studies approach to consider them as artists and activists whose tools are education as well as information. In other words, I take into consideration how they put their lives in danger, how they study and research their work in order to call attention to matters beyond the theatrical, closely relying on anthropological methods, and how they use site specificity in their work when needed.[6]

Their exploration of aesthetic beauty through ethnographic studies of the people and places they want to stage makes their work one of the most important artistic contributions within contemporary theater. In other words, TLS has a unique and original approach to studying and connecting people and places to their historical and political pasts through a documentary mode by also bringing out the beauty of any story they face, even those with gruesome content. I connect the study of documentary theater as it took a new form beginning in the twenty-first century together with the many relational aesthetics (to borrow Nicolas Bourriaud's term) that encompass art and politics. If, for Bourriaud, "art is the place that produces a specific sociability" and develops into a political project when it moves into the relational realm,[7] then this chapter argues that documentary theater, as a political artistic genre that convenes sociability, illuminates the possibility of imagining and understanding our present and our future as social beings. My research is grounded in theories of affect, in a sense "how we are touched by what we are near," as Sara Ahmed succinctly explains when she speaks of how emotions are "intentional in the sense that they are about something."[8] In theater, where we usually share a common space for a determined period of time, affective response to what we see, hear, smell, and sometimes even touch convenes the multisensorial in personal ways. In fact, TLS strives to explore the connectivity between affect, sociability, and relationality as important foundations in their work.

At the same time, this chapter analyzes how TLS and their repertoire manipulate the onstage role of the "real" to address issues of immigration with the assistance of border and migration studies to examine the cause and effect of human behavior and survival. Specifically, I study the intricacies of the use of documentary objects as well as a documentary mode in the retelling of stories for an audience. And while their work does not focus on the authenticity of the object as document, their study and approach to creating an artistic product is informed by documentary research. This information is then simultaneously portrayed as authentic material that allows the audience to learn and immerse itself in the story. As I wrote in the introduction to this book, studying documentary practices of twenty-first-century theater calls for attention to be paid to collection and to process as well as to invention.

Documentary theater, particularly in Mexico, has a strong tradition. The best-known example is the influential work of Vicente Leñero (1933–2014) and his true-to-form documentary plays from the 1960s and '70s. Leñero was highly influenced by Peter Weiss, and his plays were key examples of what Latin American documentary theater was at the time: "a critical manifestation of reality based on authentic events."[9] Leñero's constant search for the political, the value of the authentic, without fictional intervention, resulted in plays that often explored the tribunal form to heighten tension and authenticity for their audiences. In 1968, a year connected to violent riots around the world, including the massacre in Tlatelolco, Leñero premiered *Pueblo rechazado* (*Rejected People*) in Mexico City, which appeared only three years after Peter Weiss's innovative 1965 production *The Investigation* in Germany, the play that epitomized the documentary theater of that decade.

While Leñero made a name for himself through the use of documentary theater, other practitioners in Latin America also engaged in documentary practices.[10] Most notable among them were Colombian groups like Enrique Buenaventura's collective, Teatro Experimental de Cali (TEC), and Santiago García's La Candelaria, as well as the Peruvian group Yuyachakani, which approached group participation and political activism through documentary work.[11] Stimulated by the ongoing influential work by Antonin Artaud, Bertolt Brecht, and Peter Weiss, Latin American artists sought political expression on the stage. And while European tendencies were key for many Latin American practitioners, it is important to point out that collective group work, theater groups, and participatory performance practices were even more evident in many of these documentary groups. Augusto Boal and his *Teatro del oprimido* (Theatre of the Oppressed) method were paramount to his own work of 1960s and 1970s, as well as that of others influenced by him. This connection is evident in groups like Yuyachkani and TEC, among others, that sought to make Latin American theater a serious player in political theater.

In Mexico, Leñero was a pioneer through his dramaturgy, his research and his constant search for what he saw as authentic. With *Pueblo rechazado* and many other works, he solidified a tradition in Latin American theater in which the political stage became an important genre within theater. His Mexican disciples, including Víctor Hugo Rascón Banda, Tomás Urtusástegui, Leonor Azcárate, Sabina Berman, Hugo Salcedo, Enrique Rentería, and Antonio Zúñiga, helped consolidate Leñero's legacy as well as develop other documentary theater techniques by creating plays about historical events while simultaneously advancing the understanding of documentary theater as a more playful genre from which invention, irony, and doubt began to emerge.

Yet while Leñero was an influential playwright producing documentary theater in a traditional vein for which he achieved great success, twenty-first-century theater practitioners pursue a more nuanced and creative expression. Among the most prominent groups and playwrights working in this genre is another renowned Mexican collective, Lagartijas tiradas al sol (Lizards Lounging in the Sun). Founded in 2003 in Mexico City, these artists led by Luisa Prado and Gabino Rodríguez "develop projects as a mechanism to link work and life, to erase borders . . . and to provide meaning, articulate, dislocate and unravel what everyday practice fuses and overlooks."[12] Prado and Rodríguez add that their work is not entertainment; instead, they create "a space to think."[13] Many of their plays take into consideration the autobiographical, the role of the witness, the ambiguity of retelling someone's story, and the ongoing questions about what documents might or might not show.[14] Documentary theater practices, like the ones employed by Lagartijas, have encouraged many other groups and Mexican playwrights to tackle similar issues through the use of documentary modes. Authors like Antonio Zúñiga, Hugo Salcedo, Humberto Robles, and Perla de la Rosa show how the current issues of immigration, femicides, and drug violence lend themselves to exploratory work through theater. And although Leñero paved the way for bringing archival research to the stage, it is in the work by new theater groups and practitioners that questions how to treat fiction and authenticity that takes center stage. This is especially true for TLS.

The members of TLS could be considered "artivists," those who, according to Ileana Diéguez and Diana Taylor, explore political and cultural ways for the discussion and transformation of community issues and those who "use performance to intervene in political contexts, struggles and debates."[15] As artivists, TLS members compile information from newspaper articles, blogs, and documentary video, and connect that archival base with fictional threads to produce through the intertextuality of fiction—poems, short stories, and novels—complex plays. Their most recent work includes plays like *Amarillo* (*Amarillo*, 2009), *Baños Roma* (*Roma Baths*, 2013), *Pequeños territorios en reconstrucción* (*Small Territories under Reconstruction* 2014),[16] *Durango 66* (2015);[17] large-scale installations like *Artículo 13* (*Article 13*, 2012); the site-specific performances *El puro lugar* (*Nothing but the Place*, 2016–2017) and *Filo de caballo(s)* (*Poppy Trail*, 2018). TLS's participation in community activities takes on major social and political heft in their own development and creation process. One of TLS's main purposes is to study issues of human rights and immigration, as well as to explore topics of femicide and extermination in Ciudad Juárez, Mexico. Whereas other important playwrights and theater collectives have staged similar topics on border issues (for instance, the Mexican playwrights Hugo Salcedo, Antonio Zúñiga, Víctor Hugo Rascón Banda, and Humberto Robles, as well as the Spanish playwrights Angélica Liddell and Juan Carlos Rubio), TLS exposes fragments of the real through revision and documentary creation of the story they stage. In other words, from director Jorge Vargas to different members of the group, including Alicia Laguna, Eduardo Bernal, Raúl Mendoza, and Zuadd Ibáñez, TLS creates and critically examines intersections between the value of the archive and the artistic process of aesthetics.

What brought me to their work was not merely the topics and themes they studied, although that was a driving reason; instead, I was drawn to their approach to the document and the process of documentation via a laboratory setting in which they investigate how theater operates for them and for their audiences. While their methodology can also be attributed to what Hans-Thies Lehmann calls postdramatic, they prefer the term "progression" to describe how they work with real issues through theater. For them, progression manifests in collective creation—a process that relies on what each interpreter or actor brings with them. Although members invest in research and archival work, they also work with objects and their own bodies to process and understand the information in creative ways that underscore a phenomenological approach. This exercise of progression brings each actor's comments and thoughts to a collective forum and will later go through edits of texts and movement. This way, the group takes into account individual as well as group perspectives, along with embodied practices and textual evidence. According to Jorge Vargas, "Our artistic process is collective to bring together different points of view. I, as the director, later decide which pieces tie together better than others." However, he also adds that the group thrives on the independent artistic innovations and that each artist has a voice and a potential for considering materials that the final product will consider as a group.[18] In this way, their work is relational not just to the themes they tackle, but also in the way they rely on each other's work as a whole.

I am indebted to Bourriaud's concept of relationality because it anticipates how TLS works in and toward an understanding of community building theater. Bourriaud states that the focus of conviviality is not so much on the spectacle itself, as Guy Debord had expressed, but more on the experience of "being together" as an affective tool that attracts the audience to other modes of thinking and feeling. The spectators, both as individuals and as a group, are engaged and encouraged to give back to the community. This is made clear when Bourriaud proclaims that "art is a state of encounter" and that artistic practice is "the creation of relationships between subjects."[19] He contends that the relationship between art and the political create a micro–utopian community.[20] I should also note, however, that contrary to his theory, Claire Bishop expands the notion of how the "structure" of relational aesthetics works when "equating aesthetic judgment with an ethicopolitical judgment of relationships produced by the work of art."[21] Whereas Bourriaud relies on a "criteria of co-existence," Bishop disarms the idea of togetherness and community by questioning how the concept of a relational aesthetics can work in a truly democratic and "antagonistic" society where "relations of conflict are *sustained*, not erased."[22] Bishop's questions about the "limits of society's ability to fully constitute itself" focus on what happens when these micro societies do not have something in common and a micro-utopia is not fulfilled.[23] I bring up Bishop's relational antagonism because, although it is true that the utopian ideal of constructing a community is central to how TLS conceptualizes their work, I am aware of the impossibilities and the dangers of falling into thinking that politically committed work can form modes of belonging for all. And Bishop makes the valid point that there is a danger of romanticizing any event as fulfilling something it is not. But I am also cognizant that what is at stake in much of the work of TLS is the need to make the audience mindful of issues that bring communities together and what divides them as well.

TLS members' approach to the idea of encounter not only takes into consideration the ethnographic work done ahead of time; they also pay close attention to ideas about how bodies relate to each other and how their own work progresses through carefully observing bodies react to different scenarios. In this sense, their "progression" encompasses many layers of trial and error, of closely relying on documents and objects to tell a story that will contain some authenticity and some literary and artistic creation. As documentarians, they record their findings, but as artistic theater practitioners, they explore the creative process of imagination. Thus, they work in an ambivalent space—both in the sense of applying ethnographic studies and creating a fictional work—as they acknowledge and dismantle the authority contained in a story or object and juxtapose that practice with social and artistic ones.

Although TLS members do not see their work as postdramatic, similarities cannot and should not be ignored. Lehmann discusses how the irruption of the real has taken the theater to postdramatic forms of expression, where the lines between artistic fiction and the authentic are blurred, creating a new type of documentary theater that is highly attractive to both artists and audiences, since it opens up the possibilities of understanding the blurred lines of creation. According to his own definition, "It's not the occurrence of anything 'real' as such but its *self-reflexive* use that characterizes the aesthetic of postdramatic theatre. This self-referentiality allows us to contemplate the value, the inner necessity and the significance of the extra-aesthetic in the aesthetic and thus the displacement of the concept of the latter."[24] Thus, there is a suspension of a clear distinction between reality and the spectatorial event. As a result, when groups like TLS use self-reflexive mechanisms in their productions, their spectators are called to become less passive watchers. They instead engage in participatory performances that often force them to take charge or to reassess what they thought they knew. Again, this theater aesthetic blurs the boundaries between fiction and fact, spectator and actor that hundreds of years of theater have instilled in many of us, and instead theater retracts and raises questions when signs are no longer separated from their pragmatic embeddedness.

European postdramatic theater could be thought of as a post-Brechtian ideal to bring the *gestus* back, but instead of the political awakening Brecht stipulated, the "post-" in post-Brechtian explores the many aesthetic possibilities of doubting and questioning the political.[25] As Jorge Dubatti asserts, the "postdramatic theater" concept does not quite fit when speaking of theater in Argentina or elsewhere in Latin America.[26] Instead, Dubatti explores another ontological reading to understand what much of contemporary Latin American theater stages: a marginal and liminal sense tied to *poiesis*, the construction of something new through representation.[27] It is with this idea of the construction of a scene from the marginal or liminal that I believe Latin American theater diverges from the more hegemonic European theatrical discourse. As I indicated in the introduction of this book, the idea of collective creation, of analyzing the archive through objects, documents, and stories, was an important practice in the 1960s and '70s in Latin America. And despite the fact that there is truth in the need to see Latin American theater practitioners as different from their European counterparts and their model of the postdramatic, there is also clear evidence that what Lehmann—who has traveled to Latin America and participated in scholarly exchanges about this topic—has labeled "postdramatic," theater practitioners in Mexico and other countries in Latin America have experienced through a different vein. Their work combines new and innovative approaches to the theatrical with an exploration of the social relations and the affective sites of memory and creation that exist apart from or alongside the stage.

As a socially committed group and as "artivists," TLS centers its work on immersing itself in the topic and in the space, as Vargas did, for instance, by taking the bus from Iguala to Chicago. Some of their on-site residencies are months long, and others are more of a laboratory exploration in their own theatrical space. What remains central to their work, however, is the search to immerse themselves in a community by using theater as a tool to motivate, educate, and confront human rights violations as well as practices of oppression. Again, closely related to Boal's theories of the *teatro del oprimido*, where theater becomes the site of experimentation and possibilities, where voices regain power and where marginal bodies become visible, TLS intends to tap not just a political vein, but an affective relationship with what they create. As a group, they experience the stories they workshop together, and they exploit many different possible angles to foster that same experience for their audiences. Hence, their work encompasses what Rancière has termed "emancipation," defined as "the blurring of the boundary between those who act and those who look; between individuals and members of a collective body."[28] It is not that the spectators themselves need to become actors in the Boalian sense; instead, it is about how they can perceive and understand with their own cultural background when confronted with new modes of spectatorship.

TLS employment of these theater mechanics makes us, the spectators, aware of different social, political, and artistic issues at stake in hybrid forms like new documentary theater. TLS is known for its technical approach to creation, using many video cameras to create a panoptic effect that records, repeats, and even distorts images right in front of the spectators' eyes, manipulating and interpreting both the document/archive that they utilize as well as the stories they want to tell. To achieve sophistication in both artistic aesthetics and technical savviness, TLS works with and relies on visual artists, digital technicians, graffiti artists, and musicians who together create beauty through visual and corporeal poetics that destabilize traditional approaches to dividing notions of the authentic, the fictional, and the creative as separate categories. And while their work seems sophisticated, their aesthetics explore a low-tech, hands-on approach to creating natural effects—for instance, in *Amarillo*, when they pierce a red heart multiple times with a lit cigarette and sand spills out, creating a stream of red and movement that is both stunning and technically simple (see fig. 7). Hence, they underscore the impact the visual can have in re-creating a sense of ritual and respect when addressing gruesome topics. As Richard Schechner has stated, "Rituals are a way people remember. Rituals are memories in action, encoded into actions."[29] TLS benefits from exploring the ritualistic value of their performances by adhering to a total sensory experience, where beauty, colors, music, and movement explore ways of relating to difficult topics. In fact, their work invites the emancipated spectator that Rancière imagines, where there is a need for a different type of theater, "a theatre where the passive optical relationship implied by the very term is subjected to a different relationship . . . that of *drama*."[30] TLS aims to reveal these processes and thereby promulgate learning. They do this from their laboratory work in situ to their foundation of a theater laboratory called "Transversales," where they invite international artists to engage in conversations with local artists, to plays with less weight on acting and more emphasis on showing and documenting.[31] For Rancière, true theater means a return to action and the participation of the spectator (as opposed to the passive spectator), and his own understanding stems from what both Brecht and Artaud worked to dig out of the theater: presence and political action through movement and, in the case of Artaud, rituals. It is evident that for TLS ritual and action are at the forefront of their work.

Fig. 7. Antígona González. In Teatro Línea de Sombra's *Amarillo*. Teatro El Milagro, Mexico City, 2009. Photograph by Roberto Blenda.

The Real and the Threshold of Fiction

Argentine director Vivi Tellas has postulated that what is at stake when dealing with archives and documentary theater is the creation of the Minimal Threshold of Fiction (UMF; Unidad Mínima de Ficción), a type of expression that relates to the gray zone created when the authentic and the fictional confront each other. This UMF, in a sense, can be explored through the fragile space that we perceive when a nonprofessional actor, for instance, shows the audience their lives, collecting documentary evidence to build the story onstage, or when someone's life becomes, in a word, theatricalized. This fragile space appears when actual documents are introduced as theatrical props that make us see how fiction and documentary situate themselves at the same level in the aesthetics of the spectacle. In the specific case of TLS, its documentary practices have a strong social and political base. The gray zone they construct is through a constant intertextual relationship between literary pieces, witness reports, and at times autobiography. Unlike Tellas, who explores the everyday lives of regular people through their own storytelling, TLS brings fiction and ethnographic facts to the shared space of theatrical experience and embodies it with professional actors. For them, documentary practice means exposing the audience to the harsh reality of those human lives labeled as other, immigrant, or marginal but at a distance, and often with humor, dance, and speculation.

Visual poetics and the search for beauty are at stake when TLS creates new work. With *Amarillo*, TLS questioned their own hybrid motives as artist-activists by forcing themselves to go beyond being theater practitioners who staged regular plays, to being political artists who could visually imagine other forms of creation. According to Jorge Vargas, their art was highly influenced by the intersection of visual artists like Alfadir Luna and scholars who work closely with them.[32] Alfadir Luna is a well-known Mexican visual artist whose own trajectory emphasizes the relation between artist and audiences by focusing on affective stimuli. Since 2006, his installations have been found in public markets as well as more traditional museum settings. Through these collaborations, TLS began rethinking and recrafting the idea of authenticity that the document bears. Their influences, both as visual artists and thinkers, pushed members of TLS to view the political as well as visible/invisible lines inherent in dealing with issues of human rights and bringing those issues to their audiences.[33] In much the same way that Tellas uses her UMF concept, Luna explores how liminal actions become encoded with symbolic value and thus create a new poetic language. Luna works in the liminal space between affect and enunciation:

> To me, the artwork comes to be in that liminal field between enunciation and action, as a space in which if we stop for a second, we would be able to feel exactly where the figure of speech is employed to say that which did not exist until this symbolic language was created. On the other hand, there is the experience, the performance, the visual attractiveness and plasticity of the piece. Also, in this we can see the artwork taking form. But, for me, what really matters is to explore the space between the two of them, which is an open field and allows us to imagine and propose other possibilities. It not only raises the notion of living something as if it were already happening, as a world that has just appeared, but suddenly this field loses all correspondence with its surroundings, making us wonder why this is happening, why here? where does this belong? what is this?[34]

One of Luna's installations, *El hombre de maíz* (*Maize Man*, 2008; see fig. 8), shows the connectivity between people and art, between merchants and commerce, and between ritualistic forms and the present.[35] Its title is a clear reference to the 1949 novel *Hombres de maíz* by Guatemalan Nobel Prize–winning author Miguel Ángel Asturias, which itself recalls the Mayan myth recounted in the *Popol Vuh*. Luna's *El hombre de maíz* describes the

Fig. 8. Alfadir Luna, *Hombre de maíz*. Installation in Mexico City, 2008. Photograph by Brenda Anayatzin Ortiz Guadarrama.

indigenous world as a humanlike sculpture made in three parts: head, torso, and extremities. Ten different merchants are given the chance to glue seeds and grains to cover the whole body. Seven days before a procession that connects all the markets and merchants, the sculpture gets dismembered, and each of the ten merchants cares for their respective piece. On the day of the procession, the sculpture gets re-membered and unified in a celebration. Audience members take part in this project to experience community and the essence of being together. As Luna suggests, the action of coming together and of gluing together different extremities of this sculpture creates a living object in the present.

Bourriaud speaks of the "community effect in contemporary art" that propels a "political project when it endeavors to move into the relational realm by turning it into an issue" while foregrounding the human interaction and the "collective elaboration of meaning."[36] The focus on human relations and the collaboration of many to create art reinforces the idea that art is political and the political can be viewed through art. Luna's idea of coming together by bringing a merchant community together resembles how TLS also envisions their work. For these artists, conviviality, the idea of closeness and being together, reinvigorates the performative nature of the ritual. It is not just the fact that the audience becomes more participatory, which in a sense it does; it is also about the human and personal attribute of making art and how artists expose their work as a process.

Process, immersion, research, and participation are key not only in conceiving new theatrical works, but also in thinking how human rights are linked to the political and to the convivial. Teatro Línea de Sombra relies on a variety of avenues for telling a story and ways to relate to their audiences as well as to understand the people and communities within these stories. In what follows, I will analyze two specific examples of TLS's work, *Amarillo* and *Baños Roma*, as well as the methodology operating in the collaborative site-specific installation of *El puro lugar*.[37] These works examine the real through the ambiguous space of an archive while at the same time exploring historical evidence related to the present. TLS's approach to documentary aesthetics is not just another search for something novel; it is, instead, a way for the company to broach discussions about immigration, human rights, and their own overall social commitment.

Amarillo and the Route of the Desert

The title of TLS's play draws from Amarillo, the name of a town in Texas, with a history of interconnected train tracks and meatpacking plants that made this city a desirable destination for migrants from Mexico and, more recently, Central America. According to U.S. State Department data for Texas, in 2016 roughly 7,800 immigrants arrived in that state alone. Amarillo has become Texas's leading safe haven for those crossing into the United States, accepting nearly four hundred refugees in 2016—the most per capita of any city in Texas.[38] The play *Amarillo* marked a change in TLS as they began focusing on contemporary social and political issues through documentary theater techniques. Until *Amarillo*, the group had concentrated on staging plays written by other playwrights. However, their shift to a more collaborative and political venue catalyzed new work and the group as one of the leading politically committed forces in contemporary Latin American theater. Thus, their process became geared toward a laboratory workshop that explored documents, testimony, and staging from their own immersion in border towns as well as through experimentation with theatrical forms and digital cameras.

Amarillo is, in simple terms, a play that exposes a migrant's journey from somewhere in Mexico to Amarillo, Texas. The perils of the border-crossing journey are recorded through a multimedia performance via a documentary technique (letters, film, and clothing) that touches on issues of cultural identity, human suffering, and human rights. And while the play has traveled to many different international festivals, TLS stages *Amarillo* to bring awareness of the dangers of the journey of border crossing into the different migrant shelters (*albergues*). More recently, in January 2017, as part of TLS's own project "Amarillo on the Migrant Route," the group took *Amarillo* to Saltillo, Mexico, one of the many shelters for migrants seeking to cross into the United States. There they staged *Amarillo* for hundreds of people, many of

Fig. 9. A "chapel" built by TLS members in Altar, Sonora, Mexico, at the shelter Centro de Ayuda al Migrante y al Necesitado CCAMYN, 2017. Photograph by Alicia Laguna.

whom were migrants making the journey across the border. Together with talk-backs and community work (they donated a bread oven and brought in a baker to teach them how to make bread with more natural ingredients), the group used the production to foment education about the journey, its possible perils, and what the migrants can expect in the desert. A year later, the troupe traveled to Altar and Caborca, two border towns about twenty miles apart on the Mexican side, to stage *Amarillo* in Caborca and to conduct community work in Altar.[39] Known at one time as "a migrant oasis," Altar has become both a hub as well as a trap for thousands of migrants seeking refuge before crossing the border through the Arizona desert. As organized crime has taken over, the city has become what reporters call "a high stakes gamble."[40]

TLS pushed for solidarity and togetherness, reigniting how theatrical interventions might speak to audiences in dire situations. Their community-focused work ethic motivated TLS to build a simple place where migrants could meet: a shelter baptized as a chapel by Father Cipriano, the priest overseeing it (see fig. 9). This construction is part of their work with the Centro

Comunitario de Atención al Migrante y Necesitado (Community Center for Attention to Migrants in Need), a free shelter for migrants in Altar, Sonora, run by the local Our Lady of Guadalupe Church, founded in 2000. As the matron of all border crossers, the Virgen de Guadalupe holds an important if not key space in the configuration of the border town. Her image can be found everywhere: tattoos, cups, posters, pillows, and so on. Historically, "she has symbolized the power to overcome barriers, from Mexican Revolutionaries to Chicana feminists."[41] As Luis D. León suggests, "A borderlands or mestiza consciousness . . . nurtures and becomes the birth place of the poetic impulse in religious practice throughout the Mexican Americans and beyond."[42] Consequently, her presence becomes ubiquitous, not in the strongest Catholic sense, but as a liberating figure who gives authority and power to those in need.[43]

The shelter's main objective is to assist migrants both crossing the border north and returning from their travels in the United States and looking for ways to go back to their lives back in Mexico or Central America. Although the center offered the migrants beds, showers, meals (breakfast and dinner), medical attention, human rights education, and general orientation, it lacked a chapel. TLS's commitment to the community, the migrants, and the community center plays a key factor in their artistic and human rights work. In this case, their intervention consisted of two separate projects: building "the chapel" and funding a permanent paid position for the administrator and the cleaning person, as well as a printed book with memories of the community center.[44] Through the construction of the "chapel," designed by TLS member Eduardo Bernal and visual artist Alfadir Luna, a strong borderland connection to ritual, spiritualism, and hope took center stage. Migrants who risk their lives to find a better chance on the other side cling to whatever rituals they can hold onto, and a "chapel" in Altar can be the last place of comfort before their journey.

The border town, whose agricultural economy was displaced by a mercantile one with "border crossing" merchandise, such as slippers that leave no footprints, water jugs, and backpacks, is now seeing a decrease in its business and rapidly becoming a ghost town. While the citizens of Caborca and Altar have an ambiguous relationship to migrants—they do not really want them there, but at the same time they depend on their crossings for their own livelihood—their town is now also ravaged by criminal gangs run by the narco-traffickers. Thus, fewer and fewer migrants cross the border through Altar, and the city has become a gruesome and dangerous place. According to border scholar Jason de León, since the U.S. government's Prevention through Deterrence policy was established in the 1990s, migrant crossings have been consciously rerouted through the desert and other dangerous areas, exponentially increasing the number of migrant deaths. This retrafficking "set the stage for the desert to become the new 'victimizer' of border transgressors."[45] It is striking to understand how the implementation of this policy "also illustrates the cunning way that nature has been conscripted by the Border Patrol to act as an enforcer while simultaneously providing this federal agency with plausible deniability regarding blame for any victims the desert may claim."[46] Thus, the desert becomes the enforcer, and the terrain essentially transforms itself into a grave for many migrants. The desert also presents a new understanding of how to deal with immigration: now the Border Patrol can absolve itself of any blame for accidents and deaths and instead grants the desert the role of actant; agency is now shifted onto the natural elements.[47] Migrants, then, are mere pawns in a game of hide-and-seek, where as long as other border cities do not see migrants crossing, then the problem lies somewhere else: the highly dangerous and punishing desert. Altar, a city that borders the Sonoran Desert, becomes the last refuge for many seeking to cross. TLS's intersectionality between art and social commitment exposes a deeper understanding of the border, the journey, and the perils that the natural setting of the desert may bring to any human who tries to cross it—especially as migrants are dehumanized in the political and geographical space of the Sonoran Desert.

The dry, bare space of the desert transited by many migrants as the Goliath to be conquered instead turns out to be a potential stage for their own death. Gloria Anzaldúa has argued that "a borderland is a vague and undetermined place created by the emotional residue of an unnatural boundary. It is in a constant state of transition. The prohibited and forbidden are its inhabitants."[48] It is precisely this contentious space encapsulating the anxiety and the misgivings of a town that is in between, or, in Anzaldúa's words, a place "where the third world grates against the first and bleeds."[49] But the strain in this town is created not only by the ambiguous relationship between the inhabitants of Altar and Caborca vis-à-vis the migrants, but also by a powerful, ever expanding criminal group that has made these towns their base for drug trafficking. The border is also an open wound, or, in Giorgio Agamben's words, "a state of exception in which application and norm reveal their separation and a pure force-of-law" that "marks a threshold at which logic and praxis blur with each other and a pure violence without *logos* claims to realize an enunciation without any real reference."[50] In more recent studies, Sayak Valencia examines the (in)visibility of bodies on the Mexico-U.S. border. Referencing to the title of her book, *Gore Capitalism*, she signals that bodies become "targets of necropolitics," as they are part of what she sees as a "critical commodity, since this is what gore capitalism advertises."[51] As such, she posits that "there is a hyper-corporalization and a hyper-valorization applied to the body," and the market has made a profit off this commodity.[52]

There is an emptiness the desert leaves behind through the migrants' journeys that we never know about, or that we might only hear if a body is ever found. Giving voice to these unseen migrants has been a key element of TLS's artistic and community work. Through the design of a "memory book," Luna collects migrant narratives, memories, pictures, and interviews to create a depository of the lives of so many that go unnoticed. This book serves as an artistic manifestation of witnessing, bringing more information to the community, the migrants, and those interested in learning about the dangers of border crossing. Luna's work consists of a participatory event in which the community and TLS elaborate a visible and tangible production of memory by exploring what they want to keep in the book. Through this event, they bring forth the shelter's encoded memory via the visual arts. The book transmits knowledge and a connection to the community as a collective memory taken from the refugees that pass through the shelter. The participatory nature of this project exposes the agency and empathy of those involved in the center and through their own lived experiences a new narrative is formed. Thus, this memory book combines the voices of those migrants who have gone by the shelter and serves to tell something about the ephemeral transition of their lives.[53]

Can You See Me? Do You Really See Me?

Staged for the first time in 2009, *Amarillo* has now been performed in national and international festivals, and TLS has been invited to attend multiple premiere theater festivals.[54] As a result, the piece has also gained recognition for its production quality and longevity, although it has barely been studied by scholars. Centered on documentary evidence gathered from fragments of films provided by the Centro de Documentación de Voces contra el Silencio (Documentary Center for Voices against the Silence), an open and free platform to access documentary film about human rights atrocities in Latin America, TLS begins the performance by introducing audiences to their laboratory stage.[55] The voices and images from the films are projected while members of the troupe prepare their working tables at the sides of the stage by arranging photographs, cameras, clothing, and other documentary props. Influenced by Etienne Decroux and his methodology with the corporeal mime, director Jorge Vargas makes the body the center of expression. Similar to Jerzy Grotowski and his approach to "poor theater," the props are few and the actors' ferocious movement is key.[56] However, Vargas's exploration of the props or objects goes even further than that of Grotowski and Decroux. His own development of a constant synergy between objects and actors, what he has called the "intensively live object" or the "raw object" conveys a new language to relate to how bodies communicate onstage. Thus, it is not just the actor's body or the energy of the object that he centers on; rather, it is the symbiotic relationship between the two that makes his work compelling. This is an important note, because according to Vargas, his actors do not act; they "actuate" (*actoran*). In other words, bodies speak onstage through movements and pauses, accentuating their presence and their powerful relationship they build with objects onstage.

Fig. 10. Raúl Mendoza (projected on the screen) in TLS's *Amarillo*. Berlin Gastspiel Studio-FIND Festival, 2019. Photograph by Gianmarco Bresadola.

While bodies are central to how they relate to objects, spatial setting conveys the surroundings necessary for the extra surfaces carried by makeup, lights, costumes, what Grotowski characterizes as the *via negativa*. Poor theater is a technique to use the actor's body and craft as the central method onstage. He explains that "the acceptance of the poverty of theatre, stripped of all that is not essential to it, revealed to us not only the backbone of the medium, but also the deep riches which lie in the very nature of the artform."[57] However, beyond Grotowski's assertions, TLS understands that each physical action is born from a real stimulus, where the drain on the body is intensified by the interaction between the space and the object by the energy that is shared. Thus, the physicality in *Amarillo* centers on the highly affective ways of driving movement: we see the actor running, crushing his body against the wall, we sense his desperation, and we hear the eerie sounds coming from the rancher. As the pace quickens, we listen to the core questions from those marginalized voices: "Who am I?" the Everyman-like actor asks, which he answers over and over: "I am nobody." "Who do you look at if I am no one?" "No one. My name is Juan, Pedro, Fernando, Manuel, Isabel . . ." (see fig. 10).[58]

The affective role of this plea compounds Judith Butler's weighty questions about whose lives count as human and whose lives are invisible to society: "Who, in her own words, counts as human? Whose lives count as lives? And what makes for a grievable life?"[59] In a visceral and almost explosive fashion, the character's questions suggest hesitation at the core of issues surrounding the meaning of humanity and what it means to be invisible. In her illuminating research on affect, Lauren Berlant affirms that our learning to be optimistic can be devastated by cruelty and the failure to attain it. She studies how the optimistic attachment to something we may want—say, upward mobility, or in this case a fair immigration process—becomes a frayed fantasy. This cruel optimism gives way to "the ordinary as a zone of convergence of many histories, where people manage the incoherence of lives that proceed in the face of threats to the good life they imagine. Catastrophic forces take shape in this zone and become events within history as it is lived."[60] Affect studies help us rethink how artists' relationship to theatrical audiences can have a more profound and direct impact on the idea of togetherness, or what Berlant terms the "affective rhythms of survival."[61]

Berlant defines optimism as "not a map of pathology but a social relation involving attachments that organize the present. . . . Optimism is a scene of negotiated sustenance that makes life bearable as it presents itself ambivalently, unevenly, incoherently."[62] Berlant's approach to the affective is instructive because time and again Latin American theater and visual culture artists, such as TLS, demonstrate a continuous search for beauty, even in the darkest of times and spaces. They confront social events and situations from a distance, allowing themselves and us a way out, through art and the construction of beauty. But beyond what one might understand about audience response, what is central here is the way artists utilize the real and documentary frameworks as multisensorial practices that resemble our agitated lives. Multisensorial practices are also helpful for TLS when thinking about feelings and the plural perspectives on which they rely. This strategy of using affect and artistic creation to bring a sense of beauty to these stories can have different outcomes. On the one hand, theater and art make the stories bearable and, in a sense, optimistic.[63] On the other, aestheticizing violence and suffering trivializes the experience of the sufferer. It is perhaps in their methodology to documenting the lives of the invisible "others" that TLS is careful not to make a spectacle of the suffering.

In *Amarillo*, the Everyman is the only interpreter with a certain protagonist function, while the throat-singing rancher wanders around and four other women exchange roles as stage scenographers, camerawomen, dancers, and letter readers. In a desert that is sometimes enchanting and at other times deadly, it also becomes an allegorical space in nature. For instance, many migrant stories are embodied in this Everyman who takes us on a visually attractive journey through this desertscape with tragic overtones that haunt every story. Onstage, actors employ sandbags that hang from the ceiling, while the water from jugs is illuminated in an attractive, dreamy, aquatic blue, shimmering and reflecting on the floor. Throughout the play, these natural elements mark nature's persistent threat, pushing the multisensorial forward by hearing water, seeing the sand spilling out of the bags, and imagining the

Fig. 11. Jesús Cuevas in TLS's *Amarillo*. Berlin Gastspiel Studio-FIND Festival, 2019. Photograph by Gianmarco Bresadola.

ocean close by, even in a desert. The ongoing Mongolian-like throat singing together with the fluidity of the falling sand and the water make *Amarillo* a play that encompasses the act of rituals while the desert becomes beautiful, the lives of "others" become, in a sense, visible. Actors search for answers while trying to climb up the wall or engaging in lonely solo dances, exposing the real threat and desolation of this journey. The multisensorial is borne out through the vivid, colorful dresses that evoke Mexican quinceañeras, and the train whistle blowing as "La Bestia" (the train on which many Central Americans risk their lives by climbing aboard as cargo to be transported through Mexico) brings to light an omnipresent danger that the audience can both see and hear in the documentary. The screen displays the *patronas* (volunteer women who hand food to the many migrants riding atop these freight trains), while sounds of sand and water fill the enchanting space.[64] There is certainly a poetic beauty in the representation of how this play underscores the concept of hope and optimism. The use of natural objects like water and sand highlighted by hues of blue and yellow/orange colors creates an inviting atmosphere, one where, in Jill Dolan's words, "there is the possibility of a better future that can be claimed and captured in performance."[65] Not everything is hopeful and not everything we see is optimistic, but the creation of beauty from objects that usually have a different semiotic value (the lack of water, the agony of sand) makes this space enchanting, while still exposing the tragic overtones. (see fig. 11).

The poetic connections and relations that director Vargas and his team explore bring a human aspect to this multimedia play. Once the protagonist finally succumbs to the deadly desert, the women who remain as witnesses to his passing begin to speak using words from Harold Pinter's poem "Death," a poem he read as part of his 2005 acceptance speech for the Nobel Prize in Literature:

> Where was the dead body found?
> Who found the dead body?
> Was the dead body dead when found?
> How was the dead body found?
> Who was the dead body?
> Who was the father or daughter or brother
> Or uncle or sister or mother or son
> Of the dead and abandoned body?
> Was the body dead when abandoned?
> Was the body abandoned?
> By whom had it been abandoned?
> Was the dead body naked or dressed for a journey?
> What made you declare the dead body dead?
> Did you declare the dead body dead?
> How well did you know the dead body?
> How did you know the dead body was dead?
> Did you wash the dead body?
> Did you close both its eyes?
> Did you bury the body?
> Did you leave it abandoned?
> Did you kiss the dead body?[66]

When Pinter read this poem, accepting his Nobel Prize, he did so within the context of twentieth-century world atrocities committed by the United States and Britain during interventions in different international affairs. Paying close attention to Latin American countries that suffered dictatorships sponsored by the U.S. government, his speech proclaims the lack of moral sensibility with regard to human life. In the same vein, TLS uses fragments of this poem as poetic ritual in a Greek chorus fashion, exposing what happens in many deaths that go unnoticed. With clear references to the protagonist's words, where the Everyman character openly questions if we, the audience, see him, if we, the audience, know his name, *Amarillo* relates Pinter's poem to the ongoing tension between lives that matter and lives that are invisible to others. Emphasizing this tension, and in a theatrical manner, the female actors look at the audience pointedly as they walk around, and as they approach the proscenium, they keep asking, "Who was the body?," "Have you seen the body?," "Was the dead body found"?[67] This scene mirrors the opening act of the play, where the Everyman actor watches the spectators as they enter the stage, watching us watching him. This time, though, the questions are a direct punch aimed at the audience, making us hear those words, making us see the situation.

In its essence, *Amarillo* is a performance of failure to cross the border; however, it is a new way of telling through documentary means (testimonies on video, photographs, letters, poems, and blogs) but also through the creation of a dramatic story arc that is never fully realized. There are no characters, not even a story of one person, nor even a particular event. No one actually makes it to the other side of the wall at the back of the stage. What we find are endless numbers of truncated stories, fragments, and pointless deaths, retold through a visual poetics. This combination of unfinished documentary and narrative arcs makes this play more than a political statement on immigration rights. Instead, it becomes a way to show how art and the aesthetic hope of creation and its social relation might stimulate us to understand one another, to see each other, to make the cruelty of life bearable, to be affected, in a way, by optimism.

TLS relies on its artistic and digital methods to seek other ways of communicating information about border crossing, trauma, and accidental deaths. Through the combination of sounds of water, sand, and the ambiguous figure of the throat singer, the last scene explodes with an artistic collage of fused images that play with our perception of colors (yellow, blue, orange, green) and shapes. Bodies become shortened and elongated shadows, water jugs are a beam of blue light that seems to invite us with the hope of life. In a darkened space, the use of only a few of these colors and shadows encourage the audience to imagine other ways of visualizing the border. In this darkened room, the back screen turns a bluish green with yellow stains, resembling a painting by Jackson Pollock. With the help of digital and graffiti artists, digital distortions manipulate what cameras on the ceiling record, combining images in such a way that the landscape becomes fluid, welcoming, yet extremely abstract and imaginary. Ultimately, images are bright, colorful, and attractive, yet the depiction of death hangs subliminally in this collage because the body of the Everyman lies at center stage. While the collage is not always the same, digital artists bring out different possibilities by playing with photographs, paintings, and visual distortions.

Since 2012, the company has incorporated photographs from Cadillac Ranch, suggesting a cemetery-like space. Cadillac Ranch is a public art installation in Amarillo, Texas, created in 1974 by Ant Farm visual artists Chip Lord, Hudson Marquez, and Doug Michels. It consists of ten mid-twentieth-century Cadillacs half-buried in the ground, nose-first, in angular fashion. The automotive relics stand in the middle of an open field, visible from the highway and approachable by car. Today, they continue to evolve as an artistic center even though they are stationary, because graffiti is allowed on the cars, and anybody can leave their imprint on them. The image of the Cadillac

Ranch, then, becomes part of TLS's ensemble of colors, patterns, and shapes, and they distort photographs of the buried Cadillacs, which are transformed into circular headstones. This distorted collage of a tombstone is accompanied by a beautiful ritualistic sound. The cemetery-like space becomes even more emphasized when the throat singer gives the audience his last salute while sand resonates as it falls from the many bags that hang above the stage. Amid this eerie beauty, the body of the dead migrant lies on the stage, darkened by shadows. Through this culminating scene, visual and digital forms of display combine with aural stimuli to ritualize the death of those unnamed and unclaimed immigrants who still lie in the desert and to pay them respect.

It is noteworthy to emphasize that this play has been performed since 2009, with the same crew. Even as actors physically push their bodies to extremes moving, jumping, dancing, running, and throwing themselves against the back wall, they remain committed to this project and to being and staying together. As a play that has become a symbolic artistic product of a story about immigration, *Amarillo* is TLS's central and most prolifically produced work. Thus, when compared to other documentary plays discussed in this book, it becomes the most polished and visually elegant example. In a variety of personal interviews, both actors and producers of *Amarillo* have made a point about understanding the important messages that it fosters and how they are now more interested in taking *Amarillo* to the migrant routes as a production that creates connections and interrelations. Raúl Mendoza, the main actor in *Amarillo*, made clear that at one point, this play had lost its meaning for him after seeing that the migrant cause had been worsened by the Trump administration's politics. While he considered leaving the troupe because of personal issues with this topic, Mendoza decided to return to his role once TLS made more of a political and social commitment to migrant needs and issues. And although his body aches from the physical demands of this play, where he constantly throws himself against the wall with fruitless effects, he sees it as his own embodied contribution to a much-needed debate on the rights of migrants.[68]

Baños Roma and the Depths of Ciudad Juárez

If with *Amarillo*, TLS focuses their attention on the migrants' journey, *Baños Roma* explores the current ghostly state of the border town of Ciudad Juárez, a center of unresolved femicides and drug traffickers.[69] Since the early 1990s, thousands of women have been kidnapped, tortured, raped, and/or killed in Ciudad Juárez and the surrounding areas. According to the National Institute of Statistics and Geography, in 2016 alone, 2,813 women in Mexico were murdered, the highest number in the last twenty-seven years. In 2002, the Interamerican Commission on Human Rights wrote a special report about the murders in Ciudad Juárez, stating that two hundred women had been brutally killed since 1993 and more than five hundred other women had disappeared without a trace. Their study concluded that the majority of the victims were *maquila* (factory) workers who had to take buses late at night or in the early hours of the morning, making them vulnerable prey. This investigation spurred over five thousand people to sign a petition stating that "since 1993 women who live in Ciudad Juárez are afraid. Afraid of going out on the streets and walking back and forth to work. Fear at ages 10, 13, 15 or 20; it doesn't matter if they are girls or women."[70] Some bodies have been recovered, with marks of rape, mutilation, and torture. Others have never been found. Marcela Lagarde, former Mexican government representative and chair of the Special Commission on Femicide (created in 2004 to address murders of women in Cuidad Juárez), highlights femicide as a genocide and a crime of the state. Influenced by theorist Diana Russell, who coined the term "femicide" through a feminist lens, as to conceptualize gender violence through power relations, Lagarde contributes to the term "femicide," defining it as

> a minimal visible part of violence against women and girls, and it occurs as the culmination of a situation characterized by a systematic and repetitive violation of human rights against women. The common denominator is their gender: women and girls are cruelly violated solely because they are women.
>
> [una ínfima parte visible de la violencia contra niñas y mujeres, sucede como culminación de una situación caracterizada por la violación reiterada y sistemática de los derechos humanos de las mujeres. Su común denominador es el género: niñas y mujeres son violentadas con crueldad por el solo hecho de ser mujeres.][71]

As a legal term, "femicide" exposes the marginal status as part of an oppressed gender. According to sociologist Julia Estela Monárrez Fragoso, the subaltern state of these *fronteriza* women and girls allows to become victimized through a patriarchal culture that perpetuates a state of impunity and illegality.[72] Sergio González Rodríguez links what he calls "femicide machine" to the U.S. militarization of the border and the constant drug wars between cartels. He defines the term as "an apparatus that didn't just create the conditions for the murders of dozens of women and little girls but developed the institution that guaranteed impunity for those crimes and even legalized them."[73]

To compound these femicides, in 2006, then president Felipe Calderón, headed one of the strongest fights against the drug lords, which fomented an all-out war between the state and the narcos. Ciudad Juárez, the headquarters for some of the Juárez and Sinaloa cartels became a city at war. So, whereas we know that most women killed in Juárez worked in the *maquilas*, without a family to protect them from assassins, it is difficult to know whether the narcos were responsible for some, any, or all of their deaths. What is known is that many women have disappeared, and that violence and crime have increased because of the drug trafficking. As a result, Ciudad Juárez became a ghost town. Thousands of families fled the town fearing violence, abandoning the city as their last resort, and criminals made their way into the city. In her illuminating study, Pátricia Ybarra sees the long-lasting neoliberal practices to the ongoing femicide as a "condition with a profound genealogy and a durational obstinacy that refuses to end."[74] While she explores work done by Latinx theater practitioners that for the most part evade documentary practices and instead choose more nonrealistic plays, she analyzes how artists employ misogyny as a provocative tool onstage.

TLS was first attracted to a 2009 newspaper story written by Juan Manuel Vázquez for Mexican daily newspaper *La Jornada*. Vázquez interviewed Cuban Mexican boxer José Angel Mantequilla Nápoles, now deceased, about his life, his gym for teenagers named Baños Roma, and what it was like to live in the gruesome state of Ciudad Juárez.[75] Captivated by his life story and by the fact that one of their actors was a former boxer, TLS decided to travel to this border city. As a group they spent six weeks researching and documenting stories in Ciudad Juárez, as well as spending hours interviewing Mantequilla Nápoles. In a similar fashion as they did with constructing a chapel in Altar, TLS's research for this play involved a social aspect. To theatricalize Mantequilla Nápoles's story, they felt they needed to give back by renovating his gym (which was in utter ruins at the time). They also created a small booklet titled *Non Negotiable*, more like a fanzine, an amateur publication, with pictures from Mantequilla's life as a boxer as well as a compilation of the before-and-after pictures of the renovated gym. This booklet also serves to record and document their research and social intervention. Mantequilla Nápoles, who suffered from dementia and had long memory lapses, is himself a ghostly figure that fades in and out of different video fragments that TLS uses to frame the performance. Thus, his presence takes on allegorical overtones of what Ciudad Juárez represents today, an absent, empty city that cannot remember its own past and identity. When the audience enters the theater, we see a graffiti artist erasing Mantequilla Nápoles's face with white paint. His face fades away in front of us while the artist calmly coats the back wall with white paint. Employing their laboratory technique, actors Alicia Laguna and Zuadd Atala use live cameras to record, project videos on screens, and physically move props while they tell us the "true" story of Mantequilla Nápoles's life.

Featuring live music, three working tables, boxing bags, five actors, and one live musician, *Baños Roma* explores the theatricality and performativity in telling this retired boxer's story, stating from the beginning that "when a story is retold, it is already altered."[76] Although the group relies on authentic documentary material, this evidence does not guarantee veracity, as the quote suggests. Moreover, what appears to be a first-person narration of documentary material, such as "These are the shoes that Mantequilla's wife gave me" or "This is the letter that Mantequilla received," is destabilized by the artist-actors as they toggle between fact and fiction. As a result, this strategy of putting fact and fiction into tension destabilizes our faith in the archive, making the document a piece of evidence that becomes instead a questionable prop.[77] Mantequilla's loneliness is palpable when on the video screen he states, "I don't exist anymore," while a chronology of his life and the successes of his career are superimposed with photos, graphics, and statistics.[78] The group focuses on his well-known 1974 fight with Argentine boxer Carlos Monzón. Under the auspices of French actor Alain Delon, Monzón and Matequilla Nápoles met for a historic and highly anticipated fight. This encounter caught the attention of Julio Cortázar, who wrote a short story titled "La noche de Mantequilla," in which the fight takes place in the context of disappearances that were occurring in the 1970s in Argentina under the military repression. The explicit intertextuality of Mantequilla's life, as it is shown through photos, video, and performance onstage, is augmented by Cortázar's own literary intertext, written about another time and space. Fact and fiction intermingle as TLS stages a story within a story within a story.

The heft of this play can be seen in the combination of testimony acquired during their residency, their use of intertextual literary pieces like Cortázar's short story, fragments of Miguel Delgado's film *Santo y Mantequilla Nápoles en la venganza de la llorona* (*Santo and Mantequilla Nápoles in the Revenge of the Crying Woman*, 1974), as well as Argentine Spanish theater artist Rodrigo García's take on a boxer's life in his play *Prometeo* (*Prometheus*, 1984), and Myrna Pastrana's testimonial short novel *Cuando las banquetas fueron nuestras* (*When the Sidewalks Were Ours*, 2011), about the current violent state of Ciudad Juárez. The intertextual fusion of these literary and visual pieces conveys the imagination and glorious past of both a boxer and a once flourishing city like Ciudad Juárez. It also confronts the current issues of desperation and desolation in that city. *Baños Roma*, then, is a way to connect ideas, facts, and fiction about a city surrounded by violence. Alicia Laguna states that "all of a sudden, to us everything seemed to have a similarity, an affinity with the ex-champion's city. Paris, Ciudad Juárez, the ex-champion, Ciudad Juárez, Baños Roma" (De pronto, todo nos pareció que había una semejanza, una similitud con la ciudad del ex campeón. París, Ciudad Juárez; el ex campeón, Ciudad Juárez; Baños Roma).[79] There is an obvious globalized aspect to this exposure of Ciudad Juárez, where boxing, Paris, and literature come together to tell another story, one, perhaps, of a more humane and successful past. Consequently, this entangled approach to scripting Mantequilla Nápoles's life shows how documentation and creation can blur. And while the main narrative arc seems to focus on reconstructing the events of Mantequilla Nápoles's life and boxing career, Ciudad Juárez becomes a central character as well.

The (In)Visibility of Bodies

In documentary theater practices, autobiographies and staged biographies abound. TLS relies less from using witnesses as interpreters, or people telling their own life stories, as other playwrights and theater groups have done. However, the autobiographical mode is brought in through the interviews conducted with Mantequilla Nápoles that we hear through letters and we see through video fragments on the screen, as well as a photograph that actor-boxer Jorge León found of his own young mother with Mantequilla Nápoles. The real-life connection to this famous boxer is yet another technique to documenting lives onstage. The same newspaper clip written by Juan Manuel Vázquez for *La Jornada* in 2009 is mentioned by actors on the stage as a catalyst for their work. In this news story, his life, his fight against Argentine boxer Carlos Monzón in Paris and the imminent decay of Ciudad Juárez were tied together, linking Paris to Ciudad Juárez, and linking Mantequilla Nápoles to his own ghostly memories of himself and of the city where he used to live. Mantequilla Nápoles's portrayal of himself as a boxer who helps Santo, the *lucha-libre* style (freestyle) masked Mexican hero who ends the curse that La Llorona has placed on the Mexican people, marks his popular cultural appeal in the 1970s. While the audience can see fragments of this film, a sign stating "Heroes are needed here" adds a haunting image to the situation being portrayed. The image of boxing, then, becomes a frame for the film's actors. We see this frame in fragments of Mantequilla Nápoles's life and fights, and also on the physical stage, through an increase in the number of punching bags that populate the stage, as well as scales that constantly carry and record the weight of the boxer while a computer screen marks the time each round lasts. At the same time, songs by Johnny Cash (such as "The Beast in Me") played and adapted by musician and saxophonist Jesús Cuevas contribute a sonic representation of the effect of physical violence on a human body.[80] Interestingly, the visual poetics of this play use the perpetual presence of the boxing bags in a way that makes this violence visible and accepted; in the meantime, the "invisible" violence against women goes unnoticed. There is constant tension between recounting Mantequilla Nápoles's boxing days and revealing Ciudad Juárez's spiral into violence. In a first-person narration, actors come forward as witnesses to offer their own perceptions about the danger they experienced during their residency (being constantly questioned by the police, being followed by police cars and by people driving or walking behind them). The retelling of their own stories is framed by the addition of boxing bags around them, augmenting the proliferation of violence. These bags hanging lifelessly onstage, symbolizing bodies, invite further interpretation. As the performance progresses, images of boxing become darker and more violent.

Documenting the life of a once successful boxer whose own body shows the aches of age and fighting brings to light the dark impact boxing can have on a person. However, his story also serves to explore a life of boxing portrayed as "accepted violence onstage," whereas violence against female bodies goes unmarked, unprocessed. The life of the boxer is narrated through the exploration of what the body can and cannot sustain in the ring. With a clear intertextual addition from García's play *Prometeo*, the actors relate the world of boxing through weight and characteristics. With a rhythmic sequence, they toss around scales, and they repeat how their weight designates them into each category: "Light Flyweight, up to 106 pounds; Flyweight, up to 112 pounds; Bantamweight, up to 119 pounds," to which another actor adds "In boxing, a man is just a body. For fight promoters the man is just a body. The boxer isn't a man; he is his weight class: welter weight, straw weight, full weight, light weight" (Para el boxeo el hombre es un cuerpo. Para los promotores de combates entre hombres, el hombre es un cuerpo. El boxeador no es un hombre, es un wélter, un paja, un peso completo, un peso ligero).[81] Although *Baños Roma* opens up an intertextual dialogue with García's play, it does not delve into the world of the boxer himself. Instead, the world of boxing becomes mixed and blurred through the biographical lens of Mantequilla Nápoles's story. By viscerally focusing on the idea of the body, its weight, and the mere onstage presence of scales, the group calls for the actual essence of a body to take center stage. Thus, the constant repetition of the boxer's weight and class exposes a system of how bodies are seen and labeled in the official world of boxing, contrasting it with the bodies of women, which seem to evaporate, as they are given little if any weight.

The weight of bodies relates to more than just boxing. In a highly aesthetic way, TLS makes a point about how bodies can perpetuate and instigate heavy violence, especially that of gender violence directed toward women. One scene centers on how two males tell jokes, share beers with the audience, and make audience members laugh through mundane sports stories. Simultaneously, a woman dances in the distance. After the laughter dies down, they watch her and encourage each other to "go dance with her."[82] As soon as one of them approaches her to dance, the scene quickly changes to grotesque, unwanted movements, and the violent rhythms end with her body on the floor. Although their symbolic violent movements never become actual violence and are instead framed as a dance, in the end the female body lies heavily breathing, suggesting and amplifying both distance and proximity to fact and fiction. A spotlight moved on a pulley by one of the actors is lowered and focuses attention on her body while the two men smoke and watch her closely without shame. Two, maybe three minutes transpire between the laughter and this last scene. A camera zooms in to capture her shoe, and multiple screens show various fragments of this shot. This graphic scene demonstrates how staged biographies reveal to us different patterns of the real in the theater and how the audience relates and reacts to these patterns. Susan Sontag, who has written about the consequences of violent images in our virtual times, states that "something becomes real—to those who are elsewhere, following it as 'news'—by being photographed. But a catastrophe that is experienced will often seem eerily like its representation."[83] Through a photographic scene, TLS invites us to see an image frozen in time, to make us see. In this way, photographs "record the real," and the recording, itself made and played through a machine, "bear[s] witness to the real."[84] A still frame of a shoe that semiotically connects to the heavy weight of the many disappeared women in the desert freezes the image. Nothing else happens onstage, except for the breathing body of the actress that we see outside the frame of the screen and the actors who smoke and focus their gaze on her. Thus, TLS connects the idea of "less polished pictures . . . [that possess] a special kind of authenticity" and opposes it with the act of watching a live scene as an audience member.[85] This binomial between screen shots and staging creates a dynamic for how the audience actually sees and where its attention is focused. If the search for the authentic comes out of an unpolished frame, then this scene exploits this medium to bring together the visual and the visceral.

Necrotheater and the Visual Culture of Death

In Mexico's violent context, artists have used the image of death in various ways. Playwrights Hugo Salcedo and Víctor Hugo Rascón Banda have been more graphic at times in their work to call attention to atrocities.[86] Teresa Margolles, a Mexican conceptual artist and photographer, has relied on strong images of death, even to the point of utilizing body parts in her installations. Similarly, scholars in the field of theater have studied how some practitioners rely on "necrotheater" by which "an act of death is constructed in a spectacular fashion looking for terrifying effects."[87] In her illuminating study, Ileana Diéguez links the so-called period of death during President Felipe Calderón's government (2006–2012) to what she dubs "necro-theater" in a general sense, a visual brutality where bodies were staged in public spaces, producing "bodily texts of terror."[88] The visual catastrophes that Mexico has undergone after Calderón declared "a war on drugs" expose the strong, and I would dare say furious use of the spectacle of suffering as a demonstration of power. Sadly, in Mexico death scenes are not just part of the artistic performance field; rather, they are heinous public demonstrations, where bodies hang from bridges, headless torsos are found on the streets, and decapitated heads show up in Acapulco and other tourist cities. In this light, Diéguez astutely studies how these atrocities invoke a visual spectatorship that brings horror and fear to public spaces and public behavior. However, what is most striking, perhaps, is not the visual component of the gruesome bodies we see, but what this type of hypervisibility also implicitly posits about those bodies never seen—the ones that disappear without a trace, many of them without a name.[89]

While TLS does not create "necrotheater" as Diéguez describes it, it does borrow from the concept by compiling a montage of images about death that at once expand and challenge the audience's imagination. At the same time, however, TLS shies away from the spectacle of death to produce an opposite effect. In *Amarillo*, for example, TLS employs *poiesis* as a creative method to reveal possible angles and multivalent power structures. The spectacle of death is absent in their work; instead, they provide the audience with glimpses, fragments, staged photography, letters, and testimonies of the society that has been left behind. Through their documentary technique, they animate a story within a story, thus framing for their audiences the larger unanswered questions about Ciudad Juárez, the women of Juárez, and who was and still is behind the many disappearances. The audience gets "punched" with this information through their ritualistic sense of theater—their artistic manifestation of optimism in music and dances that portray the beauty of the lives of others takes place, after all, in a space of violence and death. At the end, together with a saxophonist, the graffiti artist closes the play by redrawing Mantequilla Nápoles's face on the white wall, so his print, art's imprint, refuses to give up its space and instead makes a mark on us, those who watch the creation and erasure of images before our eyes.

While the premiere of *Baños Roma* cast actor/boxer Jorge León, the restaging of the same play in 2017 was quite different.[90] The original play based its core content on biography and a documentary method to the plot, so it became an intriguing new play when the main actor was no longer part of the group. The replacement of an actor in a documentary play is rendered more problematic than simple recasting when they explore their own testimony and witnessing, adding to the foundation of the performance. Due to personal issues, León was forced to leave the troupe, but his departure compelled remaining members to search for another protagonist. The new actor, Gilberto Barraza, was definitely not a boxer; he did not embody the same physicality one would expect from a boxer. Instead, Barraza brought a fresh documentary perspective to the play, as an ex–drug dealer who lived in Ciudad Juárez and whose scarred face shows some of the tough choices he made in life. While boxing is still at the center of the plot, and Mantequilla Nápoles's story is still the focal point, the city of Juárez is now brought to life through this new actor. Barraza's life, his endurance, his vivid and personal narrative about the narcos and his own role as a drug trafficker turn this border town into a gruesome ghostly figure, exposing what some of its inhabitants still carry as leftover residue from violent acts.

In an intimate narrative, he talks to the audience about his tattoos, speaks candidly about his drug trafficking, and also reminisces about what Ciudad Juárez was like during his childhood. He remembers how people used to swim in the Rio Bravo and how the city was alive with people walking on the streets. He continues:

Over the years, in a city that still cannot be named, the streets were abandoned, outside lounge chairs were brought in, doors and windows were closed. Music from the bars gradually disappeared. And in this city of red sunsets, parties were moved inside the houses. Public space was lost, but songs and karaoke flourished inside private spaces.

[En el transcurso de los años, en una ciudad que aún no puede nombrarse, las calles se quedaron solas, metieron las poltronas a las casas, cerraron puertas, las ventanas. La música de los bares paulatinamente se apagó. Y en esta ciudad de atardeceres rojos la fiesta se trasladó al interior de las casas. Se perdió el espacio público pero en el espacio íntimo floreció el canto y se instaló el karaoke.][91]

To emphasize this private space in people's homes, the group echoes Barraza's words by inviting a local band or members of the audience to take part in a karaoke song. Used as comic, audience-inclusive relief, TLS also makes us aware of shifts in community practices that have resulted from the violence and the lack of safe access to the outside, even to one's own front yard. In this way, a major aspect of the play involves making spectators aware of spatial relations and how alert they are to dangers in their own lives.

The loss of public rights to the city, which encompasses daily civic life and activities like walking on streets, or going to markets or parks, reflects the circumstances of present-day Ciudad Juárez's inhabitants. Economic transformations also contribute to a loss of freedom, and fragments from Myrna Pastrana's novel *Cuando las banquetas fueron nuestras* find their way onto the stage through one of the actor's dialogues. Holding and pointing to Pastrana's book, the actor recites the following quote:

The maquiladoras arrived in the'60s, and they changed the face of the city and movement for its inhabitants, who from then on dressed in industrial uniforms. There were not enough women workers to cover the three shifts; that is why it is no coincidence that in the '90s they began placing big signs at plant entrances offering jobs, bonuses for perfect attendance, bonuses for punctuality, Christmas bonuses, gym memberships, pool memberships, daycare and transportation stipends; incentives to attract the work force.

[La maquiladora llegó durante los años sesenta, cambió el rostro de la ciudad y el movimiento de gran parte de sus habitantes, que de ahí en adelante vistieron con bata industrial. No se daba abasto ni contratando operadoras los tres turnos; por ello, no era casual que, en la década de los noventa, colocaran a la entrada de las plantas mantas con grandes letras ofreciendo: bono por contratación, bono por asistencia, bono por puntualidad, bono navideño, gimnasio, alberca, guardería y transporte; incentivos para atraer mano de obra.][92]

In a first-person narrative, actors relate their personal impressions to their experiences in the city by weaving in fragments of Pastrana's novel. In a more direct quote, actors relate to the author's strong conviction when they read, "We lost our sidewalks, and in doing so, we lost every connection between the city and the people" (hemos perdido nuestas banquetas, y al hacerlo, hemos perdido toda conexión con la ciudad y su gente).[93] Another actor provides a grotesque visual summary of what the city is today: "The city is filled with signs of disappeared women. I found it curious that ads soliciting women for table dancing were right next to them, as if done on purpose" (El centro está repleto de carteles de mujeres desaparecidas, lo que me pareció curioso es que al lado de muchos de estos, como si fuera a propósito hay cartulinas solicitando chicas para el table dance).[94] TLS correlates the story that the Juarense actor Barraza witnessed by showing how Ciudad Juárez was an economic hub in the 1990s and later became a death trap and vacant city. As with Cortázar's intertextual short story about Mantequilla Nápoles, TLS surveys the city through literature. Similarly, Pastrana's novel is brought in as another narrative line, fomenting its presence as yet one more document that tells the story of a once successful and energetic city.

The emptiness of Ciudad Juárez is also documented by the remains in the city: its abandoned dogs. Aided by digital artwork and video art, stories of hundreds of thousands of now stray dogs become a visually powerful exploration of what actually occurs to people's pets when they leave. And while the screen distorts drawings of dogs, a voice offstage adds that "we are a hundred thousand, we are on the streets. We are a street gang. We are a pack. The rest packed their bags . . . locked their doors and threw the keys away in the trash. We barked, we howled and we madly paced in circles on the patios. Our collars were useless . . . one hundred thousand of us. That's how this city became filled up with our howls" (Somos cien mil, estamos en las calles. Somos la clica de las calles. La manada. Hicieron las maletas . . . Cerraron la puerta y echaron las llaves en la basura. Ladramos, aullamos, dimos vueltas enloquecidas en los patios, salimos por los agujeros a la calle. Los collares no nos sirvieron de nada. 100 mil. Así se pobló esta ciudad de aullidos).[95] Tribes of dogs now rule the city, and the general sense of abandonment is magnified by the new symbolic power of what these once-pets are now: wild dogs in search of survival.

The abandoned city is the main focus, but Mantequilla Nápoles's story and the changes to Ciudad Juárez offer new perspectives for storytelling as they are transformed by the actors. Theatrically, the change in actor from Jorge León to Gilberto Barranza called for rewriting and reformatting the main connection to Mantequilla Nápoles's story in the play. While the original script invited a kinesthetic link through the boxer's body, his movements, and his own biographical narrative, a refashioning of the play aligned space and place more closely with the central focus on the city. Scenes that before seemed peripheral to the story now became fundamental. For instance, in one scene, an actress dances over sawdust that comes from the inside of one of the boxing bags. Speaking directly to the audience, she begins to trace streets, avenues, and commercial centers in Ciudad Juárez. She draws and redraws a map of the city she remembers, tapping her shoes and extending her legs from one end to another. Her movements are carefully controlled, but her map, which is also enlarged and seen on the overhead screen, is inexact. Even though she draws a street, she rapidly erases it to show another one, and another one. Names come and go. Her dancing shoes tap on the sawdust, spreading it around. With her legs moving in expanding circular motions, she creates and re-creates her own recollection of the city. Street names are invoked and new movements erase previous ones, as if the same construction of the city gets quickly forgotten by new movements, new sand, and newly vacant places. Thus, Ciudad Juárez gets redrawn and reimagined through theater. This superimposition of layers offers us a view of Ciudad Juárez as an ambiguous city that can only be conceived by way of fragments and secondhand stories. It is an ephemeral city that disappears before our eyes. For Michel de Certeau, "the act of walking is to the urban system what the speech act is to language or to the statements uttered. . . . It is a process of appropriation of the topographical system on the part of the pedestrian . . . a spatial acting-out of the place."[96] He explains that this system implies *relations* in order to foment "walking as a space of enunciation."[97] Embodying the map by dancing steps over sawdust that clearly marks and erases each drawing creates a haunting relation between the past and the present, fact and fiction, and the understanding of a city that gets both reenacted and lost in the process of performance and violence. And while this mapmaking scene was part of the original play, its centrality in recounting the role of the city is gained through the new actor's biographical link as he tells us his own story of living there.

The topic of Ciudad Juárez as a ghostly city was key in the work of TLS for this particular production. During their residency, team member Alicia Laguna explored the elusive and almost mythical history of a bar called La Brisa.[98] The bar was razed in the 1990s and is currently an empty lot. However, when intact as a standing building, it served as a meeting point for prostitutes who taught lessons about sexually transmitted diseases like AIDS and for intellectuals, artists, and writers who met for *tertulias* and progressive activist meetings. As the actress dances in the shifting sawdust, she mentions La Brisa and wonders whether prostitutes and intellectuals truly met there or if, as with everything else about Ciudad Juárez, it is part of a story that was buried in the sand. Through *Baños Roma*, documentation of Ciudad Juárez becomes the basis for understanding the history behind the city's decay as well as the birth of many myths and stories that will continue to be retold.

Violence becomes the vehicle linking these plays. The violence of migration in *Amarillo* and the violence of Ciudad Juárez in *Baños Roma* compels audience members to see the fragmentation of a society in quite different forms. Another vicissitude of this type of violence is portrayed when TLS joins forces with local artists in Veracruz to speak about the local violence that has wrapped Veracruz in the last decades.

El puro lugar: In Situ Documenting

While documentation for TLS has mainly been a way to research topics they find compelling, works like *El puro lugar* (*The Pure Place*) centers on historical facts through the activation of performance in a tourist-like experience divided into six different site-specific installations that took place between 2015 and 2016. An in situ, urban documentary installation, *El puro lugar* allows for one hundred spectators divided into groups of ten and distributed over four days. While the hope was that the same spectator would take part in all the installments, other spectators could also take their place. Each actor drives and also walks ten spectators at different times and to different locations around the town of San Bruno of Xalapa, Veracruz, a city filled with violent history, as I will detail below. There were three focal and obligatory locations for all spectators to go: the factory of San Bruno, the Zapotito chapel, and a small dormitory room where students were once attacked.

Divided into six different episodes or installations, *El puro lugar* combines archives, testimony, and photographs with a very personal and semiprivate spectatorship experience. All episodes last around sixty to ninety minutes; some take place in the abandoned factories or schools, while others are staged in the small dorm room. Thus, six installations bridge multiple times and places to focus on atrocity and violence of Xalapa. A coproduction between TLS and the Actors Organization of the University of Veracruz (ORTEUV), this work incorporates geographical and historical fieldwork undertaken by director Jorge Vargas, Alejandro Flores Valencia, and Luis Mario Moncada regarding three different instances of historical violence in Veracruz, the largest city on the Gulf of Mexico. In 1924, ten workers from the textile factory in San Bruno, Xalapa, were kidnapped and murdered. Because this was a factory with a history of leftist union workers, this crime was never solved, and the workers were never found. The thematic thread of violence is documented via events all linked to places in Veracruz in various ways: the textile factory where these workers were killed, presumably for having Marxist ideals; twelve actors in Oscar Liera's play, *Cúcara y Mácara*, who were violently attacked by a right-wing group due to the play's controversial nature in regard to religion in 1981; and finally the small dorm where eight students from the University of Veracruz were attacked and beaten by the police in 2015 for being considered radicals. All of these events are reactivated through testimonials, performances, and visits to the places where these atrocities took place. The intersectionality of violence aligns different temporal and geographical contexts in order to rethink and question history, its archival process, and audience positionality. The three separate incidents are connected by geography, violence, and political antagonism.

Maybe more than the product itself, the call to participants gives us a true understanding of the activist context of this work:

> In spite of the systematic violence perpetrated against the people of Veracruz over the last years
>
> In spite of the institutional production of fear
>
> In spite of the lack of guarantees safety for Mexican citizens
>
> In spite of the fact that it is not recommended that anyone decry injustice and corruption, go out for coffee at night, be in the wrong place, wear a miniskirt, carry a Mexican flag, get into a taxi, go to a protest, stare at the Government Palace for more than five minutes, take photographs (selfies not included), express yourself if you are over sixty years old, promote land rights, celebrate a birthday, chat on the stairs of a church, write, research, report, be a student, be an academic, be a journalist or just a regular citizen.
>
> In spite of all this, the ORTEUV and Teatro Línea de Sombra (TLS) summon an ad hoc community of citizens to collaborate in the making of a theatrical work by periodically going to a space marked by violence: the room where eight students from the Universidad Veracruzana were beaten in the middle of the night of June 5, 2015. We call this artistic and theatrical action Nothing But the Place.
>
> [A pesar de la violencia sistemática ejercida en los últimos años contra la población veracruzana.
>
> A pesar de la producción institucional del miedo.
>
> A pesar de que nada garantice seguridad a los ciudadanos mexicanos.
>
> A pesar de que no sea recomendable enunciar la corrupción y la injusticia, salir a tomar café en la noche, estar en el lugar equivocado, usar minifalda, portar en la calle una bandera del país, subirse a un taxi, asistir a una manifestación, mirar fijamente al Palacio de Gobierno durante más de 5 minutos, tomar fotografías (que no sean selfies), manifestarte si tienes más de 60 años, promover la defensa de la tierra, celebrar un cumpleaños, conversar en las escaleras de La Parroquia, escribir, investigar, reportear, ser un estudiante, ser un académico, ser un periodista o ser un ciudadano común.
>
> A pesar de todo esto, la ORTEUV y Teatro Línea de Sombra (TLS) convocamos a formar parte de una comunidad temporal de ciudadanos que colaboran con la construcción de una pieza escénica asistiendo periódicamente a un espacio marcado por la violencia: el

> cuarto donde 8 estudiantes de la Universidad Veracruzana fueron batidos a golpes la madrugada del 5 de junio de 2015. A esta acción artística y escénica la hemos llamado El puro lugar.][99]

The convocation goes on to explain how *El puro lugar* aims to transform a violently charged space into a place of memory and life. Its mission is to bring attention to the atrocities committed and disregarded, like a conscious act of erasure, to inspire citizens to reclaim their city and their right to inhabit their towns without fear of retaliation by the government or other groups. It is also a call to arms. This temporary assembly of citizens has been summoned to witness and denounce the violation of rights and to demand their restitution.

These installations destabilize the primacy of the written text as a form of cultural expression, emphasizing instead the significance of embodied forms of transmission of meaning and knowledge through temporally and spatially framed "scenarios," as Diana Taylor has succinctly studied.[100] As participants in this performance, spectators ride a car, walk the city, and are trapped in rooms where they see and hear testimony from the actors, some of whom were actual victims of the violence perpetrated in 1981. They are always accompanied by their actor-guide, who gives them maps and historical background to each installation. The three violent events are woven together through the city of Xalapa. As documents are brought in, history is retold and audience members hear firsthand the stories of these actors as they (re)trace their steps in a factory and (re)draw the map of the city with added anecdotes and urban histories from locals. Each episode is related to the others in some way through violence, but they can also stand alone.

TLS's methodology of working with in situ historical buildings, using a ratio of one hundred spectators to ten actors/guides (first episode) and highlighting the sense of space, both in open format and in a small room, delves into speculations of the veracity of the document in the past and today. In Xalapa, Veracruz, a city overcome by narco-violence, this kind of staging brings to the fore an intersectionality of atrocities committed in different times and places. Xalapa becomes a geographical axis for questions regarding how we live with constant and brutal violence. These questions are enacted through sites and installations that use documents of compounded violent acts. *El puro lugar* challenged spectators not only to participate but also to become participants.[101] As theater scholar Marvin Carlson remarks, the activation of the audience is a productive venue to create something new. He states, "We are now at least equally likely to look at the theatre experience in a more global way, as a sociocultural event whose meanings and interpretations are not to be sought exclusively in the text being performed but in the experience of the audience assembled to share in the creation of the total event."[102] Throughout the yearlong, six-episode work, participants were asked to confront their fears and leave them behind, as can be gauged by the call for participation. This, in turn, increased the cohesiveness among members of the group. Participants were challenged to engage with their bodies in a space charged with violent history to take part in a performance that demanded answers for injustices and impunity. In this way, their bodies perform a political act. For instance, in the first episode, "100 Spectators: 100 Journeys," each audience member rode in a car with a private guide (ten actors took ten participants at different times). They all converged at the textile factory where ten workers were kidnapped and killed in 1924. Here spectators listened to stories, viewed installations about violence, played Foosball, and heard Ignacio Córdoba sing a rap song about the atrocities that occurred in this now abandoned place. People milled about the empty factory where communist murals featuring images of Che Guevara decorated the walls. Politics and space were further conflated when a member of the theater group of the University of Veracruz drove by in a car and announced over a megaphone that "a ghost inhabits San Bruno." This claim established a close link to the *Communist Manifesto* and the idea of the specter of communism in Europe.[103] Calling attention to the ghosts also reinforces the ongoing silence that seems to enable the cyclical violence in this town.

Some installations took place in the dorm where the eight students were assaulted in 2015. Only eight people were allowed at one time to hear testimonies offered by survivors and to see video recordings, clothing, and even the remains of the room that were recovered from the trash and recycled by artists who encapsulated the debris in glass boxes. These boxed artifacts tell the story in yet another format, a museum-like showcase of the remains of a violent intervention against students. Audience members listened to music, viewed video installations, and heard survivors speak, as the tight space of a small dorm suggested the idea of proximity and the desperation these eight students underwent in such a small place. Other installations contained a more private encounter, as was the case with "If the Walls Spoke," where only the same one hundred spectators were permitted to enter the same dorm room one at the time. This dorm room held a collection of different materials used in previous spaces but were now displayed together as a private museum exhibit, in what participant Geraldine Lamadrid Guerrero called an "archaeological autopsy."[104] In her study, she claims that artists involved with *El puro lugar* became historians and archaeologists so that they could collect pieces of historical violence and transform them into art. Whatever artists found in the trash—fragments of clothes, pieces of students' possessions—became part of the archaeological exhibit.

For citizens of Xalapa, fear of violent retaliation for asking too many questions meant participants needed to construct a new space to learn the history and its documents. Antonio Prieto Stambaugh, who participated in this event, wrote that this fear is part of what he refers to as "troublesome memory."[105] As artists bring back the past through live performances in places of trauma, they affect spectators in a visceral fashion. From a Freudian angle, Prieto

Stambaugh argues that this type of remembering in historical places engages spectators in both personal and collective memories through new ways of seeing and engaging an already known place. Stambaugh, a scholar who lives in Veracruz, has a personal connection to the ubiquitous violence in the city and understands why people are afraid. Although hundreds of citizens have left Veracruz due to the incessant violence, he sees this type of work as a public call to action for those who remain. In a sense, exploring place and space, both in a historical vein, as well as in real time with a group of participants, forces the question of who sees and what they get to see. Documentary material exhibited in glass displays in traumatic spaces where victims recount their stories forces audience members to return to these places and probably think of them for the first time through a lens that connects them as spaces of violent encounters for abuse and murder.

A call to action emphasizes the idea of communal togetherness in a live mode in much the same way that theater does. These qualities can help eliminate or attenuate the fear that each individual brings with them. *El puro lugar*, then, forms part of this call to action for its audiences. Spectators view real documents on-site while listening to firsthand survivors relate details from these atrocities. As a part of this temporary community, audience members and TLS walk through a space marked by a violent encounter to see, hear, touch, and in a sense be affected by the stories they hear as they reinvent the space through a live collective performance. In a less staged way, the theatricality of these events comes to life through actors' bodies and voices as they remember the story of violence in Xalapa alongside the audience members.

Cultural production in the context of Mexican violence has taken many forms and includes the well-known examples of *narcocorridos* and narconovels. For TLS, art is at the center of their research, and while they might have utopian ideals of how to best represent violence onstage, they implore their audiences to see anew. Echoing this idea, Ileana Diéguez argues, "We must imagine a narrative about bodies that are never found, a narrative about those bodies that no one knows where they are, or if they are even dead."[106] TLS speculates with the ambiguity Diéguez suggests above to create a poetic landscape not of death, per se, but of the absence and gaps that these lost lives represent. For TLS, morbid images are not the point; rather, they operate within the possibilities the future holds. The real in their work is moored precisely between the fictional setting of a theater stage and the actual stories they tell—a place of ambiguity. Through a relational method, however, they combine the idea of "being-together," as in a communal theatrical encounter, with human interactions in their various social contexts to clearly define a new mode of documentary onstage. This relationality becomes important as an affective tool when purely political documentary methods give way to artistic introspection.

When this occurs, the idea of relationality pushes the boundaries of the senses and can affect audiences in more profound and possibly more political ways than before. This gray zone—an ambivalent space created by the supposed authenticity of the archive—becomes a productive space that brings art and politics together in more nuanced and critical ways. As Claire Bishop states, "Intersubjective relations serve to explore and disentangle a more complex knot of social concerns about political engagement, affect and inequality."[107] The intersubjectivity or convivial capacities of a community at risk of being detained just for being together becomes a clear form of political engagement where activism propelled by social concerns turns to the affective. TLS's methods shy away from a didactic documentary practices; instead they foment a creative way to think of issues of relationality, both as theater practitioners and as political activists who search for collaboration and participation. In a sense, as their methodologies have evolved into documentary theater, they have pushed TLS to more multivalent and committed practices that involve understanding human relations vis-à-vis political and social situations. Through their poetic exploration, TLS's work stands out, calling for new ways of spectatorship where collaboration and integration are key to artistic practice and activism.

Chapter 4

✦

Memory Sites

Guillermo Calderón's Excavation for the Truth

> Don't be taken in when they pat you paternally on the shoulder and say that there's no inequality worth speaking of and no more reason for fighting.
>
> —Peter Weiss, *The Persecution of Jean-Paul Marat*

In the morning of June 17, 2013, four thieves with connections to the Chilean leftist political movement Frente Patriótico Manuel Rodríguez (FPMR; Manuel Rodríguez Patriotic Front), robbed a branch of Santander bank in the Pudahuel neighborhood of Santiago de Chile.[1] Armed with M16 rifles, they succeeded in stealing a large amount of money, but three of the four were quickly apprehended after a police chase.[2] The fourth alleged robber, Jorge Mateluna, was caught later in the surrounding area. An FPMR member born in 1974, Mateluna had been imprisoned for armed robbery from 1992 until 2004, though it was largely believed that he had actually been imprisoned for his revolutionary tactics and leftist affiliation with FPMR. Mateluna was automatically a suspect, since he was an ex-convict with connections to a leftist group and in the past had committed armed robbery. However, he claimed to be innocent, and evidence also pointed to his lack of involvement. This story is the heart of Guillermo Calderón's play *Mateluna* (2016), in which he portrays the event using documentary material (security video footage and court hearing audio) to denounce the injustice of implicating and finding him guilty of a crime that evidence gathered by Calderón and his actors proves he did not commit. Jorge Mateluna was convicted and sentenced to sixteen years in prison, and at the moment of writing this chapter, he is still serving his sentence.

Mateluna is the most political play that Calderón has staged to date, not only because of the story line but also because the troupe takes a political stand by condemning the Chilean justice system for its incompetence. Guillermo Calderón, playwright, director, and screenwriter, is a central figure in Chilean theater. He is considered a star of a new generation of postdictatorship playwrights and directors in Chile.[3] His first play, *Neva*, opened in 2006 at the Santiago a Mil International Theater Festival, and since then his productions have received positive critical acclaim, earning him prestigious awards and festival invitations.[4] The main premise of Calderón's work is that he uses theater as a forum for political debate on issues of human rights abuses or impunity. In an interview, he explains that "Chilean theatre is always very political, which is important, because when other spheres depoliticize, it's vital that theatre remains critical."[5] As a playwright, Calderón's political plays are text-driven; the focus is not the stage, props, or even actors' movements but, rather, language and what the words can mean in and out of the theatrical context. But as a director, he is keenly attentive to the creation of the mise-en-scène, first trying out some of his ideas onstage, and then writing out the details of how he conceives his plays.[6] The published versions of his plays do not provide many details regarding onstage directions and dramatic action. His trademark style combines bare stages and simple lighting, and he equips his actors with wireless microphones that convert the theater into a quasi-private space, creating an intimate relationship between actors and audience where every whisper, every sound, and every facial movement is key.

Calderón employs the documentary mode and the blending of the real and fiction onstage to tell a compelling story. Most of his plays question how dramatic fiction may contribute to the political debate outside the theater. This chapter studies the influence that his later plays have had in Chile and abroad in documenting human rights abuses, the erasure of political memory following the Pinochet era (1973–1990), and the impotence of a rigged justice system. I will focus on four plays that showcase memory politics and the need for political action: *Villa+Discuruso* (*Villa+Speech*, 2011), *Escuela* (*School*, 2013), and *Mateluna* (2016). Each play relates in its own specific way to post-dictatorship memory politics. Calderón's reliance on documentary practices advances topics that explore the ongoing debates about memory museums and militant groups during and after the Pinochet regime. His political commitment drives him to seek out hidden and forgotten political stories. Using documentary methods to explore a judicial case in the framework of the theater leads us to look at how some of his plays, specifically *Mateluna*, might resonate beyond the fictional setting. The staging of *Mateluna* does not simply provide context and primary sources supporting his innocence; the play also foments a movement beyond the theater to find Jorge Mateluna innocent of a crime that Calderón and his troupe believe he did not commit.

In a recent interview after *Mateluna*'s opening in Santiago de Chile in 2017, a radio journalist asked Calderón why he was willing to allow his name and the names of his actors to be used in support of Jorge Mateluna, someone with a contentious and questionable past.[7] The question made specific reference to how some in the cast, especially Francisca Lewin and Daniel Alcaíno, had rallied in his favor, even making public appearances in his name.[8] Before Calderón had a chance to respond, the reporter pushed further, asking, "Isn't this dangerous for your reputation?"[9] I find this question key when thinking about how the public values what artists such as Calderón and his actors bring to the stage, and how political action and solidarity can be perceived as problematic. As the radio interviewer makes clear, what is of primary interest to her listeners is not only a conversation about the political message of the play, or just a discussion of the play's aesthetics, but, rather, the effect that the playwright's politics might have on the reputation of those involved in the production.[10]

This is not the first time Calderón has made a strong political commentary on memory politics in Chilean democratic society. Already with his plays *Villa+Discurso* (2011), he inserted his own view that former torture sites and centers of human rights abuses during the Pinochet era should be rebuilt as memory sites. These two plays, staged in tandem and with the same three actors, were first performed at Londres 38, the first central detention and torture site in Chile, where about one hundred people are thought to have been disappeared and many others were held captive.[11] *Villa* refers to Villa Grimaldi, Chile's largest and most infamous detention and torture center, which operated as such from 1974 to 1978. The second play, *Discurso*, is a play on words, since *discurso* means both "speech," as in the presidential speech, and "discourse," as in conversation, or the type of language one uses. This introspective reveals Calderón's attempt to work through the complex ideas about what a memory park should look like. Grounding his work in the lively debates that had taken place on how to rethink Villa Grimaldi in the post-Pinochet era, Calderón offers his own take on the memorialization of Chile's dictatorial past.

Villa+Discurso

The first play, *Villa*, is a debate about the reconstruction of the former torture and detention center Villa Grimaldi as a Park for Peace. Staging the play in Londres 38 fuses site-specific performance with other palimpsests of memory. *Discurso* imagines an apologetic and apocryphal farewell presidential speech by Michelle Bachelet, Chile's first female president, who was detained during the dictatorship. Both plays deal directly with issues of memory politics, truth and reconciliation, and the transitional years from the Pinochet dictatorship to democracy and beyond. Calderón incorporates concrete political and historical references in both plays, but he quickly infuses them with fiction, humor, and even parody regarding the role of archives in our understanding of recent historical data. In particular, *Villa+Discurso* address the dominant role of political discourse in influencing memory politics and the decision-making process involved in creating memorials. The choice of Londres 38 as a backdrop to *Villa+Discurso* serves to revive the past through site specificity, drawing attention to how audiences relate to the piece, and also how performance can recodify our understanding of a historical place through the theatrical event. Signaling Londres 38 as an ex–torture site engages audience members directly with the original site of violence and alerts them to the human rights' discourses that have been central to the conversation on how to reenvision and repurpose the former torture center.

In a postshow interview conducted at Londres 38 audience members of Calderón's *Villa+Discurso* expressed a variety of sentiments. When asked, "What did you think of the play?" members responded by revealing the deep impact of the play. Some said that being present at Londres 38 in itself was telling enough because the place was haunted by past trauma; others were more reflective in their thoughts and maintained that a play like Calderón's relates directly to memory politics, to issues of torture, and that the silence made them want to learn more and even enabled them to recover repressed memories. One audience member believed that plays like these bring issues of historical memory to the foreground, making younger generations aware of a still-silenced past.[12] *Villa+Discurso* affected Chilean audience members deeply through resuscitating the traumatic acts of torture and disappearance during the Pinochet era that had been hidden, forgotten, or buried somewhere in the past. As Cathy Caruth explains when speaking of trauma, "The event is not assimilated or experienced fully at the time, but only belatedly, in repeated *possession* of the one who experiences it. To be traumatized is precisely to be possessed by an image or event."[13] While many in Calderón's audiences might be too young to have experienced these atrocities firsthand, the plays force different generations to grapple with political and historical memory. For older viewers, what they see is part of a lived history; for younger ones, it's what they have (or have not) learned about their own country's recent past.

The choice of Londres 38 as a backdrop to *Villa+Discurso* serves as a revival of the past, and as a site-specific place that affects not just how the audience relates to this piece, but also how performance can recodify our understanding of a historical place through the theatrical event. Detention centers in both the city of Santiago and its surroundings should be made a topic of conversation in this recontextualization of sites.

Mike Pearson and Michael Shank write:

> Site-specific performances are conceived for, mounted within and conditioned by the particulars of found spaces, existing social situations or locations, both used and disused. . . . They rely, for their conception and their interpretation, upon the complex coexistence, superimposition and interpenetration of a number of narratives and architectures, historical and contemporary. . . . Performance recontextualises such sites: it is the latest occupation—their material traces and histories—are still apparent.[14]

Occupying Londres 38 with political plays helped reinterpret the past and the present through performance. While Londres 38 functioned as the first stage for Calderón's plays, they were also staged in other former torture centers, such as José Domingo Cañas, Villa Grimaldi, and in former concentration camps in cities including Buenos Aires, Montevideo, São Paulo, Brasilia, Guadalajara, Madrid, and Sarajevo.[15] As Karen Till suggests, "Places are never merely backdrops for action or containers for the past. They are fluid mosaics and moments of memory, matter, metaphor, scene, and experience that create and mediate social spaces and temporalities."[16] The site-specific aspect of these plays triggers mediation of social spaces by encompassing places with a haunting history and a play that deals with a similar topic. By staging *Villa+Discurso* in different former concentration camps around the world, the plays have responded well to the global need to render a narrative and connect live action to places where atrocities occurred. Even though the plays are specific to Chile and Chile's history, they have become nomadic performances, and in doing so they have dealt directly with human rights issues, both at the local and international level.[17]

In his revealing book *Memorial Museums: The Global Rush to Commemorate Atrocities*, Paul Williams exposes the fine line between a memorial and a museum, expressing concern about "how the mission, audience, educational strategies, and generational framing of memory seeks to function as a memorial."[18] Because there are similarities between what a historical museum and a memorial of atrocities aim to accomplish, he contends that memorial museums which fuse these goals contain authenticity and, thus, the power to display "tangible proof in the face of debate about, and even denial of, what transpired."[19] While a memorial museum calls for "tangible proof," there is also a need to understand that, in many cases, the only proof of the past is an empty carcass of a building, and in many others, not even a building, just the space where the building once stood. The intentional erasure of memory of atrocities committed at the hands of a dictator is a common denominator in the postdictatorship years in a wide array of countries.[20] The tremendous growth of these museums in the last ten years has also created a heated debate on how to define them. Since memorial museums are "dedicated to historic events commemorating mass suffering of some kind,"[21] Patrizia Violi makes a distinction between site-specific memorials, which she defines as trauma sites, and those memorial museums constructed anew, like the Holocaust Museum in Washington, D.C., or the Museo de la Memoria in Chile. This differentiation is helpful because trauma sites have the power of presence, of being the place where violent acts took place, of embodying memory. Even though there might not be any "tangible proof" besides the space itself. In contrast, memorial museums seek to contextualize these atrocities with historical, testimonial, and documentary material.[22]

In Chile, memory of the Pinochet years and beyond has been an increasing and active focus of recent scholarship. A range of studies, such as Steve Stern's look at Chile's history as a "memory box of Pinochet's Chile," Tomás Moulián's "whitewashed Chile," Nelly Richard's "emptying of remembrance," and Michael Lazzara's "memory lenses," have made valuable contributions to the study of memory politics in postdictatorship Chile.[23] While Moulián suggests that there is a lack of words to express what life was like during the Pinochet years, he quickly connects what he sees as silence or forgetting to a way for the capitalist system to take over Chile, its society, and its past—a whitened Chile with no blood on its hands.[24] Lazzara explains that "when there is an intentional smoothing over of trauma (in this case, by the state), the fact that something important has been forgotten or eclipsed . . . can be all the more salient."[25] What these studies tell us is that there is an obsession with memory and the past, in part due to the conscious knowledge that amnesia affects the present and the future. The issue of memory discourses in Chile's transitional years resonates with Calderón's work and to the construction and reconstruction of memorial museums, something that makes people aware of their own history, culture, past, present, and future—in other words, what Andreas Huyssen would term "active remembrance."[26] For Calderón, theater can make people aware of spaces that they might not have known about or seen before, spaces of memory that might have been silent or erased from the public eye. Joanne Tompkins argues that "the practice of site-specific performance has the potential to (re) invigorate both 'place'/ 'site' and 'performance.' "[27] *Villa+Discurso* reinvigorate place, site, and performance by exposing memory sites as palimpsests whose symbolic meaning needs to be decoded. Villa Grimaldi is no exception, and theater is one possible way to attain understanding.

Villa Grimaldi

Villa Grimaldi has lived many transformations and has seen a variety of changes throughout its lifetime. Built in the nineteenth century in the hills near the edge of the Santiago, Villa Grimaldi was first conceived as a beautiful Spanish colonial–style villa with mosaic pools and bountiful gardens that appealed to Chile's elite. In time, the luxurious villa changed hands, and during the presidency of Salvador Allende it was transformed into a restaurant and a meeting place for artists and intellectuals. From 1974 until 1978, the Dirección de Inteligencia Nacional (DINA; National Intelligence Agency) acquired and transformed the space into the largest and best-known interrogation, detention, and torture center of the dictatorship. It has been estimated that more than 4,000 people were imprisoned at Villa Grimaldi, of whom 226 were disappeared.[28] From its inception until it was inaugurated as Peace Park in 1997, this site has accumulated many layers, many lives, many functions. In 1987, near the end of the dictatorship, the villa was sold to a construction company with the aim of building new condominiums. Buildings were torn down, leaving almost no evidence of the former villa. Was the

Pinochet regime trying to erase all traces of their past crimes? Were they perhaps trying to counteract possible survivors' testimonies? Were they just after a general politics of silencing? Or were they trying to do all of that and meanwhile make a profit? Their intention will never come to light; the project was quickly stopped, and in 1990 the villa was handed over to the new democratic government. Although the site was recovered, by 1990 most of the buildings in the villa had been torn down; what remained was thus a silent ruin of the past. It has been left to a diverse collective of social activists, the Agrupación de Testigos Sobrevivientes de Villa Grimaldi (Group of Survivor-Witnesses of Villa Grimaldi), the Asamblea Permanente por los Derechos Humanos de Peñalolén y La Reina (Permanent Committee for Peñalolén and La Reina's Human Rights), and neighborhood and Catholic associations to recuperate the former detention center and to stop the continuing erasure of memory.

Even though the state was officially granted this land in 1994, the political stage of the transitional years seemed to be regulated by a politics of amnesia, as the desire to forget the past and move forward were quite evident. In a presidential speech, Patricio Aylwin made a telling comment that reflected the politics of the time: "For the good of Chile, we should look toward the future that unites us more than to the past which separates us. . . . [Chileans should not] waste our energy in scrutinizing wounds that are irremediable."[29] Chile's traumatic memory politics of amnesia are well grounded in this speech, and it has been left to neighbors, human rights activists, and survivors of the villa with their own memories and actions to shed light on the past of Villa Grimaldi. Details of how the villa was to be redesigned tell us that there were three proposed alternatives: a staged reconstruction of what the space looked like as a torture site; a site of ruins with a monument to honor the memory of the victims; and a new Park for Peace, honoring life and changing the villa's image from a death trap into a space for peace and hope. The last project succeeded, however subtle pieces of the three projects can be found in the villa, since some replicas of the villa's past have been added to the park. For instance, there is currently a wooden box that resembles the isolation cells where prisoners lived. There is also a replica of the "Torre de los Suplicios" (Tower of Cries), where victims spent hours in isolation, and a Wall of Names memorial area with a list of victims. Close to the entrance, inside a small glass box, stands a model of the main house that was used as the primary administrative office by the DINA. In addition, other subtle and controversial elements around the villa include the recycled mosaics that used to belong to the main house where victims were tortured and are now used as decorative signs around the villa and in fountains, or the rose garden, where names of female victims are staked among roses. The Peace Park project prevailed mainly because of support from survivors and victims' families, but also because the government approved of the idea of a "park conceived as a space of reconciliation" and thus granted financial support.[30] As the Villa Grimaldi Web site explains, the mission statement of the Corporación

Parque por la Paz (Peace Park Committee) responds to the need to preserve the history and memory of the villa and those who suffered under state terrorism and to spread and encourage human rights awareness. It also states that Villa Grimaldi is a place that promotes both commemoration and symbolic reparation in a democratic society.[31] In 2004 Villa Grimaldi Peace Park was declared a National Historic Monument.

Through theater Calderón offers a behind-the-scenes look at the debates surrounding how the villa needed to be rethought, reimagined, and redesigned. Three young women, all named Alejandra, are in charge of deciding what to do with the site. While the play is informed by some of the ideas considered during the debates on how to approach the villa, the play quickly turns into a nondocumentary theater piece that, when layered on top of the site, creates a multilayered memory palimpsest. Andreas Huyssen suggests that "an urban imaginary in its temporal reach may well put different things in one place: memories of what there was before, imagined alternatives to what there is."[32] While the idea of palimpsest is highly textual, reading the urban space through this lens offers us, as Huyssen puts it, a way to see the city as a lived space that can shape our collective imaginaries.[33] As we are still uncovering new information about sites of atrocities hidden for decades, the ensuing question of a geography of trauma sites is more embedded in our collective thinking today. How difficult is it to face the past when a country has lived through some of the worst human atrocities? What are the most appropriate paths to work through trauma?

Calderón pushes the boundaries of what is real, what is fiction, what is serious, and what can be playful in his treatment of subjects of death, torture, trauma, memory, and reconciliation. By using Villa Grimaldi, the topic of the first play, and Londres 38, where *Villa+Discurso* were first staged, Calderón makes a conscious effort to bring discarded and obscured stories out of their historic and geographic marginality. In a sense, the backdrop of Londres 38 (or any other site-specific location) becomes the document that haunts the audience, since it fuses site-specific place, performance, and memory. Calderón's technique of utilizing bare stages and designing up-close-and-personal spaces—where actors and audiences share an intimate, proximate space—helps emphasize the relationship between the personal and theater, the intimate and the individuality of each audience member.[34] In the specific case of *Villa+Discurso*, the use of site-specific trauma fits well with Calderón's zeal for exposing the rough edges of the stage, for joining fiction and the real, and for exhibiting political ideas on the stage.

Villa

The stage is almost bare; one banner toward the back displays a chronology of the political history of Chile.[35] One table, three chairs, a pitcher of water,

Fig. 12. Left to right, Carla Romero, Macarena Zamudio, and Francisca Lewin in Guillermo Calderón's *Villa*. Sarajevo, 2012. Photograph by Pola González Durney.

a few glasses, and three actresses occupy the stage, illuminated by regular house lights. The focal point is a small architectural model that sits on the table. This model, which is a replica of a bigger one that sits in the Villa Grimaldi Peace Park, functions in two ways: as a sign of what Villa Grimaldi once was, and as an anachronistic and ambiguous prop, because the play starts with foundational debates about what to do with the villa and ends with the description of the Peace Park that currently stands. Still, the model is a clear referent for Villa Grimaldi and draws the audience's attention to the building. The three Alejandras, played by Francisca Lewin, Macarena Zamudio, and Carla Romero, also seem to conceal some information: Are they the same person divided into three characters? Are they different women with similar lives? Is the past history a connecting thread, thus explaining the use of the same name? (see fig. 12). One possible theatrical technique could be the use of the same three actresses to play Michelle Bachelet. Joanne Pottlizer explains that the name Alejandra is a direct reference to Marcia Merino, known as "La Flaca Alejandra," who was a member of the ultra-leftwing MIR (Revolutionary Left Movement). After being detained and tortured, she conspired with the DINA and became a traitor to her own fellow members of the MIR.[36] If this is the case, I wonder how this fact resonates with audience members who might be oblivious to this reference and what effect Calderón intends to accomplish by using this name and its possible signifiers: anonymity? Militant activism?

As the play unfolds, we become aware that they are three distinct women and that at least one of them lies; in fact, all three of them may be untrustworthy. The Alejandras have been chosen to form a committee to decide whether the villa should be reconstructed or whether a museum should be built instead. Nevertheless, the three characters seem reluctant at first to be part of this committee; they often ask, "Why are we the committee?" If the Alejandras are in constant disagreement on what to do, it does not seem to make sense to keep voting, to form a committee. Questions about how committees can work in such an instance prove that there are many angles and perspectives to the same issue, and their debates seem redundant and inefficient. Later in the play we learn that the three Alejandras are daughters of survivors of the villa who were systematically raped, and as products of those rapes, they become second-generation survivors and narrators. As second-generation narrators, their experiences come not from firsthand witnessing, but instead from documents or family stories, likening their experience of memory to postmemory. For Marianne Hirsch, postmemory is "defined through an identification with the victim or witness of trauma, modulated by an unbridgeable distance that separates the participant from the one born after. . . . Postmemory would thus be *retrospective witnessing by adoption*."[37] In other words, the memories and experiences from first-generation witnesses are so strong that they become second-generation memories. However, I would also contend that Calderón pushes the ancestral link between these three survivors and their mothers through the violent acts committed against their bodies. In turn, their experience is more than second-generation, but still less than first-generation. The emphasis yet again on the liminal state of these survivors is accentuated by how these women were conceived. They embody that violence in a different way, defying the generational lines. In other words, by being born as consequence of rape, the three Alejandras have an intimate and closer relationship to what their mothers experienced.

Nevertheless, the play opens in an almost absurdist, Beckettian form, in what it looks like a circle, a repetition of a previous act now repeated for yet another time. The lack of information or of disclosure among the three characters fragments their communication. They all seem to have their own memories of the villa and ideas about what they should and should not do with it. Their replies often consist of one- or two-word answers. They vote for choice A or choice B, and at this point, the audience is not aware of what those choices refer to. In an interesting switch, one of the Alejandras votes with a Mapundungun word, *marichiweu*, that means "ten times we will win," which sparks a long enigmatic dialogue and controversy about how to vote and what it means to resist such a vote. Even though the three characters bring humor to their (mis)understandings of the vote, it is clear that Calderón alludes to real-life choices and debates that took place before the Peace Park was designed. The characters later suggest that there are actually three choices: choice A, to reconstruct the villa as it was; choice B, to build a museum; choice C, to design a Peace Park. From here to the end, the play circles around the idea of how to imagine the villa, how to think of it either as an artificial reconstruction of the site, as a museum, or as a Peace Park and how to better expose Chile's tormented past.

With colloquial Chilean speech that conveys a register of everyday life, *Villa* makes a direct commentary on why Villa Grimaldi is now a Peace Park and advances a possible criticism of how the park was envisioned. For Calderón, "the park is beautiful in the springtime with all the flowers in bloom. How can such a horrible place be remembered as something so beautiful? It is a contradiction."[38] This contradiction is the basis for this play, and through theater, the three characters act out each possible solution for what the site could or could never have been in what amounts to three monologues that represent each particular option. The metatheatrical technique of exposing what each character symbolizes makes information about the villa more public, blends historical facts with interpretation, and functions as a commentary on how memorial museums and sites of torture are conceived in Chile. However, if for Calderón the Peace Park is too beautiful and instead creates a contradiction, others don't share that point of view. For instance, Macarena Gómez-Barris argues that "the site helps fill in the history of the dictatorship's violence with a popular and alternative account of events and practices, details and stories that have been evacuated from the dominant public sphere."[39] It is obvious that Villa Grimaldi fosters different debates and interpretations of what the Peace Park can and cannot epitomize. However, Calderón brings out the theatricality, the actual representation, of how and why Villa Grimaldi is a difficult—if not impossible—space to represent. As with his theater oeuvre, where he works hard to avoid having his plays seen as cultural objects, *Villa* offers a metacommentary on museum practices and reinforces the ambiguity that memorial museums can convey by calling all historical narratives related to the park into doubt, thus making *Villa* one of his most political plays yet.

The question of how to factor absence into the transmission of memory remains. Through playful metatheatrical technique, Calderón initiates a debate about how Chile learns about its past, how society is negatively affected by the lack of knowledge, and how the hyperconstruction of museums can underestimate the story to be narrated. He succinctly expresses how a narrative about a horrific place like Villa Grimaldi gets constructed by emphasizing the idea of who can speak of what happened and who bore witness. Dori Laub argues that the story of the Holocaust "is inhabited by the impossibility of telling, and therefore, silence about the truth commonly prevails."[40] How then can the theater, and, in Calderón's own words, political theater, delve into the issue of telling? If Villa Grimaldi Peace Park "allow[s] for a meaningful reinstatement of the microhistories of political repression, resistance, and its memory,"[41] the audience must decide which microhistories will register. The play presents a variety of issues about competing histories, the repressors, and their actions, and the present and future aspects for the reconstruction, museum, or Peace Park options. In the reenacting of what "could have probably happened," issues of absence come alive. Silencing is a key factor in this play, and it becomes evident through references to cover-ups of what the character Alejandra (Carla) refers to as the "perfect crime" the military wanted to hide before leaving the villa: "But no, Colonel. If we leave the villa locked up, or covered up with branches, they might find it anyway. We might get caught. Some Swedes or Dutch might come and say: 'Hey, look at this house.'"[42] The impossibility of knowing exactly what transpired in Villa Grimaldi during the dictatorship leaves the playwright with enough room to create a possible alternative narrative. From there, the suggestion of reconstructing the villa as it was presents the audience with the idea of imagining (through artificial means), but also with the impossibility of certainty: "I'd paint the walls with muddy water, with another palette of colors in the background. Tones like sepia. And I'd buy all the paraphernalia. I'd buy a metal bed, I'd buy cables and sockets, I'd buy uniforms, I'd buy clothes with collars, I'd buy the smell of shit. To create a sort of realist Disneyland reality."[43] The constant use of the conditional seems to suggest that Villa Grimaldi is in need of props to create fiction, as if it were a theatrical stage. The undertones of consumerism, sparked by the need to purchase materials, help the audience devise what a "real" reconstruction would look like. Even with the most realistic touches, *Villa* appears to render an image of pure artificiality, like a cartoonish amusement park.

Although none of these ideas were actually considered for the new design of the Peace Park, Calderón makes an interesting connection between the roles of the survivors and their places as witnesses and possible tour guides of the park. With an indirect reference to survivors that act as guides, the play points out how even a survivor who relives his tormented past as a guide carries a hue of artificiality: "I'd find some survivors from the original villa so they could be like guides to hell. Like Virgil. And I'd ask those guides to pause in the places where they were locked up or where they screamed the most. Like they can't keep talking or stop themselves crying."[44] The well-known survivor Pedro Alejandro Matta, who in real life conducts tours and has published a guidebook titled *A Walk through a Twentieth-Century Torture Center*, narrates his horror story while pointing and detailing specific moments of his life in the villa. For Diana Taylor, Matta's presence as a survivor tour guide embodies the buried stories of the villa by bringing them back to life through his narrative, suggesting that mimesis and empathy help us, the visitors, both imagine the space and wonder about the authenticity of his act: Can theater and embodied performance reenact the past?[45] Similarly, for Calderón the survivor also falls into the pretend or make-believe setting by reenacting the past through his theatricality or embodied performance. The end product is even compared to a set of a TV show that people might want to visit. Alejandra (Carla): "You have to go. They rebuilt it. It looks a bit fake. Like it's from tv. They painted the walls with muddy water. It's so shocking. You have to go."[46] The staging of the villa through its artificial walls, smells, props, and even survivor-actors, points out that a constructed narrative about absence can be dangerous. Even if the real survivor tells his or her story, he or she is still acting during the period of the visit, and thus the narrative always falls short of truth-telling.

In January 2010, President Michelle Bachelet inaugurated the new Museum of Memory and Human Rights in Santiago (Museo de la Memoria y Derechos Humanos). The museum has three concrete mission statements: to create a visible space where people can learn about human rights abuses under the dictatorship from 1973 to 1990; to honor the victims and their families; and to promote political and ethical reflection in order to strengthen national unity and thereby present such abuses from ever happening again.[47] Nevertheless, Calderón points out that Chile is still in need of a cultural debate and understanding of human rights: even during the museum's inauguration, the conservative press criticized the Bachelet government for not telling the "true story" and for not making any reference to the failures of Allende's government, which created an opening for a dictatorship.[48]

A polemically different metacommentary about the museum comes through *Villa*, when Alejandra (Francisca) performs her idea of what a museum of Villa Grimaldi would be like.[49] With a clear reference to the aforementioned Museum of Memory, it is evident that the issue of transmission of absence is still at stake. Alejandra (Francisca) relates to the architectural style of the current Museo de la Memoria, where the color white prevails and a transparent image of glass overtakes the place. As when Moulián suggests that Chile has undergone a whitening of memory, the repetition of white, according to Alejandra (Francisca), resembles a hospital, detaching the audience from the aesthetic of a museum. She states: "Because of course you're in a museum which is, like, white, sort of with mirrors, like an international architecture competition, which is basically the aesthetic of modern-day capitalism."[50] She points out that this museum would offer, through Mac computers, a close-up on the lives of the victims with an easy click on their pictures:

> And you can click on the name and everything about that person appears. Photos of her as a girl, her family, who her boyfriend was, whether she liked to eat edible seaweed, if she used to come home eating the bread when she was sent out to buy groceries, all that. And if you do double-click on villa, click-click, a description comes up of everything that actually happened to her in the villa. Click. Who she hugged. Click. Who she spoke to. Click. Who she helped.[51]

Technology exposes the lines between private and public spaces; in addition, it once again promotes artificiality, even if visitors are supposedly dealing with documentation of the disappeared.

Even though the topic at hand is traumatic and at times the images the characters relay are indeed gruesome, Calderón sprinkles the scenes with humor. The audience is constantly going back and forth between traumatic images, sad interchanges, and funny commentaries or extravagant ideas. For instance, the sobering topic of rape is prevalent throughout the play, because the three Alejandras born in Villa Grimaldi are the children of women raped by the guards. In a grotesque theatrical imagination of the villa as museum, Alejandra (Francisca) evokes the possibility of adding an installation with a dog: "But why a dog? Oh. Gee. Oh. Well. Because they raped them with dogs. Yes. With dogs. And that says it all. Yes. And that's where it ends. So . . . you say what was this museum trying to say to me?"[52]As disturbing and controversial as this installation might be, the scene fuses violent acts against women through the presence of dogs with direct references to dogs raping women during the dictatorship while also adding some grotesque humor, since Alejandra (Francisca) quickly comments that she is aware that in order for this installation to be successful, the museum should acquire different dogs so that they can take turns performing, since, after all, they also have rights and they should be able to have breaks to comply with the law.

The politics of amnesia, of silencing, during the transitional years, are evident in Calderón's work. In the words of Alejandra (Macarena): "When the old regime ended, there was no president running to the villa . . . That never happened. It didn't happen. There was no president kneeling or clutching a fistful of earth saying: I swear that this shall not pass into history like a one-night stand."[53] Alejandra (Macarena) describes her theatrical interpretation of the Peace Park as a "camposanto" (graveyard) as a collage pastiche mixture of potpurri, and as a Chilean Pompeii in Peñalolén that was built while Chilean society was looking the other way. Whereas these words come from a theatrical character, they are indeed some of the comments made by critics of the park. In particular, Calderón makes direct references to the incongruence between a trauma site and the beautiful gardens. He criticizes how one section of the park, where women were raped by the military, is now renamed and redesigned as a rose garden. The names of the female victims are now stakes among the flowers, which leads Calderón to wonder whether "one would also like to remember [the space] as a place where a person was killed. Instead we see a flower, as though reborn into life. I don't think anyone thought much about that when they were planning the memorial. They wanted to do something fast, but the theoretical problems remain, and those problems are still discussed and disputed."[54] Thus, the Peace Park in the play is relayed as something unfinished or rushed. In reference to the combination of signs, such as the rose garden, or the mosaics that now adorn part of the ground of the villa, Alejandra (Macarena) states that they are "symbolic symbols. A great mysterious puzzle."[55] While the Peace Park might not make sense, or it might be too beautiful to relate a story of horror, Calderón creates a fluid connection between the specific site and performance, and thus exposes how theater can engage with the place and the audience congruently. The play points to circularity; it has no definite end, as there is no real decision made about the future of the villa. However, it is clear that these women are strong, that even though they might be products of rape and thus have a troublesome relationship with their own mothers and the past, they are empowered to go on with their (theatrical) lives. At its conclusion, the play makes a direct reference to President Bachelet, who herself was captured but later became the first woman president of Chile. The three Alejandras put on white jackets, each with a presidential sash of a single color, one red, one blue, and one white. They become President Bachelet and *Discurso* begins.

Discurso

Calderón wrote this play while in residence at the Royal Court Theater in London in 2009. Even though it follows *Villa*, Calderón explains that this work was conceived beforehand in order to give *Discurso* a context or framework and to make a stronger connection between Bachelet's presidency and her past as a survivor of the dictatorship. This apocryphal farewell speech executed by the same three actresses from before emphasizes Bachelet's successes and failures in a modest, humble manner while exposing the uncertainty regarding whether or not she was or was not tortured during the dictatorship. Correspondingly, Bachelet's character ambiguously states, "I would even forgive my torturers. Had they tortured me" and "[y] hubo crímenes contra mi cuerpo. O no" ([and] there were crimes against my body. Or not).[56] In this long monologue, themes of memory politics, forgiveness, the dream of socialism, dictatorship, exile, capitalism, love, and patriotism, among others, come to life. In the play, at times, Bachelet's humble appearance becomes a cliché, as when she states: "I am so optimistic that I feel like a glass of milk" (a symbol of Allende's socialist initiative, which provided a glass of milk to every child in Chile, now becomes a metaphor for this president's body).[57] At other moments, her political views seem stronger: "Maybe capitalism is only a dark phase in human history. Maybe another story will come in which everything will be cooperation" (Quizás el capitalismo sea solo una etapa gris en la historia humana. Quizás después venga otra historia en la que todo sea cooperación).[58] While this is a fictitious speech, Calderón has stated that this is what he wishes Bachelet had said. However, even though it includes playfulness and humor, as a theatrical piece *Discurso* tends to ramble on and, at times, loses some of its dramatic tension. However, as a political speech, this play offers a narrative, a look back at a convoluted Chilean history, and thus, it provides a testimony, albeit a fictitious one. In contrast to *Villa*, where there is a need for narrative, testimony, and evidence, *Discurso* displays an embodied historical figure who is willing to ramble on about her past as citizen and president of Chile.

If during *Villa* the transmission of absence and its representation are at stake, here, Bachelet seems to fill in the void through the long monologue that covers almost every important historical point from Allende's government to her own. Diana Taylor has cogently analyzed the ways that performance can transmit traumatic memory. Specifically, she points out how performance and protest resemble trauma in their nature of "repeats," and that both trauma and performance are felt in the present. Thus, they take "place in real time, in the presence of a listener." Performance, then, "helps survivors cope with individual and collective trauma by using it to animate political denunciation."[59] In this case, the survivor is the president, and although ambiguous about her past as a detainee, she makes strong references to overcoming the torturous past, while not forgetting what happened. She looks to other venues and possibilities to become an active political body, and in doing so she tells her side of the story from her official post as president: "One could build an awful resentment. And try to slowly pick up the pieces . . . or one could do what I did and become the President of the Republic. Be the first woman . . . be the first tortured president. Or not tortured" (una puede desarrollar un resentimiento espantoso. Y tratar de recuperarse lentamente . . . o una puede hacer lo que hice yo misma. Convertirme en Presidenta de la República. En la primera mujer . . . en la primera presidenta torturada. O no torturada).[60] If the transmission of trauma is in need of a listener in the present time, this apocryphal speech focuses on the possibilities for change while constantly calling attention to the ongoing silencing of the past. How do post-traumatic memories express the nuances of this character's speech? Can this play help those who suffered trauma cope? We can only speculate about the theater's ultimate effects. However, it is clear that Calderón dares to tell a story in a matter-of-fact way, as a monologue that addresses a range of themes from torture, exile, and assassinations, to the most mundane issues of dieting, hairstyle, and current social events.

Discurso fits in an in-between place, a place of ambiguity in which individual and collective memories are in constant tension. If the three Alejandras in *Villa* are second-generation, and therefore there is an evident distance between what they know and how they attained that knowledge, in *Discurso* Bachelet provides the audience with a firsthand, albeit fake, testimony. However, her individual memories of what happened seem at times even blurrier than those of the three Alejandras before. Alison Landsberg's conception of "prostheic memory" fits well with Bachelet's character: "Prosthetic memories are neither purely individual nor entirely collective but emerge at the interface of individual and collective experience. They are privately felt public memories that develop after an encounter with a mass cultural representation of the past, when new images and ideas come into contact with a person's own archive of experience."[61] President Bachelet as a theatrical character may confront spectators with their own individual and collective memories of the past, but she also questions what audience members might or might not know about the president. In this sense, the play creates a liminal space where both collective and individual memories are negotiated. Through a fictitious speech, however, Calderón reinforces the idea that "images and ideas come into contact with the person's own archives." In this case, her ambiguity about her own past is contested, exposing the fissures in the role of her own testimony. The embodied historical figure of the president explores how memories can and cannot be trusted, since after all, she never really opens up about her own past as a possible (or not) victim of the dictatorship.

Escuela and *Mateluna*

Returning to the journalist's question about Calderón's commitment to Jorge Mateluna, "Isn't this dangerous for your reputation?" seems to be out of focus, or more precisely, not in sync with what Calderón has proposed in recent work. Nevertheless, *Mateluna* does force critics to acknowledge the ways in which he moves beyond the confines of the theater to make a political stand in favor of defending Jorge Mateluna's innocence and highlighting the corrupt legal system. When the play is over, different human rights organizations wait outside to give more information about the case, encouraging the audience to learn more and even mobilize in favor of justice. Pamphlets and information about Mateluna's innocence provide the audience with an opportunity to take action and get involved in the "Mateluna Inocente" project.[62] Both an extension of and supplement to the staged play, this form of advocacy outside the theater doors offers just another example of how Mateluna's cause spills out into the streets and beyond the theatrical framework.

Mateluna is metatheatrical and intertextually rich, combining fragments of the play *Escuela* (2013) with other fictional plays: *Vaca* (*Bomb*, 2014), *Comunicado* (*Public Service Announcement*, 2015), and *Estética* (*Aesthetics*, 2016).[63] *Escuela* serves as the only actual play that directly informs *Mateluna* for a very specific reason. When Calderón was creating *Escuela*, he invited Jorge Mateluna as an adviser to explain how the underground militant groups worked during the 1980s. As a past member of the FPMR, with knowledge about weapons and bomb designs, Jorge Mateluna served as a resource for understanding the difficult topic of clandestine urban guerrillas. As with every play, Calderón demands a critical spectator who can decide on his or her own about what they see onstage. His plays employ an anachronistic approach to entice the audience to learn about Chile's recent past.[64] His constant back and forth between the past and the present enables him to work with dimensions of real events by also editing how much fiction enters the stage.

Escuela, set in 1987, centers on the taboo topic of guerrilla warfare and the concealed methods militant groups used to try to overthrow Pinochet. Staged with few props, a blackboard, a slide projector, and a few chairs, this school teaches students how to make bombs and how to shoot firearms. Five actors are *encapuchados* (*capuchas* are face masks made by folding a T-shirt so that it covers the whole head and neck) to hide away their faces from the audience, and, in the context of the play, conceal their identities and preserve their underground anonymity in case they are caught, a clear reference to the underground world of militant groups. As one of the actor states, "Under this hood there are political ideas. And those ideas give me dignity."[65] Calderón goes further about the purpose of using *capuchas* onstage:

> For me it was very important to do this. Because these people are indeed invisible and were never considered as fighters for democracy, and instead were considered terrorists or extremists, they now live in secret. . . . As years have gone by, the identity is still not revealed because dictatorship continues to be imposed in some form. And because it is also a painful and uncomfortable topic that the play has to emphasize. And finally, because the political-military schools were like that, *encapuchados*.
>
> [Para mí era súper importante hacer eso. Porque justamente esta gente está invisible y como esas personas nunca fueron considerados como luchadores por la democracia, sino que fueron considerados como terroristas o extremistas, ellos viven en una situación actual de secreto. . . . A pesar de los años esto sigue siendo un secreto, la identidad todavía no se revela porque de alguna forma la dictadura sigue impuesta. Y también porque me parece que es un tema doloroso, incómodo y la obra tiene que enfatizar eso. Por último, las escuelas político-militares eras así, encapuchados.][66]

The political symbols become part of a documentary method to telling the story of people who fought for democracy through violence. The *capuchas* are both a theatrical prop and a charged symbol of a historical past that reverberates with how part of a generation had to behave. Sounds of leftist hymns and protest songs with clear political overtones welcome the audience members, some of whom may be familiar with the songs.[67] Whereas this play has been praised by some critics, others have found it too didactic and without any emotional substance.[68] One of the international critics notes the lack of character development and the amount of didacticism that permeates the play. While these comments are not unfounded, the criticism that the play is too didactic can be linked to Calderón's obsession with uncovering and exposing details of topics that have been designated as taboo and mainly forgotten by society. The actors—Luis Cerda, Trinidad González, Camila González, Francisca Lewin, and Carlos Ugarte—interchange roles, sometimes acting as instructors and sometimes as students. However, more than character development or the amount of didacticism involved in the play (after all, it is a play about a school), Calderón's play explores the topic of guerrilla tactics, leftist revolutionary groups, and the need to instruct new generations about the past and particularly the commonly held revolutionary ideal maintaining that violence was necessary for action.

Escuela premiered at the Santiago a Mil Festival in 2013, a year that marked the fortieth anniversary of the coup. With sold-out events through the Santiago a Mil Festival and produced by the Santiago a Mil Foundation (FITAM), the play continued touring in Brazil, Germany, Portugal, France, Greece, and the United States.[69] As Jennifer Thompson asserts, this play (and almost all of Calderón's other works) is a paradox because by relying on the FITAM (a private-public entity that produces many plays), *Escuela* uses "the same system and structures it seeks to critique and resist."[70] The medium of neoliberal politics and markets is precisely what Calderón utilizes to get his point across. But it is not so much a matter of caving into the market's pressures; rather, Calderón accepts a certain complicity with the market in order to present the public with uncomfortable topics that demand their engagement. His plays, while sometimes not international favorites, underscore the challenges of political theater in a market-driven society. He is aware of the possible alienation that political theater can produce, but nonetheless uses these plays to position the spectator in a world of revolutionaries and guerrilla warfare education. Sometimes political statements or comments are central to Chile; at other times the play's political commentary is relevant for any country living under dictatorial conditions.[71]

Both *Escuela* and *Mateluna* are key examples of how a very local political topic, such as underground guerrilla groups, or even a specific case of a corrupted legal system can have relevance around the world. I suggest, then, that Calderón's political commitment might be less about renegotiating with the market-driven economy, and more about appropriating the system to find a space to introduce topics that are uncomfortable but also very personal to him and actors of his generation engaged in coming to terms with the dictatorship.[72] Connecting to the past dictatorship through the theater and through Jorge Mateluna's testimony is empowering for the actors involved in both plays.

Escuela relies on Calderón's personal memory of the dictatorship, when he was a teenager, and the experiences and witness reports of others such as Jorge Mateluna. It is also a historical play that points to key elements of how the dictatorship came to an end by a plebiscite and how the neoliberal market overtook almost every aspect of people's lives. It is noteworthy that Calderón chooses a school setting to teach about guerrilla tactics, where he emphasizes the central role students may have when redefining the political stage. As was seen previously with his play *Clase* (*Class*, 2006), Calderón was influenced by student protests and mobilizations activated in massive numbers to demand better access to education. In a similar fashion, *Escuela* reinvigorates the power of students. In 2006, when Michelle Bachelet was president of Chile, students protested what they saw as an unjust educational system that stemmed from policies set up during the dictatorship. They demanded changes to the law so that education could be more accessible, as well as free bus passes and free university entrance exams. On May 30 over seven hundred thousand students poured into the streets of Santiago and other cities, confronting President Bachelet's inactions. For the first time since the dictatorship, students demonstrated publicly and in large numbers, eventually pushing Bachelet to form a commission to address their concerns.[73]

However, in 2011 students staged even bigger demonstrations, demanding an end to the "market education" in favor of free tuition. With a new center-right president, Sebastián Piñera, the topic quickly became centralized on economics and how the government could not afford tuition-free universities. As the movement gained momentum, leader Camila Vallejo suggested renationalizing the country's natural resource industries to reform education and meet students' demands. In an interview for the *New York Times*—the title of the piece, "Just Don't Call Her Che," clearly points to the revolutionary possibilities of someone young and attractive—she explained that "having a market economy is really different from having a market society. What we are asking, via education reform, is that the state take on a different role."[74] Students brought attention to the obsolete policies put in place during the Pinochet years that made education into a market-driven economy, even after democratic governments. With the power of national and international media behind them, students advanced their demands and refused to align with any particular political party.[75] As Thompson states, students reworked lyrics to the well-known leftist chant "El pueblo unido jamás será vencido" (The people united will never be defeated), changing it to "El pueblo unido avanza sin partidos" (The people united advance without parties).[76]

Surrounded by protest songs, *Escuela* centers on understanding how to survive in this underground world. In the interchange between students and instructor, topics of how to become connected cells, yet keep isolation and compartmentalization are central, so that "if they arrest you and torture you and break you, no one else goes down. Because you don't know anything about the rest of us. We're isolated compartments. You haven't seen our faces. This house. Where are we?"[77] The audience does not know where they are either, only that is a safe house somewhere in the rich area of Santiago.

A projector shows images of the *White Book of the Change of Government in Chile* (1973), a right-wing book published in Spanish and quickly translated into English right after the coup of 1973. Using a large font reminiscent of newspaper headlines, the *White Book* begins with an introductory note by the Secretariat-General of the government of Chile, which states, "The truth about what actually happened in Chile has been deliberately distorted before the world."[78] With subtitles that call attention to the nondemocratic nature of the elections that promoted Allende as president of the nation, or with the "social cost of Allende's experiment," this book aims to promote the military's regime ideology and the "right" to take over the nation. The book in itself is a large compilation of files, photographs, diagrams, and secret documents filled with clear right-wing thought as the "truth." The evidence-like book provides ample files to try to establish that this "truth" is the only way to national restoration. Onstage more photographs with Salvador Allende with weapons, shooting, as well as other weapons and a homemade tank are projected, and actors explain the differences between "them" and "us." According to the actors, the book promoted a psychological warfare and a reason to kill the communists who had overtaken Chile. The severity of the group's mission is prevalent when actor Marcela, as the instructor, points out the goal of the group:

> Plan Z. The popular government's supposed plan to carry out a Leninist self-coup and take all the power for itself. And kill lots of people. There's a list. The idea was that President Allende was going to organize a meal with all the generals. When suddenly: "pardon, apologies, Mr. President, telephone for you." . . . "I'll be right back." And then, between the hors d'oeuvres and the stuffed avocado, the extremists, us, we enter, and we kill all generals. And then comes the massacre and then begins the dictatorship of the . . . proletariat.[79]

As the group learns the ropes, the instructor explains the need for safe houses, for anonymity, for hiding information, and for employing violence. To them, violence is a means, a way to get things done, even at the cost of killing people.

Class struggle and the search for power become central to their discussions. While conversations and demonstrations jump from Molotov cocktails to other bombs, topics of people's struggles become palpable. Students learn the central questions about exploitation, the workers' campaign, and why they are "calling on all the people to join the fight."[80] They come forward with how their war is an illegal one, how they are extremists who decided to fight for what they see as right, to defend workers' rights, how to lose a tag or make a phone call in an emergency situation. Fear and danger are also palpable because in order to fight this "dirty war," as actors call it, they have to be willing to die, as happens with sixteen-year-old Dani, who finds no way out and detonates a bomb knowing that it will kill him.

As the play advances, we hear about different fights with similar tactics: the war in Libya, the war by Mao and Ho Chi Minh, as well as the Cuban Revolution and the sway that Fidel Castro had over these guerrilla groups. The international wars provide a framework for understanding that there are other possible ways to engage in combat. Marcela, the instructor, makes this clear when she states:

> I really think we can win. The Chilean armed forces are cowards. They kill civilians and hide. They're traitors. They kill their own

> generals. And they're anti-patriots. A foreign country asks them to kill Chileans and they do it. Because all of that, I think we can beat them. We can. But we don't want to kill them all. We just want to destroy them morally.[81]

It is perhaps a heavy-handed play for an audience not familiar with Latin America's recent past. After all, this play takes information from a member of a militant group that had similar intentions, built bombs, and tried their best to overthrow the government. It also relies heavily on details about the coup, the militia groups, and the military junta. Documentary evidence, mainly through photographs, evokes a certain tribunal theater platform where facts are presented to be seen and discussed. And as Ángeles Donoso Macaya argues when thinking about documentary photography, "One can't think about the history of the resistance to the dictatorship, nor of the history of political struggle throughout this period, without considering the political space that the documentary practices of photography opened up."[82]

Nevertheless, *Escuela* is also a play that utilizes the stage as an ethical barometer. How far can we go to reach our goals? Or how distant are we from this type of warfare that we find ourselves uncomfortable with, looking around the audience to see other people's reactions? In the world of neoliberal markets, are we even capable or willing to give up our comfort to fight this type of war? As the play nears its conclusion, students find out that combat is no longer needed, that the dictatorship can come to an end through a plebiscite to democratically decide whether Pinochet stays or goes. In that plebiscite, which took place in 1989, people had two choices: vote yes to keep Pinochet in power, or vote no to oust him. To the cheers of many, the "no" vote won, forcing Pinochet out of power. However, *Escuela* makes a direct statement about power negotiations behind this vote, proving once more that real democracy did not win.

> MARÍA: Yeah. But that plebiscite is a sham. Now the dictatorship tells us that if we vote no, we can have free elections and choose a president. They want us to believe that that's a victory for the people. But it's not. Because that plebiscite is actually a fraud. Because what they really want is to strengthen the political and economic model that they used force to impose. And to do that, they need to legitimize it as democratic. They don't want to continue on as a dictatorship. They don't want the Yes option to win. They want the No to win . . . but it's going to be a false democracy. The same oppression but with a white hood . . . so our slogan for the coming election is going to be this: Vote Yes. Vote No. They both are shit, and we know. Vote Yes. Vote No. They both are shit, and we know.[83]

A false democracy lingers as a symbol of a lost battle. The negative outcome of what will happen in Chilean politics during the transition to democracy is central. But the play also emphasizes the role students can have in learning about the past, in joining groups and resisting with what they can, or at least understanding what the struggle symbolized.

Six months after the premiere of *Escuela*, the cast was on tour with this play and learned that Jorge Mateluna had been arrested for robbing a bank in Pudahuel. This was a tremendous blow, partly because Mateluna had been an adviser to them when creating *Escuela*, but also because since his release from prison in 2004, he had married, had two children and was involved in artistic and cultural activism. Robbing a bank seemed totally out of character for Mateluna. Calderón explained that after receiving a phone call about this news, they were in shock.[84] Shaken by this news and the consequences of the event, the troupe decided to create a documentary play that expands the views on guerrilla warfare as well as on the present state of Mateluna and the injustice of a legal and judicial system that put him in jail for a crime that evidence proves he did not commit.

Mateluna is the most documentary play that Calderón has written up to now. It premiered in Berlin in 2016 at the festival "The Aesthetics of Resistance—Peter Weiss 100" at the Teatro HAU Hebbel am Ufer.[85] With clear reference to Peter Weiss, who, as stated in the introduction of this book, utilized documentary theater as a political tool, this play makes use of evidence-based theater. It is also the most documentary in the sense of using the theater as a forum to bring up evidence that could, but ultimately does not, exonerate Jorge Mateluna.[86] According to Guillermo Calderón, the cast felt a personal responsibility to Mateluna, and also a political responsibility. The play intended to intervene at the political level as well but failed.[87] If *Escuela* exposed the hidden world of guerrilla warfare, *Mateluna* clearly denounces a police state and a judicial system that convicts someone without proof, and despite clear signs of tampered evidence. A play in two acts, *Mateluna* brings forth the need to tell a story about a person who falls victim of a crime he did not commit, but also about the many injustices that took place against a generation that fought against Pinochet's dictatorship. As Calderón explains in the program book for the play's premiere:

> During the Chilean dictatorship (1973–1990), several political organizations on the left decided to organize an armed struggle against the military regime. . . . Thousands of young people joined the armed resistance because they wanted to fight for a more dignified way to live, and to die. Yet the struggle did not only aim to overthrow the dictatorship, it also sought to establish a new kind of popular democracy, and with it a new economic system that was designed to bring social justice to all members of society . . . yet this victory was never achieved.[88]

Fig. 13. In alphabetical order, Luis Cerda, Andrea Giadach, Camila González, Francisca Lewin, María Paz González, and Carlos Ugarte in Guillermo Calderón's *Mateluna*. Publicity still. Santiago de Chile, 2016. Photograph by Fundación Teatro a Mil.

All actors are once again *encapuchados* (see fig. 13), a clear sign of armed resistance status. With a Mac computer on a table in the front of the stage with the screen facing the audience, we see how a member of the cast controls and manages what we will see on the large screen that is overhead at center stage. As with *Escuela*, songs frame the play, but this time what we hear is not political chants; rather, the play begins with a song by Cuban songwriter Silvio Rodríguez, whose songs became associated with the Cuban Revolution.

Actor Francisca Lewin, wearing her *capucha* in *Mateluna*, speaks directly to the audience and shares her story:

> In 2013 we staged *Escuela*. This play showed the inside of urban guerrilla clandestine schools in Chile during the 1980s. Our goal was to give visibility to thousands of young people who fought against dictatorship. Young people who have been erased by the official history. We invited people who actively fought during this time to come to our rehearsals. One of those people was Jorge Mateluna, a thirty-nine-year-old man who participated in the guerrilla schools. He came and told us his story. We incorporated his story into our play.
>
> [En el año 2013 estrenamos la obra *Escuela*. Esta obra mostraba cómo eran las escuelas clandestinas de guerrilla urbana en Chile

durante los años ochenta. Lo que queríamos era darle visibilidad a los miles de jóvenes que se prepararon para luchar con todos los medios en contra de la dictadura. Jóvenes que fueron borrados por la historia oficial. Para crear la obra invitamos a nuestros ensayos a personas que lucharon activamente durante esta época. Una de esas personas fue Jorge Mateluna. Un hombre de 39 años, que participó en las escuelas de guerrilla. El vino a un ensayo y nos contó su experiencia. Nosotros tomamos su historia y la incorporamos a la obra.][89]

The intertextuality and metatheatricality between *Escuela* and *Mateluna* are clear from the start. Actors show part of *Escuela* on the screen with no audio, while another actor recites the lines live. The brief interplay serves as part of a documentary frame to show why *Escuela* is so crucial to understanding the actors' involvement with Jorge Mateluna. Actor Francisca Lewin presents a quick chronology, explaining that the cast was staging *Escuela* abroad when they heard the news about Jorge Mateluna's imprisonment. Francisca adds: "Jorge declared his innocence from the start. And we believed him" (Desde el primer momento Jorge se declaró inocente. Y nosotros le creímos).

The use of real documents and evidence follows their statements and provides the audience with a "real video" of the "real Jorge Mateluna," where we see a lineup of five prisoners. Then the play takes a step backward, however, and instead of following a chronologically forward documentary approach to their story, *Mateluna* shifts and explores three separate apocryphal stories to frame what the leftist groups were like and what their ideology and goals were. The three apocryphal plays are *Vaca* (*Bomb*, 2014), *Comunicado* (*Public Service Announcement*, 2015), and *Estética* (*Aesthetics*, 2016). In *Vaca* there is a sense of capturing the ideology of the generation that lived under the dictatorship, the one that has been either silenced or disappeared, but there is also a temporal distance between the past and the present. We see six actors *encapuchados*, sitting in a circle, trying to learn how to make a real bomb. With a dark sense of humor, their instructor says that in order to make the bomb more lethal, one of them has to defecate in a can. We hear that in earlier times, the young guerrilla members created bombs to fight and even kill people; today the young ones just want to make noise bombs, and they only threaten using the internet. The old revolutionary who has come to "teach" the young generation about how to make a bomb, who clearly stands as Mateluna, exclaims: "I belong to another century. . . . When I returned [from prison] there was no more people's power. . . . I got ready for a war that never was" (Yo soy de otro siglo. Cuando volví [de la prisión] no había poder popular. . . . Yo me preparé por años para la guerra que nunca fue).[90] Imagining Mateluna and his generation is one of the foundational premises of this play—how to think of him in his own world, in his own time. Actor Francisca later states:

> *Vaca* was an exploration of the relationship we thought Jorge had with violence. Mateluna, of the dictatorship generation. Mateluna, of the disappeared generation trying to make a living in a new world. In this world. This is why we imagined Jorge Mateluna in a meeting with young anarchists who want him to make them a bomb. That imagined relationship with younger revolutionaries allowed us to show an isolated Jorge Mateluna. A lost soldier of a war that never arrived.
>
> [*Vaca* fue una exploración de la relación que nosotros pensábamos que Jorge tenía con la violencia. Mateluna, el de la generación de la dictadura. Mateluna, el de la generación desaparecida. Mateluna tratando de vivir en un mundo nuevo. En este mundo. Por eso nos imaginamos a Jorge Mateluna en una reunión con jóvenes anarquistas que quieren que él les fabrique una bomba. Esa relación imaginaria con revolucionarios más jóvenes nos permitió mostrar a un Jorge Magteluna aislado. Un soldado perdido de una guerra que nunca llegó.][91]

The capacity to "imagine" the world known to Mateluna but lost in today's society permeates the apocryphal plays. This metatheatrical exercise calls attention to the act of imagining as a way to portray art as a possible answer. But once again their theatrical exercise is doomed. Actors "kill" Jorge Mateluna in an explosion and claim that they failed to understand Jorge Mateluna's fight.

In representing the world of underground guerrilla tactics, where facts and fiction get clearly blurred, a song features the transition from one fake play to another. "A Little Respect" by the English duo Erasure—a queer 1980s pop song—at first seems out of place. But as we listen to the lyrics, we understand how the song invites audience members to think about "love" and "respect" for one another. In addition, Calderón states that the idea behind using this song was to build a "memory of the case, so that each time the song plays anywhere, the spectator remembers that Jorge Mateluna is serving an unjust prison sentence."[92] Moreover, when it aired, the pop song became a symbol of resistance for homosexual men who live with AIDS.[93] I would also add that the song serves as a temporal bridge between generations. Even though the song became popular in the 1980s, it is still widely listened to in Chile and other countries, thus connecting different sites and generations. In a metatheatrical twist, actor Francisca confesses to the audience that "the audience" complained about having a song in English and they questioned why they kept it. In response, the cast moves forward with the play and projects *Comunicado*, another apocryphal metatheatrical technique to emulate a guerrilla-like video communication where three "guerrilleros" speak to a camera, in their usual *capucha* attire, speaking about leaving the armed battles behind and leaving violence behind. As one of the actors claims, they decide to give up the fight "because we know that our strategy has not worked. The enemy won the people's hearts. Also, the objective conditions no longer exist for the real resurgence of a revolutionary fight" (porque hemos reconocido que nuestra estrategia no funcionó. El enemigo se ganó el corazón del pueblo. Además ya no existen las condiciones objetivas para el surgimiento de una verdadera lucha revolucionaria).[94]

The documentary angle in *Mateluna* relies on exploring the world of a generation that fought for their beliefs. What Calderón creates with these apocryphal plays is a way to look back, to delve into the world of guerrilla warfare, and to also show how their goals never came to fruition. It is perhaps in *Estética*, the last apocryphal play, where the cast draws on a long genealogy of revolutionary wars, spanning from the medieval Swedish war against the feudal system, Engelbrekt, to the Spanish Civil War, Stalin's invasion of Poland, and the Soviet Union, to build a frame. Actors join as intellectuals who talk about different wars against oppressive systems; they bring up Weiss's book *The Aesthetics of Resistance* as a prop that explores different possible perceptions of dictatorships. Nevertheless, the idea behind this long scene is to demonstrate, as actor Andrea states, that those who have fought against fascism have fought in vain. And she adds: "Our victory is to simply show our desire for liberation" (Nuestra Victoria es simplemente mostrar nuestra voluntad de liberación). An actor plays the role of Bertolt Brecht, emphasizing the function of theater and politics, as well as the inefficacy of intellectual speech with regard to actual political change.

As the three apocryphal plays come to an end, the role-playing and hypotheticals of a more just world come to a halt. The idea of how to imagine Jorge Mateluna in his world of underground guerrilla tactics is no longer feasible. Mateluna is now in jail, held against factual documents that prove his innocence. Yet he still participates in this play by sending a letter that the cast reads aloud on the stage. Mateluna states that in the past, during his previous conviction, prisoners listened to Silvio Rodríguez's songs, full of revolutionary flavor; today they listen to reggaeton, calling attention to the olden days of true guerrilla prisoners.

According to Cristián Opazo and Carlos Benítez, the first act uses false information to confront a passive audience that confuses art with politics, while the second act presents false evidence that questions the judicial system's equation of armed resistance during the dictatorship and criminal activity.[95] In other words, Calderón works to bring forward someone's testimony as a way to keep his story alive. Similarly, Steve Stern speaks of the need to make "emblematic memories [that] involved not merely differences of perspective and experience but struggles for legitimacy and primacy."[96] *Mateluna* introduces how authentic documents work to validate someone's innocence and thus centralizes the need to "legitimize" his, her, their life in terms of their participation in political activism.

After the first act, which is the longest part of the play and serves, as I mentioned before, as the frame to encapsulate Mateluna's political life, actors switch to a nonfictional play, using evidentiary proof, mainly videos and audios from the bank, the prison lineup, and an audio recording from the court that Mateluna's legal team gathered and shared with the cast. As with many other plays discussed in this book, the cast here relies on reenactments to stage their story. By intercalating the video from the bank robbery, where the audience clearly sees four individuals going into the bank, actors reposition themselves as documenters who try to understand the event. They show the videos, they pause them, and they speak directly to the audience, providing them with information that is not audible through the screen. As documenters of this event, they re-create their own video of the street pursuit. The screen shows fast movements through a camera in one of the actors' cars; the streets quickly become a dizzying laberynth of Mateluna's police chase. To this video, the cast adds that there is no evidence to tie Mateluna to the robbery, except that the police themselves testified that he was guilty because they chased him and caught him. "Do cops lie? Can they plant or imagine evidence?," one of the actors questions. In a not-so-subtle way, actors postulate that someone's past marks their present. Since Mateluna was a member of the FPMR, then it made sense he was the one.

The last few minutes of the play become evidence-based documentary theater. One of the actors claims, "We believe the police are lying. But not only do we believe it, we have proof" (Nosotros creemos que carabineros están mintiendo. Pero no solo creemos que están mintiendo. Tenemos pruebas).[97] The video footage from the prison lineup comes up to contrast evidence with conviction. We see five prisoners. They say that number five is Jorge Mateluna. But it is Alejandro Astorga, one of the thieves who confessed to his crime (and stated that Mateluna did not take part in the act). The false identification goes to the judge. Actors play an audio where the judge questions the policeman who wrote down the report and clearly says, "This is not Jorge Mateluna, and you know it." The judge even says, then, that this is not true. But he signs the sentence anyway. The policeman is not punished, and Jorge Mateluna is condemned to prison. Actors end the play by showing a photograph of Jorge and playing, once again, a "Little Respect."

In *Acts of Activism: Human Rights as Radical Performance*, D. Soyini Madison speaks of the effectiveness and affectiveness of performance as a "tactic and as emergent" in the struggles of human rights and social justice.[98] The word "tactic" is central as "*creating a means and a space from whatever elements or resources are available in order to resist or subvert the strategies of more powerful institutions, ideologies, or processes*."[99] I would call attention to how documentary theater answers to tactics of empowerment. In other words, Calderón and his cast choose to tell Jorge Mateluna's story not just from a personal point of view; they take advantage of real footage and real audio to bring up the discrepancies and deceit the legal system has used to condemn this person.

Much as in Lola Arias's *Mi vida después* and *El año en que nací*, actors throw chairs around while music overtakes the stage. Words are not enough to retell the agony of unjust actions that have taken the lives of people away. As Opazo and Benítez point out, we, the audience, are now on the bench.[100] It is our turn to do something, to get involved. With a clear reference to how to rethink ourselves within ethical advocacy, Madison states that "to be an advocate is to feel a responsibility to exhort and appeal on behalf of another or for another's cause with the hope that still others will gain the ability to respond to your advocacy agenda."[101] While the play makes a call to the audience's ethics, the cast tries to bear witness to their own exploration of the facts. But even evidence is not enough, and Calderón uses the basic premise of documentary theater to destabilize a conviction that took place with clear manipulation of facts. Although it is clear that legal documents are introduced as evidence and are central to the play, Calderón does not claim that the veracity of either the document or the theater can succeed. On the contrary, from the beginning, failure looms onstage. Neither the actual evidence nor the reenactments through theater can successfully defend Mateluna.

In today's post-truth society of selfies, reality shows, and the overconsumption of media, Calderón offers another option. His constant search to understand how the political past has refashioned the present political arena in Chile has taken him to rethink the role of documents and evidence-based theater. As he puts it, they and everybody else have failed Jorge Mateluna.

CONCLUSION

On a warm November night in 2016, my sister and I attended the play *Las ideas* (2015) by Federico León in Buenos Aires.[1] Walking into Zelaya, León's then home and atelier in the Abasto neighborhood, the playwright lured audience members to stroll through the backyard into his small theatrical space in the back. Critics had already described the play as an impeccable scenic machine, pure theater, and brilliant.[2] But I was intrigued by how León constructed a play about upstaging the real, about questioning and confronting what is fictional, what is real, and what is made to look like both. In this play, León and Julián Tello are two artists that evoke the art of creating, of rehearsing something that might or might not end up being a play. With constant use of technology, a Ping-Pong table, laptops, and music, this play becomes a central player in positioning the self as creator in front of an audience that is constantly made to think that what the actors are doing is actually real: phone calls that interrupt the scene, typing new scenes, reenactments of animals dressed as other animals on the screen, filming the scene and playing a video of the scene right after it and making the audience part of the projection. While relying on technological precision, the play nonetheless generates a sense of precarity. The two actors are wearing shorts and sandals; they are relaxed, smoking a joint, as if it were a lazy Sunday afternoon; the Ping-Pong table becomes the screen for the projections, and the main camera that is used to film is at level with the first row of the audience, making it part of the spectatorship. Actors question the cost of putting on a play, how much money they have to spend on whiskey every time they drink it onstage, what type of play they are creating. They make a budget and in so doing they postulate the possible ways of making props appear as "real" when they are not. Is it real whiskey they are drinking? After all, it would be too costly to drink whiskey every night. Is it a real joint they are smoking? How much are they also playing with the discourse of the real onstage to make the audience feel like they are being offered a behind-the-scenes glimpse of how a play is put together?

The real in the theater has emerged as a way to respond to the many ambiguities, doubts, and questions people have regarding shifting paradigms of truth, reality, and information. Staging real people, speaking of real events, and proclaiming some sort of truthful connection to audiences has provided the self with a new light to envision the world they live in. As Jenn Stephenson suggests when discussing documentary theater in Canada, this type of theater "appeal[s] to our contemporary yearning for authenticity, for unmediated contact, for truth, for the real."[3] Artists that use the genre of documentary constantly explore the limits, the edges of theatricality to question the value of information, and thus reality itself becomes a question.

Yet there is also room for artists to confront the idea of the authentic. León, for example, plays with the audience, making us take a break from the seriousness of facts and the truth. Instead, he postulates a play that makes us laugh about the weight we automatically put on what the theater can deliver. In a personal interview, León commented that he was interested in creating a play where the real and fiction commingled in a creative way. He was adamant not to break the fourth wall, not to use his real name as actor onstage, something that is common in documentary practices. In this refreshing exploration, both actors show the process of creation: Julián is the artistic one, León the rational one, yet they are both constantly in flux.[4] Laptops are handled by the actors onstage, yet we start wondering how much control they actually have. Is it just a play about creation and the excavation of that process? Is it the experience of the real that is not? The idea is to make the spectator think that the laptops are managed by the actors, right before our eyes, when in reality they are pretending, as much as anything else we see. The constant aura of failure, of something possibly going wrong, as they move their laptops, as they record their live performance, and as they constantly manipulate their own understanding of what they (as actors) should be performing, seems to point to what lies beyond failure or beyond the "poetics of failure," as Sara Bailes has argued. As postdramatic theater techniques make use of failure as a way to make other connections between actors and spectators, between the play and its possible reception, it is within the realm of understanding the political ramifications of implying and relying on failure on the stage as a possible political contestation. As Nicholas Ridout states, "It is precisely in theatre's failure, our discomfort with it, its embeddedness in capitalist leisure, its status as a bourgeois pastime that its political value is to be found."[5] In documentary theater practices, and as many of the plays studied in this book demonstrate, proposing failure as a possibility offers artists and audience members an unsettling yet attractive paradigm. And, as Ridout argues, working with the possibility of failure pushes the political value of theater itself.

Over the course of this book, I have considered a variety of artists and playwrights that expand the idea of new documentary theater in the twenty-first century. The variety with which they each worked with the real, from objects-turned-props, the autobiographical onstage, to migrant stories and political prisoners, manifest that the lines between the fictive and the real are a productive and prolific way to create art in a world where everything is put to question. Documentary theater is also a medium with which to appeal to personal, political, and social issues that are either invisible or left aside. The value of objects onstage, the energy they bring—the "vibrant matter" they offer, as Jane Bennett states—expands the affective side of the theater, where everyday people take time to tell us their stories onstage, and we, the audience, take time to listen to them. Or, in more political cases as when we hear a generation in the aftermath of the Argentine dictatorship and how the children (now adults) struggle with their own memories, recollections, and narratives of the time. The autobiographical quality of much of documentary theater explores the self as part of a generational network. As Julie Ann Ward argues in reference to Mexican collective Lagartijas tiradas al sol, "The idea of family, and the insertion of the self into a generational network, emerges as a way of understanding the nation."[6] It is precisely the infusion of documentation in the theater, its use, and its questioning that the new approach to documentary theater brings forth as a way to understand, learn, cry, and also laugh at how stories are constructed, and how history has formed some of lives of the performers, and also ours.

As the title of this book contends, the unique focus of these artists is on people's lives, on the central role testimonial stories bring to the theater, and on how evidence can proclaim and also contest hegemonic narratives. New strategies of documentary theater still search for social and political answers that may help fill silences or correct misinformation. Objects, bodies, and archives become the raw material that motivate the stories. Bodies "actuate," as director Jorge Vargas from Teatro Línea de Sombra claims. In other words, they discover through movement, pauses, and action another language that documents and explores the undecipherable. Objects and archives bring in their own veracity, their own being; yet performers make use of them from a different point of view, allowing for distortion, manipulation, and editing so that objects become props that help question facts and the past. And as I have analyzed in each chapter of this book, there is a stunning range of interpretations of how documentary theater can help understand the idea of self in today's society, how it can proclaim a new mode of testimony, and how it can provide the artists and audiences with a platform to highlight the many gaps that are left unspoken or invisible.

As I tried to exemplify with León's case, though, it is difficult to predict how this practice will continue to develop. Perhaps artists like León make us wonder about the value of the real and how many steps we are willing to take to believe (or not) what we see as documentary. Documentary theater practices have certainly morphed and changed ever since Edwin Piscator came out with his first use of technology onstage. New stages are populated with both images and technologies that help distort those images. Documentary practices such as twisting or upstaging the real—the practices we see in León's work—might well pave the way for provocative and compelling new plays.

NOTES

Translations by the author are accompanied by the Spanish. Published and professional transaltions are not supplemented with the Spanish.

Introduction

1. *Baños Roma* was part of the XV Iberoamerican Theatre Festival in Bogotá, Colombia (2016).

2. Beatriz Catani, "Fragmentos de una conversación," in *Acercamientos a lo real: Textos y escenarios*, ed. Óscar Cornago (Buenos Aires: Ediciones Artes del Sur, 2007), 14.

3. Cecilia Sosa, "La máquina del tiempo," in Cornago, *Acercamientos de lo real*, 208.

4. Peter Weiss, "Fourteen Propositions for a Documentary Theatre," *World Theatre* 17, nos. 5–6 (1968): 375.

5. Peggy Phelan, *Unmarked: The Politics of Performance* (London: Routledge, 1993), 148.

6. Jane Bennett, *Vibrant Matter* (Durham, N.C.: Duke University Press, 2010), 9.

7. Marlis Schweitzzer and Joanne Zerdy, "Introduction: Object Lessons," in *Performing Objects and Theatrical Things*, ed. Marlis Schweitzzer and Joanne Zerdy (Basingstoke, England: Palgrave Macmillan, 2014), 2.

8. Rebecca Schneider, "New Materialisms and Performance Studies," *TDR: The Drama Review* 59, no. 4 (Winter 2015): 7.

9. Diana Taylor, *The Archive and the Repertoire: Performing Cultural Memory in the Americas* (Durham, N.C.: Duke University Press, 2003), 19.

10. Diana Taylor, *The Archive and the Repertoire*, 5.

11. Diana Taylor, *The Archive and the Repertoire*, 19.

12. Rebecca Schneider, "Performance Remains," *Performance Research* 6, no. 2 (2001): 105.

13. Andrew Sofer, *The Stage Life of Props* (Ann Arbor: University of Michigan Press, 2003), 3.

14. Sofer, *The Stage Life of Props*, 9.

15. Shaday Larios, "Teatro de objetos documental: Derivaciones del teatro de objetos hacia lo documental," *Titeresante*, August 18, 2016, http://www.titeresante.es/2016/08/teatro-de-objetos-documental-derivaciones-del-teatro-de-objetos-hacia-lo-documental-por-shaday-larios/.

16. John Willett, *The Theatre of Erwin Piscator* (New York: Holmes & Meier, 1979), 50.

17. As John Willett states, Piscator's use of technology relied on front, back, and overlapping projections; these were seen as the actual "literary element" of his plays. See Willett, *The Theatre of Erwin Piscator*, 113.

18. Willett, *The Theatre of Erwin Piscator*, 118.
19. Willett, *The Theatre of Erwin Piscator*, 120.
20. Bertolt Brecht, *Ges. Werke Schriften zum Theater*, 1967, 104, quoted in Willett, *The Theatre of Erwin Piscator*, 186.
21. Weiss, "Fourteen Propositions," 379.
22. Weiss, "Fourteen Propositions," 379.
23. Hans-Thies Lehmann, *Postdramatic Theatre*, trans. Karen Jürs-Munby (London: Routledge, 2009), 27.
24. Lehmann, *Postdramatic Theatre*, 33.
25. Lehmann, *Postdramatic Theatre*, 103.
26. Lehmann, *Postdramatic Theatre*, 55.
27. In *Mi vida después* (2009) by Lola Arias, actor Viviana Falco uses the information gathered during the play as evidence against her own father for appropriating Juan Cabandié as his own son. Falco is able to use this information to testify against him, something that has never been allowed before. For more information, see chapter 2 in this book: "Reenactments: The Autobiographical at Play in Lola Arias."
28. Augusto Boal, *Theatre of the Oppressed*, trans. Charles A. McBride, Maria-Odilia Leal McBride, and Emily Fryer (London: Pluto Press, 2008).
29. Pedro Bravo Elizondo, *Teatro documental latinoamericano*, 2 vols. (Mexico City: Universidad Nacional Autónoma de México, 1982), vol 1, 20. *Pueblo rechazado* was based on real events that took place in the Benedictine monastery in Cuernavaca, Mexico, when founder and Prior Gregorio Lemercier, going against the Church, begins to conduct psychoanalysis to help determine whether members were suitable for priesthood. In 1967, the Vatican Tribunal gives him an ultimatum to stop conducting psychoanalysis. He rejects it, and the monastery is ultimately closed down. The case was reported in detail in the press. For more information about this specific play, see Tamara Holzapfel, "*Pueblo rechazado*: Educating the Public through Reportage," *Latin American Theatre Review* (Fall 1976): 15–21. See also Juan Villegas, *Historia multicultural del teatro y las teatralidades en América Latina*, Colección teatrología, dir. Osvaldo Pellettieri (Buenos Aires: Galerna, 2005).
30. While there is no concrete evidence of direct influence from Weiss, it is important to note that Leñero used the tribunal setting to unveil details of the trial against Prior Lemercier.
31. I would like to note that many of the collective groups (teatro colectivo) worked with documentary modes but that I do not equate documentary theater to collective theater creation.
32. Bravo Elizondo, *Teatro documental latinoamericano*, 1:14.
33. Silka Freire, *Teatro documental latinoamericano: El referente histórico y su (re)escritura dramática* (Buenos Aires: Ediciones Al Margen, 2007), 22.
34. Jenn Stephenson, *Insecurity: Perils and Products of Theatres of the Real* (Toronto: University of Toronto Press, 2019), 10.
35. Carol Martin, *Theatre of the Real* (Basingstoke, England: Palgrave Macmillan, 2013), 12. Martin explores the term "theater of the real" as a criterion for describing any kind of theater that works with or uses documents (ranging from a theater that works with witnesses, judicial or tribunal cases, a theater of facts, autobiographies, and that which is referred to as reenactment theater, e.g., battle re-creation).

36. Martin, *Theatre of the Real*, 14.

37. Jacques Derrida, *Archive Fever: A Freudian Impression*, trans. Eric Prenowitz (Chicago: University of Chicago Press, 1996), 29.

38. Jean Baudrillard, *Simulacra and Simulation*, trans. Sheila Faria Glaser (Ann Arbor: University of Michigan Press, 1994). I specifically dialogue with how Baudrillard situates simulation as opposed to representation.

39. Derrida, *Archive Fever*, 36.

40. Sherrill Grace, "Theatre and the AutoBiographical Pact: An Introduction," in *Theatre and AutoBiography: Writing and Performing Lives in Theory and Practice*, ed. Sherrill Grace and Jerry Wasserman (Vancouver, B.C.: Talonbooks, 2006), 14.

41. Jill Dolan, "Geographies of Learning: Theatre Studies, Performance, and the 'Performative,' " *Theatre Journal* 45, no. 4 (1993): 431.

42. Grace, "Theatre and the AutoBiographical Pact," 15; emphasis in the original.

43. Philippe Lejeune, *On Autobiography*, trans. Katherine Leary (Minneapolis: University of Minnesota Press, 1989), 5.

44. Lejeune, *On Autobiography*, 126.

45. Lejeune, *On Autobiography*, 128.

46. Lejeune, *On Autobiography*, 22; emphasis in the original.

47. Susan Bennett, "3-D A/B," in *Theatre and AutoBiography: Writing and Performing Lives in Theory and Practice*, ed. Sherrill Grace and Jerry Wasserman (Vancouver, B.C.: Talonbooks, 2006), 34.

48. Bennett, "3-D A/B," 34.

49. Lola Arias, "Footnote," in *Lola Arias: Re-enacting Life*, ed. Jean Graham-Jones (Aberystwyth, Wales: Performance Research Books, 2019), 43.

50. Nicholas Ridout, "Welcome to the Vibratorium," *Senses and Society* 3, no. 2 (2008): 224.

51. Ridout, "Welcome to the Vibratorium," 224.

52. Ridout, "Welcome to the Vibratorium," 230–231.

53. Jill Dolan, *Utopia in Performance: Finding Hope at the Theatre* (Ann Arbor: University of Michigan Press, 2005), 5.

54. Carol Martin, "Bodies of Evidence," in *Dramaturgy of the Real on the World Stage*, ed. Martin (Basingstoke, England: Palgrave Macmillan, 2010), 11; Diana Taylor, *The Archive and the Repertoire*, 20–23.

55. Paola Hernández, "Biografías escénicas: *Mi vida después* de Lola Arias," *Latin American Theatre Review* 45, no. 1 (Fall 2011): 121.

56. Alison Forsyth and Chris Megson, eds., *Get Real: Documentary Theatre Past and Present* (Basingstoke, England: Palgrave Macmillan, 2009), 2.

57. Pamela Brownell and Paola Hernández, eds., *Biodrama / Proyecto Archivos: Seis documentales escénicos* (Córdoba: Papeles Teatrales, 2017), 9.

58. Brownell and Hernández, *Biodrama / Proyecto Archivos*, 9; emphasis in the original.

59. Vivi Tellas in discussion with the author, July 27, 2016.

60. Brownell and Hernández, *Biodrama / Proyecto Archivos*, 25.

61. See Ileana Diéguez Caballero, *Escenarios liminales: Teatralidades, performances y política* (Mexico City: Toma Ediciones, 2014), where she dedicates one chapter to the work of Mapa Teatro in Bogotá, Colombia. This theater collective

works as urban ethnographers who seek to document the lives of those living on the margins of poverty in the city. On the same lines, see Diana Taylor's "Performing Ruins," which studies this group's intervention in the city of Bogotá as a way to document ruins of the past and to make people's testimonies from a marginal community, now razed by the government, come to life. See also Lagartijas tiradas al sol's website, http://lagartijastiradasalsol.com.

Chapter 1

1. In an interview, Vivi Tellas explains her methodology thus: "I always look for people who have some sort of connection to the representational." She cites this "connection" as one of the factors that creates the idea of a fragile contour between the person's body and the spectator. Juan José Santillán, "Cómo poner la vida sobre el escenario," Espectáculos, *Diario Clarín*, July 31, 2008, https://www.clarin.com/espectaculos/poner-vida-escenario_0_SkMztunCatg.html.

2. Members of Las Bay Biscuit include Diana Nylon, Fabiana Cantilo, Isabel de Sebastián, and Edith Kucher. Pamela Brownell, "El recorrido artístico de Vivi Tellas en los '80: de Las Bay Biscuit al Teatro Malo," *Revista Afuera*, September 15, 2015, http://revistaafuera15.blogspot.com/p/el-teatro-entre-dictadura-y-posdictadura.html. See also Alejandro Lingenti, "Vivi Tellas, el nombre de la vanguardia teatral," *La Nación*, February 22, 2020, https://www.lanacion.com.ar/espectaculos/vivi-tellas-el-nombre-de-la-vanguardia-teatral-nid2335046.

3. During the Argentine dictatorship (1976–1983), there was a clear censorship to counteract any presumed subversive act. The military junta declared an "ideological penetration" into people's way of life, and their mission was to control them in whatever means possible. Many artists chose to exile; others chose to silence themselves. For more information, see Diana Taylor, *Disappearing Acts: Spectacles of Gender and Nationalisms in Argentina's "Dirty War"* (Durham, N.C.: Duke University Press, 1997), 11–13.

4. Teatro Malo featured works by an unknown playwright, under the pseudonym of Orfeo Andrade, who was discovered by a friend of Tellas's, Marcelo Tealdi, in the library of stage designer Saulo Benavente. For more information, see Brownell, "El recorrido artístico."

5. Vivi Tellas, personal interview with the author, July 27, 2016.

6. Pamela Brownell, "Lo real como utopía en el teatro argentino contemporáneo: Prácticas biográficas y documentales. Productividad del trabajo de dirección y curaduría de Vivi Tellas en el marco de su Proyecto Biodrama (de 2002 al presente)" (PhD diss., Universidad de Buenos Aires, 2019), 16.

7. Rodolfo Biscia, "Vivi Tellas: 'Soy como una editora biográfica': Puedo editar tu vida," Cultura, *Infobae*, January 27, 2019, https://www.infobae.com/cultura/2019/01/27/vivi-tellas-soy-como-una-editora-biografica-puedo-editar-tu-vida/.

8. Alan Pauls, "Kidnapping Reality: An Interview with Vivi Tellas," trans. Sarah Townsend, in *Dramaturgy of the Real on the World Stage*, ed. Carol Martin (Basingstoke, England: Palgrave Macmillan, 2010), 246. For Tellas, people's lives are theatrical already, and that is why the documentation of their lives with the staging of their stories creates the perfect blend of theatrical archives. See Pauls, "Kidnapping Reality."

9. Martin, *Dramaturgy of the Real*.

10. Martin, *Dramaturgy of the Real*, 5.

11. Beatriz Trastoy, "El lugar del otro: Interferencias y deslindes entre discurso crítico y práctica escénica contemporánea," *Orbis Tertius* 11, no. 12 (2006): 13–14.

12. Biscia, "Vivi Tellas."

13. Marcela A. Fuentes, "El teatro como acontecimiento: Políticas de la interrupción en el teatro documental de Vivi Tellas," *Revista Conjunto*, no. 185 (October–December 2017): 44.

14. Pamela Brownell and Paola Hernández, eds., *Biodrama / Proyecto Archivos: Seis documentales escénicos* (Córdoba: Papeles Teatrales, 2017), 9.

15. The full title of this project was "Cycle Biodrama: About People's Lives." The list comprises fourteen plays: *Barrocos retratos de una papa* [Baroque portraits of a potato] (Analía Couceyro, 2002); *Temperley* (Luciano Suardi and Alejandro Tantanián, 2002); *Los 8 de julio: Experiencia sobre el registro del paso del tiempo* [8 of July: Experience through time] (Beatriz Catani and Mariano Pensotti, 2002); *¡Sentate! Un Zoostituto* [Sit down! A zoostitute] (Stefan Kaegi, Ariel Dávila, and Gerardo Naumann, 2003); *El aire alrededor* [The air around] (Mariana Obersztern, 2003); *La forma que se despliega* [The shape that spreads] (Daniel Veronese, 2003); *Nunca estuviste tan adorable* [You were never this adorable] (Javier Daulte, 2004); *El niño en cuestión* [The kid in question] (Ciro Zorzoli, 2005); *Squash: Escenas de la vida de un actor* [Squash: Scenes from an actor's life] (Edgardo Cozarinsky, 2005); *Budín inglés* [Poundcake] (Mariana Chaud, 2006); *Salir lastimado (Post)* [Getting hurt (Post)] (Gustavo Tarrío, 2006); *Fetiche* [Fetish] (José María Muscari, 2007); *Deus ex Machina* (Santiago Gobernori, 2008); *Mi vida después* [My life after] (Lola Arias, 2009—this last play permiered after Tellas was no longer director of Teatro Sarmiento).

16. It should be noted that in 2008 Proyecto Archivos was also staged as "Biodrama XIV: Archivos." Only four plays participated in this event: two of them, *Tres filósofos con bigotes* and *Escuela de conducción*, were restaged from earlier performances, and the other two, *Mujeres guía* and *Disc Jockey*, were created specifically for this event.

17. For more concrete information about the chronology and change to Vivi Tellas's biodramatic work, see Brownell and Hernández, "Introducción: Proyecto Biodrama," in *Biodrama / Proyecto Archivos*, 7–36. See also Brownell, "Lo real como utopía en el teatro argentino contemporáneo," 105–111.

18. Florian Malzacher, "Dramaturgies of Care and Insecurity: The Story of Rimini Protokoll," in *Experts of the Everyday: The Theatre of Rimini Protokoll*, trans. Daniel Belasco Rogers, Ehren Fordyce, Geoffrey Garrison, Mat Hand, Sophia New, and Walter Sutcliffe; ed. Miriam Dreysse and Florian Malzacher (Berlin: Alexander Verlag, 2008), 23.

19. Malzacher, "Dramaturgies of Care and Insecurity," 38.

20. Malzacher, "Dramaturgies of Care and Insecurity," 39.

21. The zoo of the City of Buenos Aires closed down in 2016.

22. Alan Pauls, "La bestia humana," *Radar* (blog), *Pagina 12*, May 7, 2003, https://www.pagina12.com.ar/diario/suplementos/radar/9-655-2003-03-16.html.

23. *¡Sentate! Un zoostituto* (2003), directed by Stefan Kaegi. Interpreters were Stella Maris Romero and her dog, Garotita; Enrique Santiago and his two turtles (Manolo and Julieta); María Luisa Cisale and her fourteen rabbits, with names

such as Cortázar, Bob Wilson, Sartre, China Zorrilla, Martín Fernández and his iguana named Lacan III; and Alberto Cáceres, a dog walker who shows off the dogs he walks every day.

24. Pauls, "La bestia humana."

25. For more information, see the introduction to Brownell and Hernández, *Biodramas/Proyecto Archivos*.

26. Alan Pauls, "Biodrama," in *Diccionario del pensamiento alternativo*, ed. Hugo E. Biagini and Arturo A. Roig (Buenos Aires: Editorial Biblos, 2008), 69.

27. Trastoy, "El lugar del otro," 7–8. The idea of Biodramas as a finished cycle is important here because as Pamela Brownell and I explore in *Biodramas/ Proyecto Archivos*, as of 2014 two other plays were performed under the title *Biodramas*: *Maruja enamorada* (2013) and *Las personas* (2014), thus exposing the fact that as any collection, Biodramas is still an open and a project very much alive. Two more recent Biodramas have been staged: *El niño Rieznik* (2016) and *Los amigos, un biodrama afro* (2018).

28. Vivi Tellas, "Comienza el Biodrama" (press release), Complejo Teatral de Buenos Aires, April 9, 2002, Buenos Aires.

29. Tellas, "Comienza el Biodrama," 2002.

30. Pauls, "Biodrama," explores the many strategies applied to the Biodramas: a mixture of documentary, reenactments and displays that together with a director's touch become a fruitful landscape of possiblilites.

31. According to Brownell and Hernández, *Biodrama / Proyecto Archivos*, 17–20, the fourteen plays that form part of the "cycle" are part of an "artistic macroproject" that began what would later become Tellas's signature work.

32. The economic crisis that took place between December 19 and 20, 2001, was the biggest banking default in modern history in Argentina. After two decades of neoliberalist practices that began under the last dictatorship (1976–1983) and continued during Carlos Menem's decade-long presidency (1989–99), the artificial economy exploded. As a result, "bank accounts were frozen, savings in dollars were converted one-for-one into the heavily devalued peso, unemployment surged and a little over half the population found itself abruptly below the poverty line"; Alejandro Grimson, "La experiencia argentina y sus fantasmas," in *La cultura en las crisis latinoamericanas*, ed. Alejandro Grimson (Buenos Aires: CLASCO), 192.

33. Philippa Page, *Politics and Performance in Post-dictatorship Argentine Film and Theatre* (Woodbridge, England: Tamesis, 2011), 129.

34. Óscar Cornago, "Biodrama: Sobre el teatro de la vida y la vida teatro," *Latin American Theatre Review* 39, no. 1 (Fall 2005): 5.

35. Cecilia Sosa, "Cuéntame tu vida," *Radar* (blog), *Página 12*, October 17, 2004, http://www.pagina12.com.ar/diario/suplementos/radar/9-1748-2004-10-17.html.

36. Brownell and Hernández, *Biodrama / Proyecto Archivos*, 9.

37. John Beverley, *Testimonio: On the Politics of Truth* (Minneapolis: University of Minnesota Press, 2004), 34, 35.

38. Ana Elena Puga, *Memory, Allegory, and Testimony in South American Theater: Upstaging Dictatorship* (New York: Routledge, 2008), 195.

39. Beverley, *Testimonio*, 2. John Beverley takes aim at different academics, especially David Stoll, for "producing an illusion of facticity" in regard to

Rigoberta Menchú's testimony. See David Stoll, *Rigoberta Menchú and the Story of All Poor Guatemalans* (Boulder, CO: Westview Press, 1999), 2

40. Beverley, *Testimonio*, 4.

41. Jacques Derrida, *Archive Fever: A Freudian Impression*, trans. Eric Prenowitz (Chicago: University of Chicago Press, 1996), 29.

42. Derrida, *Archive Fever*, 36.

43. Hal Foster, "An Archival Impulse," *October*, no. 110 (Fall 2004): 4.

44. Foster, "Archival Impulse," 5.

45. Nicolas Bourriaud, *Relational Aesthetics*, trans. Simon Pleasance, Fronza Woods, and Mathieu Copeland (Dijon: Les Presses du Réel, 2002).

46. Foster, "Archival Impulse," 5.

47. In five years, fifteen museums became the basis for fifteen plays to "explore the city in a different way, to relate theater with a historical setting, and to consider the political decisions certain forms of exhibitions entail." See Vivi Tellas, *Proyecto Museos* (Buenos Aires: Libros del Rojas / Universidad de Buenos Aires, 2002), where there is a short description of each play and each museum's retrospective analysis on the methodology applied, and short essays by Alan Pauls.

48. Alan Pauls, "Kidnapping Reality: An Interview with Vivi Tellas," trans. Sarah Townsend, in Martin, *Dramaturgy of the Real*, 248.

49. Pauls, "Kidnapping Reality," 247.

50. José Santillán, "Cómo poner la vida."

51. An interesting attempt in this direction is Pamela Brownell's study of Proyecto Biodrama, where she considers it as a macroproject that includes all of Tellas's biographical and documentary recent work, in all its different manifestations. Brownell identifies two periods in the development of the project: a first period with the two inaugural stages of Biodrama Cycle and Proyecto Archivos (with Tellas as curator and director, respectively); and a second period where both initial stages merge and the project begins to diversify, eventually leading to the present where all of Tellas's biographical and documentary work identifies with the name of Biodrama. See Pamela Brownell, "Lo real como utopía en el teatro argentino contemporáneo: Prácticas biográficas y documentales: productividad del trabajo de dirección y curaduría de Vivi Tellas en el marco de su Proyecto Biodrama (de 2002 al presente)" (PhD diss., Universidad de Buenos Aires, 2019), 105–111.

52. Trastoy, "El lugar del otro," 9; *Maruja enamorada* (which premiered as part of yet another cycle, Proyecto Manual, curated by Matías Umpierrez), and *Las personas* are clear examples of fused products; and while they work with archives and real people, there is also a distinct point about how these works can also be biodramas.

53. Sara Jane Bailes, *Performance Theatre and the Poetics of Failure: Forced Entertainment, Goat Island, Elevator Repair Service* (Oxfordshire, England: Routledge, 2011), 2.

54. Bailes, *Performance Theatre and the Poetics of Failure*, 4–5.

55. Bailes, *Performance Theatre and the Poetics of Failure*, 7.

56. Bailes, *Performance Theatre and the Poetics of Failure*, 9.

57. Bailes, *Performance Theatre and the Poetics of Failure*, 15.

58. Jill Dolan, *Utopia in Performance: Finding Hope at the Theatre* (Ann Arbor: University of Michigan Press, 2005), 2–3.

59. Jill Bennett, *Empathic Vision: Affect, Trauma, and Contemporary Art* (Stanford, Calif.: Stanford University Press, 2005), 23.

60. Bennett, *Empathic Vision*, 23.

61. Vivi Tellas, "Vidas prestadas," *Radar* (blog), *Página 12*, August 24, 2008, https://www.pagina12.com.ar/diario/suplementos/radar/9-4788-2008-08-30.html.

62. Tellas, "Vidas prestadas."

63. As Brownell and Hernández, *Biodrama / Proyecto Archivos*, 18, state "It is important to point out that, during this period, Tellas created her works in conjunction with the same team: Paolo Baseggio as stage designer, María La Greca as producer, Mei Iudicissa as assistant director and dramaturge. It was this collective that defined the characteristic traits of her Archives project."

64. Vivi Tellas quoted in Sosa, "Cuéntame tu vida."

65. Vivi Tellas, "Intimidad," in Brownell and Hernández, *Biodrama / Proyecto Archivos*, 37. I should note that Tellas's thought on intimacy was first published in 2007 on her own website, www.archivostellas.com.ar; this website is not easily accessible outside the country. A new website is forthcoming: www.vivitellas.com. As of the writing of this book, it is best to find it in the published book.

66. Eve Kosofsky Sedgwick, *Touching Feeling: Affect, Pedagogy, Performativity* (Durham, N.C.: Duke University Press, 2003), 17.

67. Sedgwick, *Touching Feeling*, 19.

68. In "Cuéntame tu vida," Cecilia Sosa explains the way to purchase tickets by calling over the phone or sending an email. She emphasizes the intimate space and closed circle that this created.

69. Lauren Berlant, "Intimacy," *Critical Inquiry* 24, no. 2 (Winter 1998): 282.

70. Pauls, "Kidnapping Reality."

71. Tellas, "Vidas prestadas."

72. With Teatro Sarmiento, since it is a large theater, Tellas modified the space, placing the public on the stage and with only sixty spectators. The idea is precisely to emphasize the closeness for the public, but also so that the actors feel this closeness, this intimacy. According to Tellas, space is crucial in the construction of intimacy. Nevertheless, what also stands out is that the director sought this kind of closeness not only for the audience but also for the actors themselves because, since they were not professional actors, she wanted to protect them and to not "expose them to a situation lacking a public." Sonia Jaroslavsky, "Capturar la teatralidad," *Teatro: Revista del Complejo Teatral de Buenos Aires* 29, no. 95 (August 2008): 79.

73. Menus are always thematic and have a connection to either the culture and traditions of people onstage, or a subtle reference to the topic of conversation. For instance, for *Mi mamá y mi tía*, the menu consisted of Arabic food, *Tres filósofos con bigotes* had a Greek component, and *Escuela de conducción* resembled a typical selection of food found at restaurants by the side of the road.

74. Jorge Dubatti, *Filosofía del teatro I: Convivio, experiencia, subjetividad* (Buenos Aires: Atuel, 2007), 51.

75. Leonor Arfuch, *El espacio biográfico: Dilemas de la subjetividad contemporánea* (Buenos Aires: Fondo de Cultura Económica, 2010), 49–50.

76. Bourriaud, *Relational Aesthetics*, 83.

77. Peggy Phelan, *Unmarked: The Politics of Performance* (London: Routledge, 1993), 31.

78. Phelan, *Unmarked*, 31.

79. In a recent interview, Tellas speaks candidly about using "evidence" almost as a forensic term where she is allowed to see how a story might or might not be theatrical enough to be staged. Vivi Tellas in Biscia, "Vivi Tellas."

80. Some books that feature the role of autobiography on the stage and clearly show an interest in performances of the lives of women and their forgotten stories include Sidonie Smith and Julia Watson, eds., *Interfaces: Women/Autobiography/Image/Performance* (Ann Arbor: University of Michigan Press, 2002); Julia Swindells, *The Uses of Autobiography* (London: Taylor & Francis, 1995); Lynn C. Miller, Jacqueline Taylor, and M. Heather Carner, *Voices Made Flesh: Performing Women's Autobiography* (Madison: University of Wisconsin Press, 2003). This last one engages with historical women's autobiographies as well as self-representation in contemporary art.

81. Bourriaud, *Relational Aesthetics*, 31.

82. It should be noted that Edgardo Cozarinsky, the focus of *Cozarinsky y su médico*, is a well-known director of independent films.

83. Biscia, "Vivi Tellas."

84. Claire Bishop, *Artificial Hells: Participatory Art and the Politics of Spectatorship* (London: Verso, 2012), 2; emphasis in the original.

85. Jacques Rancière, *The Emancipated Spectator*, trans. Gregory Elliott (London: Verso, 2009), 13.

86. Trastoy, "El lugar del otro," 7; emphasis in the original.

87. Marcela A. Fuentes, "Theatre as Event: The Politics of Interruption in Vivi Tella's Documentary Theatre," in *Calling Out of Context*, ed. Joachim Harrou (Dijon: Les Presses du Réel, 2017), 16.

88. Trastoy, "El lugar del otro," 9.

89. Jordana Blejmar, *Playful Memories: The Autofictional Turn in Postdictatorship Argentina* (Cham, Switzerland: Palgrave Macmillan, 2017), 4; emphasis in the original. Even though Jordana Blejmar focuses more on works created by artists of ages similar to those of the postdictatorship (those who were born between 1976 and 1983), and Proyecto Archivos clearly relies on an older generation, the similarities that can be found between play, humor, fiction, and the documentary are notable.

90. Brownell and Hernández, *Biodrama / Proyecto Archivos*, 73.

91. Susana Freire, "El género documental, a escena," *La Nación*, January 5, 2005, http://www.lanacion.com.ar/668467-el-genero-documental-a-escena.

92. Brenda Werth, "*Mi mamá y mi tía*: El arte de crear mundos íntimos," in *Biodrama / Proyecto Archivos: Seis documentales escénicos*, ed. Pamela Brownell and Paola Hernández (Córdoba: Papeles Teatrales, 2017), 81.

93. Vivi Tellas, *Mi mamá y mi tía*, in Brownell and Hernández, *Biodrama / Proyecto Archivos*, 54. All of the textual references to the works that form part of Proyecto Archivos are from Brownell and Hernández, *Biodrama / Proyecto Archivos*.

94. Tellas mentions the relationship between archery and Zen philosophy and mentions the book *Zen en el arte del tiro con arco* by Eugen Herrigel, which gave her ideas about how to think through this scene in particular. Vivi Tellas, personal conversation with author, 2016.

95. Vivi Tellas, *Tres filósofos con bigotes*, in Brownell and Hernández, *Biodrama / Proyecto Archivos*, 97.

96. Jaroslavsky, "Capturar la teatralidad," 78.

97. Vivi Tellas, *Escuela de conducción*, in Brownell and Hernández, *Biodrama / Proyecto Archivos*, 195.

98. Vivi Tellas, *Escuela de conducción*, 178.

Chapter 2

1. Jorge Dubatti, "Lola Arias: Acerca de artistas 'anfibios' y nuevo teatro documental," *Teatro Independiente La Plata Argentina* (blog), December 9, 2012, http://teatroindependientelaplata.blogspot.com/2012/12/lola-arias-acerca-de-artistas-anfibios.html. Other theater artists of her generation that, according to Dubatti, belong to the same "collective" are Federico León, Romina Paula, Mariano Pensotti, Heidi Steinhardt, and Claudio Tolcachir, among others.

2. *Mi vida después* was conceived as the last play to be part of this cycle, but by the time of its premiere, Vivi Tellas was no longer the director of the Teatro Sarmiento. For more information, see chapter 1 of this book, and Vivi Tellas, *Biodrama: Proyecto Archivos. Seis escenarios documentales de Vivi Tellas*, ed. Pamela Brownell and Paola Hernández (Córdoba: Papeles Teatrales, 2017).

3. Lola Arias, "The Work of Art Is a Parasite: Lola Arias," interview by Bertie Ferdman, trans. Ferdman, *Theatre* 44, no. 2 (2014): 31.

4. Lola Arias, "El teatro antes del futuro: Sobre *Mi vida después* de Lola Arias," interview by Pamela Brownell, *telondefondo: Revista de teoría y crítica teatral*, no. 10 (December 2009): 10, http://www.telondefondo.org/numeros-anteriores/numero10/articulo/210/el-teatro-antes-del-futuro-sobre-mi-vida-despues-de-lola-arias.html; Cecilia Sosa, "Los niños que fuimos," *Radar* (blog), *Página 12*, October 7, 2012, https://www.pagina12.com.ar/diario/suplementos/radar/9-8291-2012-10-07.html.

5. Program for *Mi vida después*.

6. *Mi vida después* traveled to many festivals, including International Summer Festival Hamburgo, Noordezon Performing Arts Festival Gronengen, Steirischer Herbst Festival Graz, Transversales, México, Festival radicals, Barcelona, FITAM Festival Internacional Santiago a Mil, Santiago de Chile, and others in Paris, Athens, Prague, Budapest, Brighton.

7. Interest in Lola Arias's documentary work has been constantly increasing, as it can be gauged by the most recent publication of her trilogy, *Campo miando / Minefield*, and other texts in English. See Jean Graham-Jones, ed., *Lola Arias: Re-enacting Life* (Aberystwyth, Wales: Performance Research Books, 2019).

8. Lola Arias, *Mi vida después y otros textos* (Buenos Aires: Reservoir Books, 2016), 9. All translations from Spanish to English are my own unless specified otherwise.

9. Arias, *Mi vida después*, 9.

10. Arias, *Mi vida después*, 15.

11. From now on, I will mainly use the Spanish title when appropriate.

12. Brenda Werth, *Theatre, Performance, and Memory Politics in Argentina* (New York: Palgrave Macmillan, 2010), 200–201.

13. I use the English title because this play was first designed and presented at London's Battersea Arts Centre and presented by the London International Festival of Theatre (LIFT).

14. *Veterans* was included in *Doble de riesgo* [Stunt double], a multifaceted installation that took place at the Parque de la memoria, an important park that houses different monuments to the victims of state terrorism, as well as a museum (Sala PAyS) with information and names of the disappeared during the last dictatorship. Situated beside the Río de la Plata, this park is a beautiful green open space that houses a variety of artwork that relates to human rights violations. *Doble de riesgo* was housed in Sala PAyS for three months, and it coincided with the premiere of *Campo minado / Minefield* in Buenos Aires. For an excellent study on this installation, see Gail A. Bulman, "Not My Choice: Feeling as a 'Productive Paradox' in Lola Arias's *Doble de riesgo*," *Latin American Theatre Review* 51, no. 1 (Fall 2017).

15. Lola Arias, "Lola Arias y las ideas detrás de *Veteranos, Campo minado* y *Teatro de Guerra*," interview by Diego Brodersen, Cultura y Espectáculos, *Página 12*, September 6, 2018, https://www.pagina12.com.ar/140206-hay-una-tension-entre-lo-artificial-y-lo-real.

16. In *Veterans*, Marcelo Vallejo is the only veteran who will go on with the subsequent projects. The other four Argentine veterans for this installation are Guillero Dellepiane, Daniel Terzano, Darío Volonte, and Fabián Volonte. The film version, *Theatre of War*, does bring in other veterans as well, however the main protagonists and the stories that are told are still done by the same six veterans from *Campo minado / Minefield*.

17. In conversation with Jean Graham-Jones, she explained to me that Arias cast a mother and her baby for this play, and when the baby had to be replaced (getting too old for the project), she recast the mother as well.

18. Arias, "The Work of Art Is a Parasite." In this interview, Arias explains her own process of becoming attracted by the real onstage: "This was a very interesting process for me, and what I became fascinated with was how to work with the real in a way in which the unpredictable and pure aspects of life—here, the baby's essence (in fact, we did the piece right until the baby could talk, up until he turned two)—can begin to infiltrate the play. Elements that can have an effect on the life of a play but that are more performative and less representational—less an idea of theater as fiction" (31).

19. According to Me Mumford, Reality Theater, first seen in the 1990s, features intersecting and different genres, among them "autobiographical, community, documentary and 'verbatim theater' " (Mumford quoted in Jean Graham-Jones, "Lo real no siempre se rehace de la misma manera: *Mi vida después* y *El año en que nací* de Lola Arias," *Apuntes de Teatro*, no. 138 [2013]: 55). For a more succinct study on how Rimini Protokoll works with "experts" and the nonactor method, see Miriam Dreysse and Florian Malzacher, *Experts of the Everyday: The Theatre of Rimini Protokoll* (Berlin: Alexander Verlag, 2008).

20. It is interesting to see how *Ciudades paralelas*, while transnational, it was not able to be fully produced in India. According to Arias, "Art Is a Parasite," 36, one of the eight installations, *Home* by Dominic Huber, was impossible, "because the notion of peeking through windows to see inside a private home is absolutely inconceivable." The same case goes for *Palacio de Justicia* (Justice Court), where a chorus is supposed to sing the verdicts. In India, due to high security, this performance was not possible.

21. This quote is taken from Rimini Protokoll's website, https://www.rimini-protokoll.de/website/en/.

22. These projects are *The Quiet Volume* [Library] by Ant Hampton and Tim Etchells; *Sometimes I Think, I Can See You* [Station] by Mariano Pensotti; *Factory* by Gerardo Naumann; *Prime Time* [House] by Dominic Huber; *In the Name of the People* [Court] by Christian García; *The First International of Shopping Malls* [Shopping center] by Ligna; *Hotel / Maids* [Hotel] by Lola Arias; and *Review* [Roof] by Stefan Kaegi.

23. In 2013, inspired by Brecht's *The Threepenny Opera*, she created a play titled *The Art of Making Money* that was performed by beggars, prostitutes, and actors from the city of Bremen. Another urban project, *Audition for a Demonstration* (2014–2017), was a durational performance that began with an ad in the newspaper and other media to reenact a demonstration that happened in the past. This type of urban participatory project exploring the relationship between politics, history, fiction, and collective memory was foreseen as a portable project that could be applied to any city. The project took place in Buenos Aires (2017), Prague (2015), Athens (2015), and Berlin (2014). For more information about these and other projects or a list of the artists who participated in *My Documents*, see *Lola Arias*, accessed December 12, 2018, http://www.lolaarias.com.

24. Lola Arias "My Documents 2020-12," https://lolaarias.com/my-documents.

25. Paola Hernández, "Biografías escénicas: *Mi vida después* de Lola Arias," *Latin American Theatre Review* 45, no. 1 (Fall 2011): 123.

26. Jordana Blejmar, "Autofictions of Postwar: Fostering Empathy in Lola Arias' *Minefield / Campo minado*," *Latin American Theatre Review* 50, no. 2 (Spring 2017): 188.

27. Lola Arias, "El teatro antes del futuro: Sobre *Mi vida después* de Lola Arias," interview by Pamela Brownell, *telondefondo: Revista de teoría y crítica teatral*, no. 10 (December 2009), http://www.telondefondo.org/numeros-anteriores/numero10/articulo/210/el-teatro-antes-del-futuro-sobre-mi-vida-despues-de-lola-arias.html.

28. Lola Arias, *My Life After*, trans. Daniel Tunnard, rev. Jean Graham-Jones, in *Lola Arias: Re-enacting Life*, ed. Graham-Jones (Aberystwyth, Wales: Performance Research Books, 2019), 47.

29. In December 2009, a judge allowed Falco to testify against her father for the appropriation of her brother, Juan Cabandié (now a congressman), because she was already doing so as part of a play. This was a crucial case for Falco and for the Abuelas de Plaza de Mayo who had been pursuing this case for five years. This case was also a landmark for allowing other children to testify against their parents. Luis Falco was sentenced to eighteen years in prison, a sentence that reflected the most severe punishment heretofore given for such a crime. However, in June 2018 his sentence was changed to house arrest. For more information, see Paula Giménez, "A la izquierda del padre," *Página 12*, March 19, 2010, http://www.pagina12.com.ar/diario/suplementos/soy/1-1283-2010-03-21.html; Victoria Ginzberg, "Con la condena más alta para un apropiador," El país, *Página 12*, May 18, 2011, https://www.pagina12.com.ar/diario/elpais/1-168409-2011-05-18.html; and "Otorgaron la prisión domicialiaria al apropiador de Juan Cabandié," Sociedad, *Perfil*, https://www.perfil.com/noticias/sociedad/otorgaron-la-prision-domiciliaria-al-apropiador-de-juan-cabandie.phtml.

30. Arias has expressed that for her the process of investigation that each actor underwent was crucial and probably the most interesting part of the project. And she adds that the play was an excuse to dig into personal and familiar memories to make something new. For more information, see Lola Arias, "*Mi vida después*: Itinerario de un teatro vivo," interview by Ana Longoni and Lorena Verzero, *Revista Conjunto*, no. 162 (January–March 2012): 6–7.

31. Marianne Hirsch, *The Generation of Postmemory: Writing and Visual Culture after the Holocaust* (New York: Columbia University Press, 2012). There has been a strong debate among scholars about how reliable and useful Hirsch's concept of postmemory is in relation to *Mi vida después*. Among the most prominent, see Cecilia Sosa, *Queering Acts of Mourning in the Aftermath of Argentina's Dictatorship* (Woodbridge, England: Tamesis, 2014); Mariana Eva Pérez, "Their Lives After: Theatre as Testimony and the So-Called 'Second Generation' in Post-dictatorship Argentina," *Journal of Romance Studies* 3, no. 3 (Winter 2013): 6–16; Werth, *Theatre, Performance, and Memory Politics in Argentina*; Graham-Jones, "Lo real no siempre"; Paola Hernández, "Biografías escénicas"; and Geoffrey Maguire, *The Politics of Postmemory: Violence and Victimhood in Contemporary Argentine Culture* (Basingstoke, England: Palgrave Macmillan, 2017).

32. Pérez, "Their Lives After," 10.

33. Pérez, "Their Lives After," 14.

34. Hirsch, "The Generation of Postmemory," *Poetics Today* 29, no. 1 (2008): 106–107.

35. Hirsch, "The Generation of Postmemory," 107.

36. Hirsch, "The Generation of Postmemory," 107.

37. Cecilia Sosa, *Queering Acts of Mourning in the Aftermath of Argentina's Dictatorship: The Performances of Blood* (Woodbridge, England: Tamesis, 2014), 127.

38. Arias, "Footnote," in Graham-Jones, *Lola Arias*, 44.

39. Arias, "*Mi vida después*: Itinerario de un teatro vivo," 7–8.

40. Hirsch, *The Generation of Postmemory*, 6.

41. Sosa, *Queering Acts*, 107.

42. Arias, *My Life After*, 61.

43. Arias, *My Life After*, 62.

44. Roland Barthes, *Camera Lucida: Reflections on Photography*, trans. Richard Howard (New York: Hill and Wang, 1982), 21.

45. Barthes, *Camera Lucida*, 55.

46. Barthes, *Camera Lucida*, 81.

47. Marianne Hirsch, *Family Frames: Photography, Narrative and Postmemory* (Cambridge, Mass.: Harvard University Press, 1997), 11.

48. Margaret Olin, *Touching Photographs* (Chicago: University of Chicago Press, 2012), 1.

49. Olin, *Touching Photographs*, 3.

50. Olin, *Touching Photographs*, 10.

51. Barthes, *Camera Lucida*, 76, quoted in Olin, *Touching Photographs*, 53.

52. Elizabeth Edwards and Janice Hart, eds., *Photographs Objects Histories: On the Materiality of Images* (London: Routledge, 2004), 2.

53. Ángeles Donoso Macaya, *The Insubordination of Photography: Documentary Practices under Chile's Dictatorship* (Gainesville: University Press of Florida, 2020), 4.

54. Donoso Macaya, *The Insubordination of Photography*, 11.
55. Edwards and Hart, *Photographs Objects Histories*, 13.
56. Barthes, *Camera Lucida*, 49
57. Arias, *My Life After*, 48.
58. Annette Kuhn, *Family Secrets: Acts of Memory and Imagination* (London: Verso, 2002), 13.
59. Kuhn, *Family Secrets*, 19.
60. Kuhn, *Family Secrets*, 151.
61. Arias, *Mi vida después*, 10.
62. Marvin Carlson, *Shattering Hamlet's Mirror: Theatre and Reality* (Ann Arbor: University of Michigan Press, 2016), 40.
63. According to Arias, the protagonists are "Viviana Hernández, daughter of a national policeman who murdered two leftist militants; Alexandra Benado, daughter of a Revolutionary Left Movement (MIR) militant murdered by the police; Ítalo Gallardo, son of a Marine trained during the dictatorship; Soledad Gaspar, daughter of Popular Unitary Action Movement militants exiled in Mexico; Leopoldo Courbis, son of a police intelligence officer who was part of Allende's government and later helped 'cleanse the institution of Marxists'; Ana Laura Racz, daughter of a MIR militant mother exiled in the United States, where she worked collecting torture-victim testimonies; Pablo Díaz, whose father was in the far-right nationalist Fatherland and Freedom movement; Jorge Rivero, son of a Pinochet supporter who was unemployed for ten years of the dictatorship; Fernanda González, daughter of a militant father in the armed Manuel Rodríguez Patriotic Front; Alejandro Gómez, son of a journalist who supported Allende and spent years in jail; and Nicole Senerman, daughter of a young upper-middle-class couple who spent the dictatorship defying the imposed curfew as they went from party to party." Arias, "Footnote," in Graham-Jones, *Lola Arias*, 43–44.
64. *El año en que nací* was also part of the prestigious LIFT programming in London in 2014, and it later toured different countries in Europe and the Americas.
65. Alexandra Ripp, "Remembering the Coup: Chilean Theatre Now," *Performing Arts Journal*, no. 108 (2014): 89.
66. Ripp, "Remembering the Coup," 88.
67. Marcela A. Fuentes, "Performance Constellations: Memory and Event in Digitally Enabled Protests in the Americas," *Text and Performance Quarterly* 35, no. 1 (January 2015): 34.
68. For a more in-depth look at these student protests, see Nicolás M. Somma, "The Chilean Student Movement of 2011–2012: Challenging the Marketization of Education," *Interface* 4, no. 2 (2012). It is also worth noting that another massive student movement took place in October 2019 to demand changes to students loans, among other changes to higher education as well as social and economic equality for Chilean citizens.
69. Graham-Jones, "Lo real no siempre," 6.
70. Daniela Contreras López, "Reclaiming Memory: Social Reconstruction through Performance and Theatre in Post-dictatorship Chile," *Journal of Applied Theatre and Performance* 20, no. 3 (2015): 288.
71. For a study on the differences between these plays, see Graham-Jones, "Lo real no siempre."

72. Carol Martin, "The Theatrical Life of Documents," *Peripeti* 21 (2014): 27.

73. Anonymous program note from the performance of *The Year I Was Born* at the Museum of Contemporary Art (MCA), Chicago, January 2014.

74. Arias, *Mi vida después y otros textos* (Buenos Aires: Reservoir Books, 2016), 124–125.

75. Arias, *Mi vida después y otros textos*, 132.

76. As an Argentine national, I will reference the islands by the Argentine name, "Malvinas," and will use "Falklands" only when it is appropriate (e.g., when referring to Great Britain). For more information on the islands, see the website of the Museo Malvinas e Islas Atlánticas del Sur, http://museomalvinas.cultura.gob.ar/.

77. Rosana Guber, *¿Por qué Malvinas?* (Buenos Aires: Fondo de Cultura Económica, 2001), 164.

78. Federico Lorenz, *Malvinas: Una guerra argentina* (Buenos Aires: Editorial Sudamericana, 2009), 56.

79. On May 27, 1982, eighteen days before Argentina surrendered, the title page of *Revista Gente* read, "We keep winning," adding the number of British helicopters, ships, planes taken down, as well as boasting of defeating the British forces.

80. It is interesting to think about the role of media in this war, a war which has often been called the last physical war of the twentieth century. While the military junta controlled media outlets, it was not a war that was covered live. Due to its distant geographic position, it was not easy for the British to record the war either, and it was also highly censored. See D. George Boyce, *The Falklands War* (New York: Palgrave Macmillan, 2005), which states, "The war would not be a television spectacle, nor even a pictorial one. Dispatches took longer to reach London than had W. H. Russell's reports of the charge of the light Brigade in 1854" (154).

81. Nine hundred seven people lost their lives, and almost two thousand more were injured.

82. See Boyce, *The Falklands War*, 171–190, which dedicates a whole chapter to "Thatcher's Britain." Thatcher's gain and loss of her popularity during and after the war is studied closely with how the British people and politicians viewed her and her party.

83. Julieta Vitullo, *Islas imaginadas: La Guerra de Malvinas en la literatura y el cine argentinos* (Buenos Aires: Corregidor, 2012), 15–16.

84. Federico Lorenz, "Testigos de la derrota Malvinas: Los soldados y la guerra durante la transición democrática argentina, 1982–1987," in *Historizar el pasado vivo en América Latina*, ed. Anne Perotin-Dumon (Buenos Aires: Edhasa, 2007), 37.

85. See Oliver Galak, "No cesan los suicidios de ex combatientes de Malvinas," Política, *La Nación*, February 28, 2006, https://www.lanacion.com.ar/784519-no-cesan-los-suicidios-de-ex-combatientes-de-malvinas. Up until the mid-1990s, there were very few associations for veterans. The first such association was the Centro de Ex Soldados Combatientes de Malvinas (Center for the Ex–Combatant Soldier of Malvinas), founded in 1982. As of 2006, the number of suicides among veterans had reached 454. This number is staggering, considering that 326 soldiers died in combat (not counting the ones who died in

the sinking of the cruiser *Belgrano*), and also when compared to the national statistics of suicides. The number of Malvinas veteran suicides is fourteen times higher than that of civilian suicides. According to César González Trejo, Malvinas veteran and founder of the Federation of the Veterans of War, many suicides were due to "demalvinization," which "was brought by a society who looked the other way, who did not remember the fallen nor did they help the ones who returned."

86. Federico Lorenz, *Unas islas demasiado famosas: Malvinas, historia y política* (Buenos Aires: Capital Intelectual, 2013), 188–189.

87. The vast amount of fiction based on the Malvinas shows the wide interest in this topic. Other fiction and nonfiction publications of interest are the documentary film *Hundan el Belgrano* (1996) [Sink the *Belgrano*] by Federico Urioste; the novels *Cuando te vi caer* [When I saw you fall] (2008) by Sebastián Basualdo, *Transfondo* [Background] (2012) by Patricia Ratto, and *La construcción* [Construction] (2014) by Carlos Godoy; and the plays *Piedras dentro de la piedra* [A rock within a rock] (2012) by Mariana Mazover (a theatrical adaptation of *Los pichiciegos*), and *Los Tururú* (2012) by Diego Quiróz. For another look at theatrical productions of Malvinas, see Noe Montez, "Performing Public Memorialization of the Malvinas War," in *Memory, Transnational Justice, and Theatre in Postdictatorship Argentina* (Carbondale: Southern Illinois University Press, 2017).

88. See Marin Laufenberg, "Tempering Trauma with Humor in Argentine Post-dictatorship Theatre: Laughing to Recover, Reimagine, Rebuild" (PhD diss., University of Wisconsin, 2017). Laufenberg writes, "While initially researched for a documentary film, the play manipulates and drastically alters the tone of that more objective material for the new audience. *Islas de la Memoria: Historias de guerra en la posguerra* by Julio Cardoso, is the end result of archival research undertaken by the Observatorio Malvinas de la Universidad Nacional de Lanus originally done for the documentary film *Locos de la bandera*. After gathering research, testimony, letters from and to soldiers, photos, other documents, and conducting interviews with families of fallen soldiers, *Islas de la memoria* was born in 2011 with a goal of connecting the youngest Argentines to a key moment of their recent history. The Teatro Nacional Cervantes was commissioned to produce this piece in conjunction with the Observatorio Malvinas de la Universidad Nacional de Lanús as an educational work that teaches while entertaining. Though the documentary follows a more solemn tone, the play bursts to life, shattering silence with laughter. By infusing humor into a serious matter, this piece finds a captivating, and lively way to teach about the Guerra de las Malvinas: drawing them close emotionally" (126–127).

89. For more information on the current theater of the Malvinas, see Ricardo Dubatti, ed., *Malvinas I. La guerra en el teatro, el teatro de la guerra* (Buenos Aires: Ediciones del CCC, 2017); Ricardo Dubatti, ed., *Malvinas II. La guerra en el teatro, el teatro de la guerra* (Buenos Aires: Ediciones del CCC, 2019); and Ricardo Dubatti, ed., *La guerra de Malvinas en el teatro argentino* (Buenos Aires: CONICET, Eudeba, 2020).

90. Blejmar, "Autofictions of Postwar," 106.

91. Arias, *Minefield / Campo minado*, trans. Daniel Tunnard (London: Oberon Books, 2017), 64.

92. While Arias worked in both countries, conducting auditions, she saw the full and final cast for the first time in Buenos Aires, right before the first round of rehearsals was to begin.

93. Lola Arias, "*Minefield* Director and Writer Lola Arias: My Shows Are Living Creatures That Evolve," interview by Tom Wicker, *The Stage*, October 27, 2017, https://www.thestage.co.uk/features/interviews/2017/minefield-director-writer-lola-arias-my-shows-living-creatures-that-evolve/.

94. Playwright Federico León staged a Malvinas veteran in *Museo Miguel Ángel Boezzio*, a short documentary play that was part of Proyecto Museos, directed by Vivi Tellas. Together with photographs and letters, this vet talks to the audience about his life during the war. For a more in-depth study, see Brenda Werth, "A Malvinas Veteran Onstage: From Intimate Testimony to Public Memorialization," *South Central Review* 30, no. 3 (Fall 2013): 83–100.

95. Lola Arias, quoted in Blejmar, "Autofictions of Postwar," 105. According to Arias, finding veterans from the British side was extremely difficult. She relied on contacting directors of previous films, such as *The Falklands War: The Untold Story*, where one of the veterans, a young Lou Armour is interviewed, but she also contacted veterans' association and military personnel. After two years of finding the right veterans to stage the play, it took many hours of conversations about how the story was going to be told, how these ex-soldiers were going to be standing next to each other. As of the writing of this chapter, the six original veterans are still touring after the premiere in June 2016.

96. Lola Arias, "Lola Arias: Interview by Elianna Kan," *Bomb*, no. 128 (Summer 2014): 64, https://bombmagazine.org/articles/lola-arias/.

97. Arias, "Lola Arias," 64.

98. Arias, "Lola Arias," 64; emphasis in the original.

99. Mercedes Méndez, "Primer film de la talentosa directora teatral Lola Arias y su personal visión de Malvinas," *Revista Ñ, Clarín*, August 31, 2018, https://www.clarin.com/revista-enie/escenarios/espacio-urbano/lola-arias-personal-vision-malvinas_0_ryff4gwPm.html.

100. The British premiere took place in May 2016 at the Brighton Festival and later, in June, at London's Royal Court Theatre as part of LIFT, the international festival that commissioned the work. As of this writing, the play is still touring different Latin American, European and Asian countries, among them France, Germany, Portugal, Belgium, Italy, Spain, Japan, Brazil, and Chile.

101. Cecilia Sosa states that while only three performances were scheduled at the Royal Court, it was expanded to a total of nine, all with standing ovations. See Cecilia Sosa, "*Campo minado / Minefield*: War, Affect and Vulnerability—a Spectacle of Intimate Power," *Theatre Research International* 42, no. 2 (July 2017): 179. For information about how different newspaper reviews called the performance "unforgettably potent," see Paul Taylor, "*Minefield*, Royal Court London: Unforgettably Potent" (review of *Minefield / Campo minado*), *Independent*, June 6, 2016, https://www.independent.co.uk/arts-entertainment/theatre-dance/reviews/minefield-royal-court-london-theatre-review-unforgettably-potent-a7067196.html. Thanks to this success, it was invited to return in November 2017.

102. Lola Arias, quoted in Graham-Jones, "The Translational Politics of Surtitling: Lola Arias's *Campo minado / Minefield*," in *Theatrical Speech Acts:*

Performing Language, ed. Erika Fischer-Lichte, Torsten Jost, and Saskya Iris Jain (New York: Routledge, 2020), 121.

103. Jill Dolan, *Utopia in Performance: Finding Hope at the Theatre* (Ann Arbor: University of Michigan Press, 2005), 27.

104. Verónica Perera, "Testimonios vivos, dramaturgia abierta: La guerra de Malvinas en Campo minado de Lola Arias," *Anagnórisis: Revista de investigación teatral*, no. 6 (December 2017): 305.

105. In September 2018, *Campo minado / Minefield* was finally staged in the Teatro San Martín, the official cultural theater center of the city. The film was released at the same time in Buenos Aires.

106. Arias, *Campo minado / Minefield*, 62.

107. This is part of Marcelo Vallejo's dialogue in Arias, *Campo minado / Minefield*, 1.

108. Graham-Jones, "The Translational Politics of Surtitling," 127.

109. María M. Delgado, "Ways of Remembering Las Malvinas/The Falklands," in *Lola Arias: Re-enacting Life*, ed. Jean Graham-Jones (Aberystwyth, Wales: Performance Research Books, 2019).

110. According to Boyce (*The Falklands War*, 66), the Argentines' uniforms were substandard and ill suited for the weather, emphasizing a disparity that could be seen between the military junta's uniforms and the low quality of their army's conscripts.

111. Arias, *Minefield / Campo minado*, 9.

112. Dierdre Heddon, *Autobiography and Performance* (Basingstoke, England: Palgrave Macmillan, 2008), 27–28; emphasis in the original.

113. Arias explains that for her "the dilemma between fiction and documentary doesn't exist. All of my work is based on the art of storytelling where fiction and reality contaminate one another" ("Lola Arias," 64).

114. Arias, "Lola Arias," 61.

115. Elizabeth Jelin, *State Repression and the Labors of Memory*, trans. Judy Rein and Marcial Godoy-Anativia (Minneapolis: University of Minnesota Press, 2003), 11.

116. For an insightful understanding of the role of autofiction in postdictatorship Argentina, see Jordana Blejmar, *Playful Memories: The Autofictional Turn in Post-dictatorship Argentina* (Cham, Switzerland: Palgrave Macmillan, 2016).

117. Lorena Verzero, "Representaciones afectivas/efectivas en Lola Arias: 'La memoria también puede funcionar como un campo minado,' " *Revista Conjunto*, no. 185 (2017): 39.

118. Blejmar, "Autofictions of Postwar," 104.

119. Heddon, *Autobiography*, 9.

120. Heddon, *Autobiography*, 10.

121. See Shoshana Felman and Dori Laub, *Testimony: Crises of Witnessing in Literature, Psychoanalysis, and History* (New York: Routledge, 1992).

122. A clear reference to this can be seen in the Truth and Reconciliation Commissions. With the creation of the National Commission on the Disappearance of Persons in 1983, the first truth commission to be recognized nationally and internationally, Argentina pioneered a way to legitimize testimony from survivors about abuses committed by the government. The subsequent publication in 1985 of the official report, *Nunca más* [Never again], incremented the value of

testimony later used in trials against the military perpetrators of human rights abuses. Similar Truth and Reconciliation Committees follows in Chile, South Africa, Peru, Guatemala, and El Salvador, all after repressive governments that left thousands of victims, deaths, and disappeared persons. To give testimony (or *dar testimonio*) was the key element of these reports and commissions. Among the vast amount of literature on this topic, the following titles are excellent studies of different cases and countries: Priscilla B. Hayner, *Unspeakable Truths: Transitional Justice and the Challenge of Truth Commissions*, 2nd ed. (New York: Routledge, 2011); Kerry Bystrom, "The Public Private Sphere: Family Narrative and Democracy in Argentina and South Africa," *Social Dynamics* 36, no. 1 (March 2010); Kathryn Sikkink and Carrie Booth Walling, "The Impact of Human Rights Trials in Latin America," *Journal of Peace Research* 44, no. 4 (July 2007); and Kevin Avruch, "Truth and Reconciliation Commissions: Problems in Transitional Justice and the Reconstruction of Identity," *Transcultural Psychiatry* 47, no. 1 (February 2010).

123. See Felman and Laub, *Testimony*; Cathy Caruth, ed., *Trauma: Explorations in Memory* (Baltimore: John Hopkins University Press, 1995); Nancy K. Miller and Jason Tougaw, eds., *Extremities: Trauma, Testimony and Community* (Urbana: University of Illinois Press, 2002); and Heddon, *Autobiography*.

124. Suzette Henke, *Shattered Subjects: Trauma and Testimony in Women's Life Writing* (Basingstoke, England: Palgrave Macmillan, 2000), xix, quoted in Heddon, *Autobiography*, 54.

125. Kuhn, *Family Secrets*, 158; emphasis in the original.

126. Sosa, "*Campo minado / Minefield*: War, Affect and Vulnerability," 186.

127. Arias, *Minefield / Campo minado*, 53.

128. Leigh Gilmore, *The Limits of Autobiography: Trauma and Testimony* (Ithaca, N.Y.: Cornell University Press, 2001), 6.

129. Gilmore, *Limits of Autobiography*, 6.

130. Gilmore, *Limits of Autobiography*, 7.

131. Arias, *Minefield / Campo minado*, 57.

132. Arias, *Minefield / Campo minado*, 58.

133. Here I am also dialoguing with Heddon, who states, "The relationship that autobiographical performances attempt to forge with the spectator seems to be particularly crucial." Heddon, *Autobiography*, 6.

134. Anthony Andrew, "Minefield: Two Sides of the Falkland's War on One Stage," *The Guardian*, November 12, 2017, https://www.theguardian.com/stage/2017/nov/12/two-sides-falklands-war-one-stage-minefield-veterans-stories.

135. In Arias, "Las ideas detrás," Arias clarifies that Gurkhas were deployed to the islands but never actually fought, adding to the myth and fear that they had decapitated, as well as cut off ears and tongues of Argentine soldiers. For a more historical view on the Gurkhas and their deployment to the islands, see Mike Seear, *With the Gurkhas in the Falklands: A War Journal* (Barnsley, England: Pen and Sword Books, 2017).

136. Lola Arias, dir., *Theatre of War* (Argentina-Spain-Germany, Documentary) A Gema Films production, in co-production with BWP S.L. (Spain), Sutor Kolonko Filmproduktion (Germany), Sake Argentina (Argentina), 2018. I thank Jean Graham-Jones, who has had a chance to see a more current performance of this play, where she observed that Sukrim feels and performs more comfortably

onstage. After years of touring this play, he now seems to rejoice in the act of the stage and seems more connected to the audience than before.

137. Méndez, "Primer film."

138. Arias, *Minefield / Campo minado*, 27.

139. Walter Benjamin, "Ibizan Sequence, 1932," in *Walter Benjamin: Selected Writings*, vol. 2, bk. 2: *1931–1934*, ed. Marcus Paul Bullock, Michael William Jennings, Howard Eiland, and Gary Smith (Cambridge, Mass.: Belknap Press of Harvard University Press, 2005), 576.

140. Arias, *Minefield / Campo minado*, 35.

141. Arias, *Minefield / Campo minado*, 36.

142. Rebecca Schneider, *Performing Remains: Art and War in Times of Theatrical Reenactment* (London: Routledge, 2011), 2.

143. Schneider, *Performing Remains*, 2.

144. Schneider, *Performing Remains*, 7.

145. Schneider, *Performing Remains*, 9.

146. Schneider, *Performing Remains*, 17; emphasis in the original.

147. Paul Taylor, "*Minefield*, Royal Court London, Theatre Review."

148. Arias, *Minefield / Campo minado*, 19–20.

149. Richard Schechner, *Between Theatre and Anthropology* (Philadelphia: University of Pennsylvania Press, 1985), 36–37.

150. Arias, *Minefield / Campo minado*, 20.

151. Joseph Roach, *Cities of the Dead* (New York: Columbia University Press, 1996), 2.

152. Roach, *Cities of the Dead*, 6.

153. Schneider, *Performing Remains*, 102.

154. Peggy Phelan quoted in Schneider, *Performing Remains*, 105.

155. Méndez, "Primer film."

156. Arias, *Minefield / Campo minado*, 64–65.

Chapter 3

1. *Filo de caballo* refers to a town in the state of Guerrero where almost all of the population works on the manufacturing of heroin or fentanyl.

2. The students were undergraduates at the Escuela Normal Rural Raúl Isidro Burgos, a teacher's college in Ayotzinapa.

3. On October 2, 1968, about fifteen thousand students from various universities marched through the streets of Mexico City to protest the army's occupation of the university campus, after students had been striking for months. At night about five thousand students, some with children, congregated at the Plaza de las Tres Culturas in Tlatelolco for a peaceful rally. However, the police and military forces attacked students and demonstrators. On September 25, 2018, a Mexican government body finally acknowledged that the attack in Tlatelolco was a state crime. Jaime Rochin, a spokesman for the Executive Commission for Attention to Victims, stated: "The use of sniper fire was a state crime, aimed at creating chaos, terror and an official narrative to criminalize the protest. It was a state crime that continued beyond October 2 with arbitrary arrests and tortures." "Mexico Calls Student Massacre Ahead of '68 Olympics a 'State Crime,'" *Democracy Now!* (2018), accessed December 12, 2018, https://www.democracynow.org/2018/9/28/headlines/mexico_calls_student_massacre_ahead_of_68_olympics_a_state_crime.

4. For more information about Forensic Architecture, see https://forensic-architecture.org/investigation/the-enforced-disappearance-of-the-ayotzinapa-students.

5. There is a vast amount of newspaper coverage on this topic; however, for more reading, see North American Congress on Latin America (NACLA), "Ayotzinapa Timeline," NACLA, https://nacla.org/ayotzinapa-timeline. This report from the North American Congress on Latin America creates a social memory of this event by compiling historical data, photographs, maps, interviews, and analysis of the event, stating: "This timeline was constructed after reviewing a total of 334 documents, which were issued by the state and non-state actors with a key role in the investigation of the disappearance of the 43 students. Main sources of information include statements from the government of the State of Guerrero, Mexico's General Attorney, Tlachinollan, the Inter-American Commission of Human Rights, the Argentine Forensic Team, and the United Nations Committee on Enforced Disappearances. In addition to these official documents, the timeline also draws from over a hundred newspaper articles."

6. For a closer study on TLS's research methods and anthropology, see Rodrigo Parrini, "Figuras del límite: documentos, etnografías y teatro," *Investigación Teatral: Revista de Artes Escénicas y Performatividad* 9, no. 13 (Apr.–Sept. 2018): 14–34.

7. Nicolas Bourriard, *Relational Aesthetics*, trans. Simon Pleasance and Fonza Woods (Dijon: Les Presses du Reel, 2009), 16–17.

8. Sara Ahmed, "Happy Objects," in *The Affect Theory Reader*, ed. Melissa Gregg and Gregory J. Seigworth (Durham, N.C.: Duke University Press, 2010), 30; Sara Ahmed, *The Cultural Politics of Emotion*, 2nd ed. (New York: Routledge, 2015), 7.

9. Pedro Bravo Elizondo, *Teatro documental latinoamericano*, 2 vols. (Mexico City: Universidad Nacional Autónoma de México, 1982), 1:24.

10. Vicente Leñero (1933–2014) was a Mexican playwright known for his documentary plays, which were influenced by Peter Weiss's fourteen propositions, encouraging a specific structure to writing in this genre. Some of his best-known earlier plays are *Pueblo rechazado* [Rejected people] (1968), *Los albañiles* [The bricklayers] (1969), *Compañero* [Comrade] (1970), and *El juicio* [The trial] (1970). He later published *Martirio de Morelos* [The martyrdom of Morelos] (1981) and *La noche de Hernán Cortés* [The night of Hernán Cortés] (1992), two controversial plays that question and demystify Mexican historical heroes. He later became known for his screenwriting in films, such as *El crimen del Padre Amaro* [The crime of Padre Amaro] (2002). He also wrote as a journalist for *Excélsior* and *Proceso*.

11. The collective creation in Colombia during the 1960s and '70s brings out some of the most important work of documentary plays done by groups. In a country where the lack of prolific playwrights has been an issue, groups like the TEC and La Candelaria became key players in national and international settings, and a pioneer in documentary practices of this era.

12. Lagartijas tiradas al sol, "Lagartijas tiradas al sol," accessed December 12, 2018, http://www.lagartijastiradasalsol.com.

13. Lagartijas tiradas al sol, "Lagartijas tiradas al sol."

14. Lagartijas tiradas al sol brings the theater and the digital world together by creating blogs as part of their work. Their trilogy *La rebeldía* [Rebel] consists of a blog *El rumor del oleaje* [The whisper of waves], where they shared

their research, and the plays *El rumor del incencio* [The whisper of fire] and *El rumor del momento* [The whisper of the moment]. The autobiographical story of anthropologist Margarita Urías Hermosillo, who participated in the revolutions of the 1960s is embodied through her daughter, Luisa Pardo. Simultaneously, the play brings attention to #YoSoy132, a social movement composed of Mexican university students who opposed the Institutional Revolutionary Party candidate Enrique Peña Nieto and the election media coverage. #YoSoy132 was a virtual movement to express support to the 131 initial protesters.

15. Ileana Diéguez, *Escenarios liminales* (Mexico City: Toma Ediciones, 2014), 128–129; Diana Taylor, *Performance* (Durham, N.C.: Duke University Press, 2016), 147.

16. *Pequeños territorios en reconstrucción* is an interactive installation-performance about the construction of the so-called City of Women in Turbaco, Colombia. This story retells how La Liga de Mujeres Desplazadas [The League of Displaced Women] built their own "city of women" as a means of escaping violence in their own cities and features Turbacan women and their children onstage as interpreters. TLS constructs a stage with cylinder blocks, pictures, video montage while some of the women and female actors retell the story of the city. Using workshops, this play was created over weeks of residency in Turbaco, Colombia, during which the company helped women build more homes. For more information about the construction of this city of women, see Theresa Delgadillo, "Artists in America Confront the Fracturing Effects of Violence," *Mujeres Talk* (blog), Ohio State University Libraries, April 19, 2016, https://library.osu.edu/blogs/mujerestalk/2016/04/19/artists-in-the-americas-confront-the-fracturing-effects-of-violence/.

17. *Durango 66* draws connections between the student protest movement in Mexico in the 1960s and the recent massacres in Mexico attributed to crime syndicates and government collusion. These include the mass murders discovered in Durango in 2011 and other recent atrocities, such as the forty-three students that disappeared in Iguala. According to director Jorge Vargas, the play focuses on actions taken fifty years ago, where social upheaval of students resulted from privatization and exploitation of natural resources. With the idea that there were extant voice recording of this event, the group seeks to document facts and fiction from this moment. Jorge Vargas (director, Teatro Línea de Sombra), in discussion with the author, May 2016.

18. Vargas, personal interview, May 2016.

19. Bourriaud, *Relational Aesthetics*, 16–18.

20. Bourriaud, *Relational Aesthetics*, 13.

21. Claire Bishop, "Antagonism and Relational Aesthetics," *October*, no. 110 (Fall 2004): 65.

22. Bourriaud, *Relational Aesthetics*, 109; Bishop, "Antagonism and Relational Aesthetics," 66.

23. Bishop, "Antagonism and Relational Aesthetics," 67.

24. Lehmann, *Postdramatic Theatre*, trans. Karen Jürs-Munby (London: Routledge, 2009), 101–102.

25. Lehmann, *Postdramatic Theatre*, 104.

26. Jorge Dubatti, *Teatro matriz, teatro liminal: Estudios de filosofía del teatro y poética comparada* (Buenos Aires: Atuel, 2016), 75.

27. Dubatti, *Teatro matriz*, 101.

28. Jacques Rancière, *The Emancipated Spectator*, trans. Gregory Elliott (New York: Verso, 2009), 19.

29. Richard Schechner, *Performance Studies: An Introduction* (London: Routledge, 2002), 45.

30. Rancière, *The Emancipated Spectator*, 3; emphasis in the original.

31. Teatro Línea de Sombra is well-known for their pedagogical focus as well as their interrelational space they have created by inviting international artists to participate in their one-week international gathering to teach and share theater methodologies. Their most recent "Encuentro Internacional de Escena Contemporánea" brought together artists from Lebanon, Belgium, and Mexico. For a more in-depth look, see Teatro Línea de Sombra, "Teatro Línea de Sombra," accessed December 12, 2018, www.teatrolineadesombra.com

32. Vargas, interview by the author, May 2016. In addition to Luna's influence, Vargas states that the intellectual work of artist-scholars like Rodrigo Parrini and Eduardo Bernal are key voices in the development of their work.

33. Vargas interview, May 2016.

34. Alfadir Luna, interview by Bernard Vienat, *Vorticidad*, https://vorticidad.org/artist/alfadir-luna-2/; English version is provided online, however Sarah Misemer edited the language for better understanding.

35. The first procession took place on September 24, 2008, at the historic La Merced market in the heart of Mexico City to reunite surrounding markets that combine religious and magical backgrounds. The markets involved are Mixcalco, Comidas, Flores, Anexo, Sonora, Sonora Anexo, Nave Menos, Nave Mayor, Desnivel, and Baquetón.

36. Bourriaud, *Relational Aesthetics*, 61, 17, 15.

37. Except for *El puro lugar*, an in situ walking installation, my analysis is based on performances attended at different times since 2016, as well as video recordings and unpublished manuscripts provided to me by TLS. All translations from the Spanish to English are my own, unless noted otherwise.

38. While Amarillo was a safe haven for many documented migrants from different nations, such as Cuba, Vietnam, Somalia, and Burma, it has seen a diminishing number of migrants beginning in 2016. And even though Amarillo is the city in Texas that allows more immigrants per capita, bigger cities in the state admit more numbers. As a state, Texas accepts more immigrants than any other state. For more information, see Patrick Michels, "The Strangers Next Door," *The Observer*, April 11, 2016, https://www.texasobserver.org/the-strangers-next-door-amarillo-refugees/.

39. Since 2013, TLS, with the support of SERTULL (a socially and humanly committed institution), has worked with other human rights organizations and has taken *Amarillo* on the Migrant Route to other important places. Some of their work can be seen in their intervention with groups such as Casa del Migrante La 72, Grupo de Mujeres Las Partronas, Casa del Migrante de Ixtepec, among other cultural and social agencies in the south, center, and north of Mexico. In 2018, they traveled to Agua Prieta, to stage *Amarillo* right on the border with Douglas, Arizona. Email from Alicia Laguna, February 2, 2018.

40. Rory Carroll, "Altar Mexico: How the 'Migrant Oasis' for Would-Be Border Crossers Became a Trap," *The Guardian*, October 14, 2015, https://www.theguardian.com/world/2015/oct/14/altar-mexico-how-the-migrant-oasis-for-would-be-border-crossers-became-a-trap. Carroll's article also explains how

gruesome the situation has become due to the presence of organized crime groups that "extort, kidnap and kill migrants," and it points out to the gravity of the situation due to drug trafficking that also incites human trafficking through this area.

41. Luis D. León, "Metaphor and Place: The U.S.-Mexico Border as Center and Periphery in the Interpretation of Religion," *Journal of the American Academy of Religion* 67, no. 3 (1999): 546.

42. León, "Metaphor and Place," 544.

43. León argues that "for most Mexican and Chicano Catholics, she is the head of a complex terrain of sacred geography delimited by saints and the sites of their apparitions" and goes on to explore how the symbolic order is constantly in flux." León, "Metaphor and Place," 546.

44. Six months after TLS's visit to Altar, the funding became available for two permanent positions at the shelter. This transaction would not have been possible without the work of Alicia Laguna. Jorge Vargas in conversation with the author, September 14, 2018.

45. Jason de León, *The Land of Open Graves: Living and Dying on the Migrant Trail* (Berkeley: University of California Press, 2015), 35. In his illuminating work, de León traces how Prevention through Deterrence was thought of as "the prediction is that with traditional entry and smuggling routes disrupted, illegal traffic will be deterred, or forced over more *hostile* terrain, less suited for crossing and more suited for enforcement." De León, *The Land of Open Graves*, 32; emphasis in the original.

46. De León, *The Land of Open Graves*, 29–30.

47. De León, *The Land of Open Graves*, 43.

48. Anzaldúa, *Borderlands/La Frontera: The New Mestiza* (San Francisco: Spinsters/Aunt Lute, 1987), 4.

49. Anzaldúa, *Borderlands*, 4.

50. Giorgio Agamben, *State of Exception*, trans. Kevin Attell (Chicago: University of Chicago Press, 2005), 40.

51. Valencia, *Gore Capitalism*, trans. John Pluecker (South Pasadena, Calif.: Semiotext(e) Intervention Series, 2018), 208.

52. Valencia, *Gore Capitalism*, 208.

53. Alicia Laguna, email message to author, February 7, 2018. According to producer and actor Alicia Laguna, in all the shelters that TLS has visited, tension and violence dominated as a result of different circumstances that threaten the migrants and the centers. Thus, shelters, community centers and churches become an overall safety net for the migrants as well as for the community itself. TLS took extreme precautions during this trip and was well aware of the possible danger they could face.

54. This play has traveled throughout Mexico and has toured major festivals and theaters in France, Argentina, the U.S., Canada, Colombia, Peru, Brazil, Spain, Finland, Russia, Korea, Slovenia, and Macedonia, among others. *Amarillo* received the Latin ACE Award for Best Foreign Production in New York, in 2012; and the Audience Award for the Best Performance of the Twenty-First Exponto International Performing Arts Festival in Ljubljana, Slovenia. My analysis of this play is based both on the video performance available through On the Boards, a script provided by TLS, as well as the live production at the Chicago Shakespeare Theatre under the Chicago Latino Theatre Alliance in October 2017.

55. For a closer look at their catalog and choices of films, see http://www.contraelsilencio.org/index.html.

56. A specific definition of props and their importance was prevalent in the program distributed during the production at The Yard at Chicago Shakespeare during October 2017 in Chicago. It states that "the objects used in staging *Amarillo* are inexpensive ones, like water jugs, sand, and candles. Some invoke the water stations in the desert, where water drums or jugs are left for border crossers along known passages. Some are components of the 'kits' people carry to cross the border into the United States—kits that commonly consist of a backpack, running shoes, tuna, lemons, pain killers, water and a loaf of bread. The border crossers walk up to 50 miles a day with just these kits for survival."

57. Jerzy Grotowski, "Towards the Poor Theatre" (ed. Kelly Morris, trans. T. K. Wiewiorowski), *Tulane Drama Review* 11, no. 3 (1967): 62–64.

58. TLS, *Amarillo* (unpublished MS, October 2016), Word document.

59. Judith Butler, *Precarious Life: The Powers of Mourning and Violence* (London: Verso, 2004), 20.

60. Berlant, *Cruel Optimism* (Durham, N.C.: Duke University Press, 2011), 10.

61. Berlant, *Cruel Optimism*, 11.

62. Berlant, *Cruel Optimism*, 14.

63. Jorge Vargas states that their artistic work is influenced by the collaboration they had in 2006 with the artistic collective, Akhe Group from St. Petersburg, Russia. Jorge Vargas (director, Teatro Línea de Sombra), in discussion with the author, September 2018.

64. One of TLS's commitments was to stage *Amarillo* for the *patronas* in Veracruz, Mexico, which they were able to do with "Amarillo on the Migrant Route" in 2014. Las *patronas* is a strong group of women who for the last twenty years have been feeding migrants for free atop the train La Bestia. This charitable institution began when two women waiting for a freight train, found themselves throwing their own groceries to migrants as they pleaded for food. Today, Norma Romero Vásquez is the recipient of Human Rights National Award, one of Mexico's most prestigious Human Rights Awards (2013) for her ongoing work with the *patronas*. Their notoriety has also made them the topic of a new documentary about their humanitarian work: Javier García, dir., *La cocina de las patronas* [Las patronas' kitchen] (2016).

65. Jill Dolan, *Utopia in Performance: Finding Hope at the Theatre* (Ann Arbor: University of Michigan Press, 2005), 3.

66. Harold Pinter, "Death," *Times Literary Supplement*, August 22, 2011, https://www.the-tls.co.uk/articles/public/harold-pinter-death-2-2/.

67. TLS, *Amarillo*.

68. Raúl Mendoza (actor, Teatro Línea de Sombra), in discussion with the author, October 21, 2017.

69. My analysis of this play is based on two separate live productions: the first one was during the XV Iberoamerican Theater Festival in Bogotá, Colombia (2016), and the second performance was at University of Wisconsin–Madison (2017). I also base my reading on an unpublished script provided by TLS. The original cast members were Zuadd Atala, Alicia Laguna, Malcom Vargas, Viany Salinas, and Jorge León. This last actor subsequently gets replaced by Gilberto

Barraza. The text is by Eduardo Bernal, Jorge Vargas, Gabriel Contreras, and a fragment from *Prometeo* by Rodrigo García. During the performance, live music is played by Jesús Cuevas. The scores are by Jesús Cuevas and Jorge Verdín. The play was directed by Jorge Vargas.

70. Inter-American Commission on Human Rights, *Situación de los derechos de la mujer en Ciudad Juárez, México: El derecho a no ser objeto de violencia y discriminación* (Washington, D.C.: General Secretariat, Organization of American States, 2003). In Spanish: "Desde 1993 las mujeres que viven en Ciudad Juárez tienen miedo. Miedo de salir a la calle y recorrer la distancia del camino de su casa a su trabajo. Miedo a los 10, a los 13, a los 15, a los 20 años, no importa si es niña o ya mujer."

71. Marcela Lagarde y de los Ríos, *Por la vida y la libertad de las mujeres: Fin al feminicidio* (Mexico City: Congreso de la Unión, Cámara de Diputados, LIX Legislatura, Comisión Especial para Conocer y dar Seguimiento a las Investigaciones Relacionadas con los Feminicidios en la República Mexicana y a la Procuración de Justicia Vinculada, 2005), 9. Marcela Lagarde y de los Ríos is the President of the Special Comision for Knowledge and Investigation Related to Feminicides in Mexico (Comisión Especial para Conocer y Dar Seguimiento a las Investigaciones Relacionadas con los Feminicidios en la República Mexicana). For more information on the mobilization by different human rights organizations about femicide in Ciudad Juárez and Chihuahua, see *Primer Tribunal de Conciencia sobre la violencia y discriminación hacia las mujeres. Casos: Cd. Juárez y Chihuahua* (Chihuahua, Mexico: La Gota Editorial, 2004); and Marcela Lagarde y de los Ríos, "Preface: Feminist Keys for Understanding Feminicide," in *Terrorizing Women: Feminicide in the Americas*, ed. Rosa-Linda Fregoso and Cynthia Bejarano (Durham, N.C.: Duke University Press, 2010).

72. Julia Estela Monárrez Fragaso, *Trama de una injusticia: Feminicidio sexual sistémico en Ciudad Juárez* (Tijuana: El Colegio de la Frontera Norte, 2009), 10–15.

73. Sergio González Rodríguez, *The Femicide Machine*, trans. Michael Parker-Stainback (New York: Semiotext(e), 2012), 7.

74. Patricia A. Ybarra, *Latinx Theater in the Times of Neoliberalism* (Evanston, Ill.: Northwestern University Press, 2018), 107.

75. Juan Manuel Vázquez, "Una vez me puse los guantes con Alain Delon," Deportes, *La jornada*, July 25, 2009, http://www.jornada.unam.mx/2009/07/25/deportes/a36n1dep. In this piece, Mantequilla Nápoles reminisces about his fight against Carlos Monzón, organized by international movie star Alain Delon.

76. TLS, *Baños Roma* (unpublished MS, October 2017), provided by Jorge Vargas to the author.

77. TLS, *Baños Roma.*

78. TLS, *Baños Roma.*

79. TLS, *Baños Roma.*

80. The music for *Baños Roma* is a combination of adapted works created by Jesús Cuevas and overseen by musician Jorge Verdín.

81. TLS, *Baños Roma*

82. TLS, *Baños Roma.*

83. Sontag, *Regarding the Pain of Others* (New York: Picador, 2003), 21.

84. Sontag, *Regarding the Pain of Others*, 26.

85. Sontag, *Regarding the Pain of Others*, 27.

86. I am referring to more violent plays like *Hotel Juárez* by Víctor Hugo Rascón Banda or *Música de balas* [Music of bullets] by Hugo Salcedo. In both cases, violent scenes are central to the plays.

87. Diéguez bases the term "necrotheater" on Achille Mbembe's definition of necropolitics, where he rethinks Michel Foucault's term *biopolitics* to emphasize, instead, the sovereign power of death. Ileana Diéguez Caballero, "Necroteatro: Iconografías del cuerpo roto y sus registros punitivos," *Investigación Teatral* 3, no. 5 (2013): 11, https://investigacionteatral.uv.mx/index.php/investigacionteatral/article/view/951/1751.

88. Diéguez Caballero, "Necroteatro," 9.

89. Diéguez Caballero, "Necroteatro," 13.

90. The production discussed here was performed especially for University of Wisconsin–Madison in October 2017.

91. TLS, *Baños Roma.*

92. Myrna Pastrana, *Cuando las banquetas fueron nuestras* (Mexico City: Ficticia, 2011), 13.

93. TLS, *Baños Roma.*

94. TLS, *Baños Roma.*

95. TLS, *Baños Roma.*

96. Michel de Certeau, *The Practice of Everyday Life*, trans. Steven Rendall (Berkeley: University of California Press, 1988), 97–98.

97. De Certeau, *The Practice of Everyday Life*, 98.

98. Alicia Laguna and Zuadd Ibañez created a performance titled *La Brisa* (2017), based on their research and experience during their residency in Ciudad Juárez. This work fuses dance and theater, where director Tamara Cuba and a cast of four women investigate the history of La Brisa, a bar known for cultural and progressive activism in the 1990s.

99. Teatro Línea de Sombra and ORTEUV, "Convocatoria: A la sociedad Jalapeña," *El puro lugar* (blog), April 8, 2016, https://elpurolugar.wordpress.com/2016/04/08/convocatoria/.

100. Diana Taylor, *The Archive and the Repertoire: Performing Cultural Memory in the Americas* (Durham, N.C.: Duke University Press, 2003), 16.

101. For more information about the participatory nature of this work, see Geraldine Lamadrid Guerrero,"Informe sobre *El puro lugar*: Recuento y preguntas," *Revista Conjunto*, no. 183 (2017): 2–13, http://www.casa.co.cu/revistaconjunto.php#arr; and Antonio Prieto Stambaugh, "Memorias inquietas en el teatro del unheimlich: *El puro lugar*, *Telecápita* (blog), 2016, https://telecapitarevista.org/2016/09/24/memorias-inquietas-en-el-teatro-del-unheimlich-el-puro-lugar/.

102. Marvin Carlson, *Places of Performance: The Semiotics of Theatre Architecture* (Ithaca, N.Y.: Cornell University Press, 1993), 2.

103. Teatro Línea de Sombra and ORTEUV, *El puro lugar*, last updated May 5, 2016, https://www.youtube.com/channel/UCsEdCtjgMUXnwAbFPXxeDTA. Fragments of each chapter of *El puro lugar* are available via the project's YouTube channel.

104. Lamadrid Guerrero, "Sobre *El puro lugar*," 10.

105. Prieto Stambaugh, "Memorias inquietas."

106. Diéguez Caballero, "Necroteatro," 13.

107. Claire Bishop, *Artificial Hells: Participatory Art and the Politics of Spectatorship* (London: Verso, 2012), 39.

Chapter 4

1. The Frente Patriótico Manuel Rodríguez was a Marxist-Leninist guerrilla organization created in 1983 to combat the military regime headed by Augusto Pinochet. The group was known for their military tactics and their knowledge of bombs and weapons. It was considered a terrorist organization by the Department of State of the United States and the United Kingdom, two countries that supported the military regime of Pinochet. For more information, see Sean Anderson and Stephen Sloan, *Historical Dictionary of Terrorism* (Lanham, Md.: Scarecrow Press, 2009), 416.

2. René Sanhueza Molina (ex-member of the FPMR) and Alejandro Astorga Valdés (ex-member of Perú's Tupac Amaru's revolutionary party) have been charged for this robbery and are each serving a fourteen-year prison sentence. In an interview, Astorga Valdés, who confessed to the robbery, denies Jorge Mateluna's involvement stating that he did not participate nor was he involved in the design of the robbery. For more information, see https://www.elciudadano.com/justicia/autor-confeso-de-asalto-en-el-santander-aseguro-a-fiscales-que-mateluna-no-participo/07/06/.

3. Juan Villegas, "El teatro chileno de la postdictadura," *Inti: Revista de literatura hispánica* 1, no. 69 (2009): 202.

4. *Neva* is one of three ensemble plays. The other two are *Clase* [Class] (2007) and *Diciembre* [December] (2008). *Teatro I: Neva, Clase, Diciembre* (Santiago de Chile: LOM, 2012). These three plays have received both local and international acclaim, making Calderón a bright star on the Chilean stage. In 2009, he was a resident playwright at the Royal Court Theatre in London, where he began writing *Discurso* [Speech], and in 2011, Under the Radar Festival invited Calderón to stage *December* at the Public Theatre in New York City. In March, 2013 *Neva* premiered in English with American actors, again at the Public Theatre. As a playwright and director, he has also founded different theater groups: Teatro en el Blanco with which he performed *Neva* and *Diciembre*, la Agrupación La Reina de Conchalí that performed *Clase*, and later Teatro Playa to perform *Villa+Discurso*. His cowritten screenplay with Andres Wood, *Violeta se fue a los cielos* [Violeta went to heaven] won the World Cinema Jury Prize for Drama at the 2012 Sundance Film Festival. He cowrote *El club* [The club], directed by Pablo Larrain, winner of the Silver Bear at the Berlin International Film Festival 2015, and nominated for the Golden Globes in the Foreign Language category. The script won the Silver Plaque at the Chicago International Film Festival. He wrote the script for *Neruda*, directed by Pablo Larraín, presented at the Quinzaine des Réalisateurs (Director's Fortnight) during Cannes Film Festival 2016.

5. Sophie Ivatts, "Guillermo Calderón on Theatre, Politics, and Pinochet's Legacy," *Pulsamerica* (October 2011), http://www.pulsamerica.co.uk/2011/10/19/guillermo-calderon-on-theatre-politics-and-pinochet's-legacy/.

6. Joanne Pottlizer, "A Serious Man of the Theatre," *Edinburgh International Festival Program* (August 2010): 6–12.

7. *Mateluna* permiered in Berlin in 2016 as part of the theater festival titled "The Aesthetics of Resistance: Peter Weiss 100." This festival called on different artists to explore topics of antifascist movements, underground guerrilla tactics, among others. In this book Weiss argued the possibility to resist fascism through the political participation by individuals.

8. Francisca Lewin and Daniel Alcaíno, together with the dean of the Law School at the Universidad de Chile, publicly supported Jorge Mateluna's defense legal team. See "Facultad de Derecho y Clínica Jurídica se suman a la defense de Jorge Mateluna," http://www.derecho.uchile.cl/noticias/140062/facultad-y-clinica-juridica-se-suman-a-la-defensa-de-jorge-mateluna.

9. Radio interview, September 2017, https://www.youtube.com/watch?v=HZwtdTbyAxE.

10. Actor Francisca Lewin, Calderón's present partner and active member of his cast, is also a well-known actor due to her work on TV. The journalist also directs the question at her, clearly pointing the fact that other cast directors might not use her because she is seen as "too political."

11. This place was the first in a long chain of detention centers controlled by the National Intelligence Directorate (DINA), which occupied Londres 38 from 1973 to 1975. However what is most striking about the ex–detention center is that it was not inaugurated as a memorial site until October 2009, and it did not gain the right to the estate until mid-2011.

12. For more information on audience members' responses, plus a short interview with the playwright, see http://www.londres38.cl/1934/w3-article-91232.html.

13. Cathy Caruth, "Trauma and Experience," in *Trauma: Explorations in Memory*, ed. Cathy Caruth (Baltimore: John Hopkins University Press), 4–5; emphasis in the original.

14. Quoted in Joanne Tompkins, "The 'Place' and Practice of Site-Specific Theatre and Performance," in *Performing Site-Specific Theatre: Politics, Place, Practice*, ed. Anna Birch and Joanne Tompkins (New York: Palgrave Macmillan, 2012), 28–29.

15. Tompkins, "The 'Place' and Practice of Site-Specific Theatre and Performance," 29.

16. Karen Till, *The New Berlin: Memory, Politics, Place* (Minneapolis: University of Minnesota Press, 2005), 7.

17. I base the term "nomadic performance" on what Lesley Ferris refers to "nomadic form" of site-specific performance, where the emphasis is "not on the actual wanderer." Instead, nomadic form is the "subversion of set conventions that defines the nomadic state, not the literal act of traveling." Lesley Ferris, "Contemporary Ekkeklemas in Site-Specific Performance," in Birch and Tompkins, *Performing Site-Specific Theatre*, 139.

18. Paul Williams, *Memorial Museums: The Global Rush to Commemorate Atrocities* (Oxford: Berg, 2007), 8.

19. Williams, *Memorial Museums*, 25.

20. I would like to point out that according to Paul Williams "more memorial museums have been opened in the last 10 years than in the past 100." In turn, he composes a list of the many memorial museums, from the Hiroshima Peace Memorial Museum (1955) up to the World Trade Center Memorial in New York (2009). Williams, *Memorial Museums*, 9.

21. Williams, *Memorial Museums*, 8.

22. Patrizia Violi, "Trauma Site Museums and Politics of Memory: Tuol Sleng, Villa Grimaldi and the Bologna Ustica Museum," *Theory, Culture and Society* 29, no. 1 (January 2012): 37.

23. I borrow these terms from a wide range of studies, mainly Steve Stern's trilogy title, "The Memory Box of Pinochet's Chile," in *Remembering Pinochet's*

Chile: On the Eve of London 1998 (Durham, N.C.: Duke University Press, 2004). Tomás Moulián's concept of the whitening of Chile through the symbolic representation of an iceberg that was transported from Chile and exhibited as a symbol of the "new" and "purified" version of the country at the World Expo in Seville in 1992 in *Chile actual: Anatomía de un mito*, 3rd ed. (Santiago de Chile: LOM, 2002); Nelly Richard's study of site-specific memorial museums, "Sitios de la memoria, vaciamiento del recuerdo," *Revista de Crítica Cultural* 23 (2001); and Michael Lazzara's *Chile in Transition: The Poetics and Politics of Memory* (Gainesville: University Press of Florida, 2006), where he approaches trauma studies through "memory lenses" that provide him different angles through which to engage with Chile's past.

24. Moulián, *Chile actual*, 38–39.

25. Lazzara, *Chile in Transition*, 130.

26. Andreas Huyssen, *Twilight Memories: Marking Time in a Culture of Amnesia* (New York: Routledge, 1995), 249.

27. Tompkins, "The 'Place' and Practice of Site-Specific Theatre and Performance," 40.

28. For more in-depth information about Villa Grimaldi, its history, its transformation, and the present-day Peace Park, visit http://villagrimaldi.cl.

29. Quoted in Julia Paley, *Marketing Democracy: Power and Social Movements in Post-dictatorship Chile* (Berkeley: University of California Press, 2001), 127.

30. Lazzara, *Chile in Transition*, 135–136.

31. The website www.villagrimaldi.cl has plenty of information about how the villa was designed and what its present and future roles are. Audio, videos, photographs, and documents provide additional information. It is also evident that the villa is a site for transnational human rights awareness. On January 19, 2013, Judge Baltasar Garzón, a renowned advocate for transnational human rights, and for his arrest of Pinochet in 1998, visited the villa to honor its fifteen-year anniversary.

32. Andreas Huyssen, *Present Pasts: Urban Palimpsests and the Politics of Memory* (Stanford, Calif.: Stanford University Press, 2003), 7.

33. Huyssen, *Present Pasts*, 7.

34. Isabel Baboun Garib, "Guillermo Calderón: Tres motivos para una poética casi trágica," *Teatro Apuntes* 131 (2010): 24.

35. This banner is part of Londres 38 as a historical site. Calderón used it as part of the specific production in Londres 38 fusing, once again, site specificity and different stories of human rights atrocities. Other productions of *Villa* did not have this timeline in the back.

36. Joanne Pottlizer, "Forgetting Filled with Memory," *Theater* 43, no. 2 (2013).

37. Marianne Hirsch, "Surviving Images: Holocaust Photographs and the Work of Postmemory," *Yale Journal of Criticism* 14, no. 1 (2001): 10; emphasis in the original.

38. Pottlizer, "Forgetting Filled with Memory."

39. Macarena Gómez-Barris, *Where Memory Dwells: Culture and State Violence in Chile* (Berkeley: University of California Press, 2009), 42.

40. Dori Laub, "Truth and Testimony: The Process and the Struggle," in *Trauma: Explorations of Memory*, ed. Cathy Caruth (Baltimore: Johns Hopkins University Press, 1995), 64.

41. Gómez-Barris, *Where Memory Dwells*, 42.

42. Guillermo Calderón, *Villa* (trans. William Gregory), *Theater* 43, no. 2 (May 2013): 72.

43. Calderón, *Villa*, 73.

44. Calderón, *Villa*, 73.

45. Diana Taylor, "Trauma, memoria y performance: Un recorrido por Villa Grimaldi con Pedro Matta," *e-misférica* 7, no. 2 (Winter 2010), http://hemisphericinstitute.org/hemi/en/e-misferica-72/taylor.

46. Calderón, *Villa*, 74.

47. For more information, visit El Museo de la Memoria's website: http://www.museodelamemoria.cl.

48. Catalina Forttes, "Guillermo Calderón en conversación: 'Chile como nación puede acabarse,'" *Mester* 39 (2010), http://www.escholarship.org/uc/item/22x9x219.

49. The names in parenthesis are those of the actresses.

50. Calderón, *Villa*, 76.

51. Calderón, *Villa*, 76.

52. Calderón, *Villa*, 77.

53. Calderón, *Villa*, 84.

54. Pottlizer, "Forgetting Filled with Memory."

55. Calderón, *Villa*, 85.

56. Calderón, *Discurso* (unpublished MS), 99. My translation.

57. Calderón, *Villa*, 77.

58. Calderón, *Villa*, 77.

59. Diana Taylor, *The Archive and the Repertoire: Performing Cultural Memory in the Americas* (Durham, N.C.: Duke University Press, 2003), 165–166.

60. Calderón, *Villa*, 107.

61. Alison Landsberg, *Prosthetic Memory: The Transformation of American Remembrance in the Age of Mass Culture* (New York: Columbia University Press, 2004), 19.

62. For more information on this project, see "Mateluna Inocente," a grassroots movement that works to clear him of this crime. https://www.matelunainocente.com.

63. *Escuela* premiered in 2013 in the Santiago a Mil Festival. The cast at the time was Luis Cerda, Andrea Giadach, Camila González, Francisca Lewin, and Carlos Ugarte. It traveled to Under the Radar Festival—the Public theater in New York, FringeArts in Philadelphia, the Museum of Contemporary Art Chicago, and the Iseman Theater at Yale University.

64. Sara Rojo, "Teatro político actual: La dramaturgia de Guillermo Calderón," *Meridional Revista Chilena de Estudios Latinoamericanos*, no. 5 (October 2015): 122.

65. Guillermo Calderón, *School*, trans. Alex Ripp (also titled *School*), unpublished MS, 39.

66. Guillermo Calderón, "Guillermo Calderón: 'Cada vez queda más claro que la dictadura nunca fue derrotada,'" interview with Melissa Gutierrez, *The Clinic*, April 18, 2013.

67. These songs include the "Himno Montonero" [Montonero hymn], the "Himno Tupamaro" [Tupamaro hymn], "El soldado boliviano" [The Bolivian soldier], and the "Himno de la Unidad Sandinista" [Sandinista unity hymn].

68. Charles Isherwood, in "Review: From Chile, *Escuela*, a Drama about Education," *New York Times*, January 17, 2016, states that this play does not stimulate his attention and is too didactic, and that no character emerges as individual.

69. Fundación Santiago a Mil, "*Escuela* de Guillermo Calderón: 'La obra es importante, siempre va a ser contingente'" (press release), Fundación Teatro a Mil, April 2, 2017, http://fundacionteatroamil.cl/noticia/escuela-guillermo-calderon-la-obra-importante-siempre-va-contingente/.

70. Jennifer Joan Thompson, "Dramaturgies of Democracy: Performance, Cultural Policy, and Citizenship in Chile 1979–present" (PhD diss., CUNY–Graduate Center, 2019), 246.

71. Some scholars have even gone further in their understanding of Calderón's political theater by labeling it "post-political." Following Rancière and Adorno's dialectic, Thompson argues that the "post" underscores his dramaturgy as dialectical in that "it contains a real political capacity (in the dissensual, Rancieran sense) that is both facilitated by and always on the verge of its cooption and de-politicization by the larger environment of post-politics" ("Dramaturgies of Democracy," 248). I concur that a postpolitics approach to Calderón's works can serve to guide our understanding of his plays, both in national and international arenas, to better understand how "the pursuit of the political in the condition of post-politics must always be a process of renegotiation and reimagination" (248). However, I would also add that by relying on the international network of theater marketability, albeit through festivals, Calderón imposes heavy political material on audiences that might not be aware of Chile's recent past. Regardless, according to Calderón, "politics sell, particularly when works come from Latin American countries" (quoted in Thompson, "Dramaturgies of Democracy," 249).

72. Calderón states that this play was important because younger generations are not aware of what happened in the country. He speaks of the invisibility of the people involved in guerrilla groups, how they were considered terrorists, and how their lives are still in some way hidden because dictatorship is still somehow imposed in their lives. For more information, see Guillermo Calderón, "Guillermo Calderón: 'Cada vez queda más claro que la dictadura nunca fue derrotada," interview with Melissa Gutiérrez, *The Clinic*, April 18, 2013.

73. For more information about students' demands and subsequent changes, see Cristián Bellei, *El gran experimento: Mercado y privatización de la educación chilena* (Santiago: LOM Ediciones, 2015); Manuel Larrabure and Carlos Torchia, "The 2011 Chilean Student Movement and the Struggle for a New Left," *Latin American Perspectives* 204.42, no. 5 (Fall 2015); Marcela A. Fuentes, "Performance Constellations: Memory and Event in Digitally Enabled Protests in the Americas," *Text and Performance Quarterly* 35, no. 1 (January 2015).

74. William Moss Willson, "Just Don't Call Her Che," *New York Times*, January 28, 2012, https://www.nytimes.com/2012/01/29/opinion/sunday/student-protests-rile-chile.html.

75. Student protests continued and in October 2019 hundreds of thousand of students protested to demand more changes to the 3 percent hike in subway fares, as well as to draw attention to the overall social and economic inequalities that persist in Chile. Protesters called for a new constitution to replace the one written during the Pinochet dictatorship. Different from the previous protests,

however, this last one became a nationwide uprising, with violent confronations with the police.

76. Thompson, "Dramaturgies of Democracy," 304.

77. Calderón, *School*, 14.

78. *White Book of the Change of Government in Chile: 11th September 1973* (Santiago, Chile: Empresa Editora Nacional "Gabriela Mistral," 1974), 3. It is also worth noting that the sale proceedings of this book are to be used to the "national reconstruction of Chile," whatever that means during the military junta.

79. Calderón, *School*, 16.

80. Calderón, *School*, 28.

81. Calderón, *School*, 53.

82. Ángeles Donoso Macaya, *The Insubordination of Photography: Documentary Practices under Chile's Dictatorship* (Gainesville: University Press of Florida, 2020), 34.

83. Calderón, *School*, 54.

84. "Mateluna Inocente—Freedom for Mateluna," YouTube video, 15:25, posted by "Mateluna Inocente," December 3, 2018, https://www.youtube.com/watch?v=V98JwBkVqcU.

85. The play is a coproduction between the Fundación Santiago a Mil and HAU: Hebeel am Ufer. The play traveled right after the premiere to Santiago at the Teatro de la Pontificia Universidad Católica de Chile.

86. In December 2018 the Supreme Court ruled against Jorge Mateluna, confirming his prison sentence.

87. Lorena Caimanque, "Guillermo Calderón sobre Dragón: 'Volví a la idea del problema de la creación,'" May 23, 2019, https://www.fundacionteatroamil.cl/articulos/guillermo-calderon-dragon/#.XPH-pbL9jys.mailto.

88. Guillermo Calderón, "When Is It Right to Stop Fighting," in *The Aesthetics of Resistance: Peter Weiss 100* (Berlin: HAU, 2016), https://issuu.com/hau123/docs/aedw_engl_issue_1_.

89. All references to *Mateluna* come from an unpublished manuscript provided by theater scholar Cristián Opazo. My analysis also relies on a live version I saw of *Mateluna* in Santiago de Chile, as well as a video provided by Guillermo Calderón.

90. Calderón, *Mateluna*.

91. Calderón, *Mateluna*.

92. Calderón, quoted in Cristián Opazo and Carlos Benítez, "A Little Respect: Mateluna de Guillermo Calderón," *Revista Conjunto*, no. 185 (October–December 2017): 14.

93. Opazo and Benítez, "A Little Respect," 12.

94. Calderón, *Mateluna*.

95. Opazo and Benítez, "A Little Respect," 12.

96. Stern, *Remembering Pinochet's Chile*, 147.

97. Calderón, *Mateluna*.

98. D. Soyini Madison, *Acts of Activism: Human Rights as Radical Performance* (Cambridge: Cambridge University Press, 2010), 2.

99. Madison, *Acts of Activism*, 2; emphasis in the original.

100. Opazo and Benítez, "A Little Respect," 11.

101. Madison, *Acts of Activism*, 11.

Conclusion

1. *Las ideas* premiered in May 2015 at Kunstenfestivaldesarts in Brussels. It later toured other European countries and in September it premiered in Buenos Aires at the International Theatre Festival, and later at Zelaya, León's own theater space.

2. Alejandro Cruz, "*Las ideas*, una impecable maquinaria escénica," *La Nación* (Espectáculos), April 5, 2016. https://www.lanacion.com.ar/espectaculos/teatro/las-ideas-una-impecable-maquinaria-escenica-nid1886110.

3. Jenn Stephenson, *Insecurity: Perils and Products of Theatres of the Real* (Toronto: University of Toronto Press, 2019), 3.

4. Personal interview with the author, January 26, 2018, Chicago. I also thank Federico León for providing a video of the play.

5. Nicholas Ridout, *Stage Fright, Animals, and Other Theatrical Problems* (Cambridge: Cambridge University Press, 2006), 4.

6. Julie Ann Ward, *A Shared Truth: The Theater of Lagartijas tiradas al sol* (Pittsburgh: University of Pittsburgh Press, 2019), 18.

BIBLIOGRAPHY

Agamben, Giorgio. *State of Exception*. Translated by Kevin Attell. Chicago: University of Chicago Press, 2005.

Ahmed, Sara. *The Cultural Politics of Emotion*. 2nd ed. New York: Routledge, 2015.

———. "Happy Objects." In *The Affect Theory Reader*, edited by Melissa Gregg and Gregory J. Seigworth, 29–51. Durham, N.C.: Duke University Press, 2010.

Anderson, Sean, and Stephen Sloan, eds. *Historical Dictionary of Terrorism*. Lanham, Md.: Scarecrow Press, 2009.

Andrew, Anthony. "Minefield: Two Sides of the Falkland's War—on One Stage." *The Guardian*, November 12, 2017. https://www.theguardian.com/stage/2017/nov/12/two-sides-falklands-war-one-stage-minefield-veterans-stories.

Anzaldúa, Gloria. *Borderlands / La Frontera: The New Mestiza*. San Francisco: Spinsters / Aunt Lute, 1987.

Arfuch, Leonor. *El espacio biográfico: Dilemas de la subjetividad contemporánea*. Buenos Aires: Fondo de Cultura Económica, 2010.

Arias, Arturo, ed. *The Rigoberta Menchú Controversy: With a Response by David Stoll*. Minneapolis: University of Minnesota Press, 2001.

Arias, Lola. "El teatro antes del futuro: Sobre *Mi vida después* de Lola Arias." Interview by Pamela Brownell. *telondefondo: Revista de teoría y crítica teatral*, no. 10 (December 2009). http://www.telondefondo.org/numeros-anteriores/numero10/articulo/210/el-teatro-antes-del-futuro-sobre-mi-vida-despues-de-lola-arias.html.

———. "Footnote." *Lola Arias: Re-enacting Life*. Edited by Jean Graham-Jones. Aberystwyth, Wales: Performance Research Books, 2019.

———. *Hotel/Maids*. Parallel Cities. https://www.rimini-protokoll.de/website/en/project/ciudades-paralelas-parallele-staedte.

———. "Lola Arias: Interview by Elianna Kan." *Bomb*, no. 128 (Summer 2014): 58–64. https://bombmagazine.org/articles/lola-arias/.

———. "Lola Arias y las ideas detrás de *Veteranos, Campo minado* y *Teatro de Guerra*." Interview by Diego Broderson. Cultura y Espectáculos, *Página 12*, September 6, 2018. https://www.pagina12.com.ar/140206-hay-una-tension-entre-lo-artificial-y-lo-real.

———. *Minefield / Campo minado*. Translated by Daniel Tunnard. London: Oberon Books, 2017.

———. "*Minefield* Director and Writer Lola Arias: My Shows Are Living Creatures That Evolve." Interview by Tom Wicker. *The Stage*, October 27, 2017. https://www.thestage.co.uk/features/interviews/2017/minefield-director-writer-lola-arias-my-shows-living-creatures-that-evolve/.

———. "*Mi vida después*: Itinerario de un teatro vivo." Interview by Ana Longoni and Lorena Verzero. *Revista Conjunto*, no. 162 (January–March 2012): 4–15.

———. *Mi vida después y otros textos*. Buenos Aires: Reservoir Books, 2016.

———. *My Life After*. Translated by Daniel Tunnard, revised by Jean Graham-Jones. In *Lola Arias: Re-enacting Life*, edited by Jean Graham-Jones. Aberystwyth, Wales: Performance Research Books, 2019.

———, dir. *Theatre of War*. (Argentina-Spain-Germany, Documentary) A Gema Films production, in co-production with BWP S.L. (Spain), Sutor Kolonko Filmproduktion (Germany), Sake Argentina (Argentina), 2018.

———. "The Work of Art Is a Parasite: Lola Arias." Interview by Bertie Ferdman, translated by Ferdman. *Theatre* 44, no. 2 (2014): 31–45.

Artaud, Antonin. *El teatro y su doble*. Translated by Equipo Editorial. Buenos Aires: Retórica Ediciones, 2002.

Avruch, Kevin. "Truth and Reconciliation Commissions: Problems in Transitional Justice and the Reconstruction of Identity." *Transcultural Psychiatry* 47, no. 1 (February 2010): 33–49.

"Ayotzinapa Timeline," NACLA, accessed July, 20, 2020. https://nacla.org/ayotzinapa-timeline.

Baboun Garib, Isabel. "Guillermo Calderón: Tres motivos para una poética casi trágica." *Teatro Apuntes* 131 (2010): 20–28.

Bailes, Sara Jane. *Performance Theatre and the Poetics of Failure: Forced Entertainment, Goat Island, Elevator Repair Service*. Oxfordshire, England: Routledge, 2011.

Barthes, Roland. *Camera Lucida: Reflections on Photography*. Translated by Richard Howard. New York: Hill and Wang, 1982.

Baudillard, Jean. *Simulacra and Simulation*. Translated by Sheila Faria Glaser. Ann Arbor: University of Michigan Press, 1994.

Bellei, Cristián. *El gran experimento: Mercado y privatización de la educación chilena*. Santiago: LOM Ediciones, 2015.

Benjamin, Walter. "Ibizan Sequence, 1932." In *Walter Benjamin: Selected Writings*, vol. 2, bk. 2: *1931–1934*, edited by Marcus Paul Bullock, Michael William Jennings, Howard Eiland, and Gary Smith, 553–690. Cambridge, Mass.: Belknap Press of Harvard University Press, 2005.

Bennett, Jane. *Vibrant Matter: A Political Ecology of Things*. Durham, N.C.: Duke University Press, 2010.

Bennett, Jill. *Empathic Vision: Affect, Trauma, and Contemporary Art*. Stanford, Calif.: Stanford University Press, 2005.

Bennett, Susan. "3-D A/B." In *Theatre and AutoBiography: Writing and Performing Lives in Theory and Practice*, edited by Sherrill Grace and Jerry Wasserman. Vancouver, B.C.: Talonbooks, 2006.

Berlant, Lauren. *Cruel Optimism*. Durham, N.C.: Duke University Press, 2011.

———. "Intimacy." *Critical Inquiry* 24, no. 2 (Winter 1998): 281–288.

Beverley, John. *Testimonio: On the Politics of Truth*. Minneapolis: University of Minnesota Press, 2004.

Biscia, Rodolfo. "Vivi Tellas: 'Soy como una editora biográfica': Puedo editar tu vida." Cultura, *Infobae*, January 27, 2019. https://www.infobae.com/cultura/2019/01/27/vivi-tellas-soy-como-una-editora-biografica-puedo-editar-tu-vida/.

Bishop, Claire. "Antagonism and Relational Aesthetics." *October*, no. 110 (Fall 2004): 51–79.

———. *Artificial Hells: Participatory Art and the Politics of Spectatorship*. London: Verso, 2012.

Blejmar, Jordana. "Autofictions of Postwar: Fostering Empathy in Lola Arias' *Minefield / Campo minado*." *Latin American Theatre Review* 50, no. 2 (Spring 2017): 103–124.

———. *Playful Memories: The Autofictional Turn in Post-dictatorship Argentina*. Cham, Switzerland: Palgrave Macmillan, 2017.

Boal, Augusto. *Theatre of the Oppressed*. Translated by Charles A. McBride, Maria-Odilia Leal McBride, and Emily Fryer. London: Pluto Press, 2008.

Bourriaud, Nicolas. *Relational Aesthetics*. Translated by Simon Pleasance, Fronza Woods, and Mathieu Copeland. Dijon: Les Presses du Réel, 2009.

Boyce, D. George. *The Falklands War*. New York: Palgrave Macmillan, 2005.

Bravo Elizondo, Pedro. *Teatro documental latinoamericano*. 2 vols. Mexico City: Universidad Nacional Autónoma de México, 1982.

Brownell, Pamela. "El recorrido artístico de Vivi Tellas en los '80: de Las Bay Biscuit al Teatro Malo." *Revista Afuera*, September 15, 2015. http://revistaafuera15.blogspot.com/p/el-teatro-entre-dictadura-y-posdictadura.html.

———. "Lo real como utopía en el teatro argentino contemporáneo: Prácticas biográficas y documentales. Productividad del trabajo de dirección y curaduría de Vivi Tellas en el marco de su Proyecto Biodrama (de 2002 al presente)." PhD diss., Universidad de Buenos Aires, 2019.

———. "Proyecto Archivos: El teatro documental según Vivi Tellas." *e-Misférica* 9, nos. 1–2 (Summer 2012). http://hemisphericinstitute.org/hemi/en/e-misferica-91/brownell.

Brownell, Pamela, and Paola Hernández, eds. *Biodrama / Proyecto Archivos: Seis documentales escénicos de Vivi Tellas*. Córdoba: Papeles Teatrales, 2017.

Bulman, Gail A. "Not My Choice: Feeling as a 'Productive Paradox' in Lola Arias's *Doble de riesgo*." *Latin American Theatre Review* 51, no. 1 (Fall 2017): 13–34.

Butler, Judith. *Precarious Life: The Powers of Mourning and Violence*. London: Verso, 2004.

Bystrom, Kerry. "The Public Private Sphere: Family Narrative and Democracy in Argentina and South Africa." *Social Dynamics* 36, no. 1 (March 2010): 139–152.

Caimanque, Lorena. "Guillermo Calderón sobre Dragón: 'Volví a la idea del problema de la creación.'" Fundación Teatro a Mil, May 23, 2019. https://www.fundacionteatroamil.cl/articulos/guillermo-calderon-dragon/#.XPH-pbL9jys.mailto.

Calderón, Guillermo. "Guillermo Calderón: 'Cada vez queda más claro que la dictadura nunca fue derrotada." Interview with Melissa Gutierrez, *The Clinic*, April 18, 2013.

———. *Mateluna*. Unpublished ms. and video.

———. *School*. Translated by Alex Ripp. Unpublished ms.

———. *Teatro I* (*Neva, Diciembre, Clase*). Santiago de Chile: LOM, 2012.

———. *Teatro II* (*Villa, Discurso, Beben*). Santiago de Chile: LOM, 2012.

———. *Villa*. Translated by William Gregory. *Theater* 43, no. 2 (2013): 65–97.

———. "When Is It Right to Stop Fighting." In *The Aesthetics of Resistance: Peter Weiss 100.* Berlin: HAU, 2016. https://issuu.com/hau123/docs/aedw_engl_issue_1_.

Carlson, Marvin. *Places of Performance: The Semiotics of Theatre Architecture.* Ithaca, N.Y.: Cornell University Press, 1993.

———. *Shattering Hamlet's Mirror: Theatre and Reality.* Ann Arbor: University of Michigan Press, 2016.

Carroll, Rory. "Altar Mexico: How the 'Migrant Oasis' for Would-Be Border Crossers Became a Trap." *The Guardian*, October 14, 2015. https://www.theguardian.com/world/2015/oct/14/altar-mexico-how-the-migrant-oasis-for-would-be-border-crossers-became-a-trap.

Caruth, Cathy, ed. *Trauma: Explorations in Memory.* Baltimore: John Hopkins University Press, 1995.

Catani, Beatriz. "Fragmentos de una conversación." In *Acercamientos a lo real: Textos y escenarios*, edited by Óscar Cornago. Buenos Aires: Ediciones Artes del Sur, 2007.

Comisión Nacional de Derechos Humanos. *Informe especial de la Comisión Nacional de los Derechos Humanos sobre los casos de homicidios y desapariciones de mujeres en el municipio de Juárez, Chihuahua.* Mexico City: Comisión Nacional de Derechos Humanos, 2003. http://www.campoalgodonero.org.mx/documentos/informe-especial-comision-nacional-derechos-humanos-casos-homicidios-y-desapariciones-muj.

Contreras López, Daniela. "Reclaiming Memory: Social Reconstruction through Performance and Theatre in Post-dictatorship Chile." *Journal of Applied Theatre and Performance* 20, no. 3 (2015): 288–291.

"Convocatoria: A la sociedad Jalapeña," *El puro lugar* (blog), April 8, 2016, https://elpurolugar.wordpress.com/2016/04/08/convocatoria/.

Cornago, Óscar. "Biodrama: Sobre el teatro de la vida y la vida teatro." *Latin American Theatre Review* 39, no. 1 (Fall 2005): 5–28.

Cruz, Alejandro. "*Las ideas*, una impecable maquinaria escénica." Espectáculos, *La Nación*, April 5, 2016. https://www.lanacion.com.ar/espectaculos/teatro/las-ideas-una-impecable-maquinaria-escenica-nid1886110.

de Certeau, Michel. *The Practice of Everyday Life.* Translated by Steven Rendall. Berkeley: University of California Press, 1988.

de León, Jason. *The Land of Open Graves: Living and Dying on the Migrant Trail.* Berkeley: University of California Press, 2015.

Delgadillo, Theresa. "Artists in the Americas Confront the Fracturing Effects of Violence." *Mujeres Talk* (blog), Ohio State University Libraries, April 19, 2016. https://library.osu.edu/blogs/mujerestalk/2016/04/19/artists-in-the-americas-confront-the-fracturing-effects-of-violence/.

Delgado, María M. "Ways of Remembering Las Malvinas/The Falklands." In *Lola Arias Re-enacting Life*, edited by Jean Graham-Jones. Aberystwyth, Wales: Performance Research Books, 2019.

Delgado, Miguel M., dir. *Santo y Mantequilla Nápoles en La venganza de la Llorona.* 1974; Barcelona: Manga Films, 2005. DVD.

Derrida, Jacques. *Archive Fever: A Freudian Impression.* Translated by Eric Prenowitz. Chicago: University of Chicago Press, 1996.

Diéguez Caballero, Ileana. *Escenarios liminales*. Mexico City: Toma Ediciones, 2014.

———. "Necroteatro: Iconografías del cuerpo roto y sus registros punitivos." *Investigación Teatral* 3, no. 5 (2013): 9–28. https://investigacionteatral.uv.mx/index.php/investigacionteatral/article/view/951/1751.

Dolan, Jill. "Geographies of Learning: Theatre Studies, Performance, and the 'Performative.'" *Theatre Journal* 45, no. 4 (1993): 417–441.

———. *Utopia in Performance: Finding Hope at the Theatre*. Ann Arbor: University of Michigan Press, 2005.

Donoso Macaya, Ángeles. *The Insubordination of Photography: Documentary Practices under Chile's Dictatorship*. Gainesville: University Press of Florida, 2020.

Dreysse, Miriam, and Florian Malzacher, eds. *Experts of the Everyday: The Theatre of Rimini Protokoll*. Berlin: Alexander Verlag, 2008.

Dubatti, Jorge. *Filosofía del teatro I: Convivio, experiencia, subjetividad*. Buenos Aires: Atuel, 2007.

———. "Lola Arias: Acerca de artistas 'anfibios' y nuevo teatro documental." *Teatro Independiente La Plata Argentina* (blog), December 9, 2012. http://teatroindependientelaplata.blogspot.com/2012/12/lola-arias-acerca-de-artistas-anfibios.html.

———. *Teatro matriz, teatro liminal: Estudios de filosofía del teatro y poética comparada*. Buenos Aires: Atuel, 2016.

Dubatti, Ricardo. *Malvinas I. La guerra en el teatro, el teatro de la guerra* (Buenos Aires: Ediciones del CCC, 2017)

______. *Malvinas II. La guerra en el teatro, el teatro de la guerra* (Buenos Aires: Ediciones del CCC, 2019)

______. *La Guerra de Malvinas en el teatro argentino* (Buenos Aires: CONICET, Eudeba, 2020).

Edwards, Elizabeth, and Janice Hart, eds. *Photographs Objects Histories: On the Materiality of Images*. London: Routledge, 2004.

Facultad de Derecho y Clínica Jurídica se suman a la defense de Jorge Mateluna," Dec 19, 2017, http://www.derecho.uchile.cl/noticias/140062/facultad-y-clinica-juridica-se-suman-a-la-defensa-de-jorge-mateluna.

Favorini, Attilio. *Voicings: Ten Plays from Documentary Theatre*. New York: Ecco Press, 1995.

Felman, Shoshana, and Dori Laub. *Testimony: Crises of Witnessing in Literature, Psychoanalysis, and History*. New York: Routledge, 1992.

Ferris, Lesley. "Contemporary Ekkeklemas in Site-Specific Performance." In *Performing Site- Specific Theatre: Politics, Place, Practice*, edited by Anna Birch and Joanne Tompkins, 135–149. New York: Palgrave Macmillan, 2012.

Fontana, Juan Carlos. "Vivi Tellas estrena sus 'Archivos.'" Espectáculos, *La Prensa*, July 30, 2008, 29.

Forsyth, Alison, and Chris Megson, eds. *Get Real: Documentary Theatre Past and Present*. Basingstoke, England: Palgrave Macmillan, 2009.

Forttes, Catalina. "Guillermo Calderón en conversación: 'Chile como nación puede acabarse.'" *Mester* 39 (2010): 57–66. http://www.escholarship.org/uc/item/22x9x219.

Foster, Hal. "An Archival Impulse." *October*, no. 110 (Fall 2004): 3–22.
Freire, Silka. *Teatro documental latinoamericano: El referente histórico y su (re) escritura dramática*. Buenos Aires: Ediciones Al Margen, 2007.
Freire, Susana. "El género documental, a escena." *La Nación*, January 5, 2005. http://www.lanacion.com.ar/668467-el-genero-documental-a-escena.
Fuentes, Marcela A. "El teatro como acontecimiento: Políticas de la interrupción en el teatro documental de Vivi Tellas." *Revista Conjunto*, no. 185 (October–December 2017): 44–53.
———. "Performance Constellations: Memory and Event in Digitally Enabled Protests in the Americas." *Text and Performance Quarterly* 35, no. 1 (January 2015): 24–42.
———. "Theatre as Event: The Politics of Interruption in Vivi Tella's Documentary Theatre." In *Calling Out of Context*, edited by Joachim Harrou, 16–35. Dijon: Les Presses du Réel, 2017.
Fundación Santiago a Mil. "*Escuela* de Guillermo Calderón: 'La obra es importante, siempre va a ser contingente.' " Press release, Fundación Teatro a Mil, April 2, 2017. http://fundacionteatroamil.cl/noticia/escuela-guillermo-calderon-la-obra-importante-siempre-va-contingente/.
Galak, Oliver. "No cesan los suicidios de ex combatientes de Malvinas." Política, *La Nación*, February 28, 2006. https://www.lanacion.com.ar/784519-no-cesan-los-suicidios-de-ex-combatientes-de-malvinas.
García, Javier, dir. *La cocina de las patronas*. Producciones Saché, 2016. DVD.
García, Rodrigo. *Prometeo*. In *Teatro de la España demócrata: los noventa*. Edited by John P. Gabriele and Candyce Leonard. Madrid: Editoriales fundamentos, 1996.
Gilmore, Leigh. *The Limits of Autobiography: Trauma and Testimony*. Ithaca, N.Y.: Cornell University Press, 2001.
Giménez, Paula. "A la izquierda del padre." *Página 12*, March 19, 2010. http://www.pagina12.com.ar/diario/suplementos/soy/1-1283-2010-03-21.html.
Ginzberg, Victoria. "Con la condena más alta para un apropiador." El país, *Página 12*, May 18, 2011. https://www.pagina12.com.ar/diario/elpais/1-168409-2011-05-18.html.
Gómez-Barris, Macarena. *Where Memory Dwells: Culture and State Violence in Chile*. Berkeley: University of California Press, 2009.
González Rodríguez, Sergio. *The Femicide Machine*. Translated by Michael Parker-Stainback. New York: Semiotext(e), 2012.
Grace, Sherrill. "Theatre and the AutoBiographical Pact: An Introduction." In *Theatre and AutoBiography: Writing and Performing Lives in Theory and Practice*, edited by Sherrill Grace and Jerry Wasserman. Vancouver, B.C.: Talonbooks, 2006.
Graham-Jones, Jean, ed. *Lola Arias: Re-enacting Life*. Aberystwyth, Wales: Performance Research Books, 2019.
———. "Lo real no siempre se rehace de la misma manera: *Mi vida después* y *El año en que nací* de Lola Arias." *Apuntes de Teatro*, no. 138 (2013): 52–65.
———. "The Translational Politics of Surtitling: Lola Arias's *Campo minado / Minefield*." In *Theatrical Speech Acts: Performing Language*, edited by Erika Fischer-Lichte, Torsten Jost, and Saskya Iris Jain, 119–130. New York: Routledge, 2020.
Grimson, Alejandro, ed. *La cultura en las crisis latinoamericanas*. Buenos Aires: CLASCO, 2004.

Grotowski, Jerzy. "Towards the Poor Theatre." Edited by Kelly Morris; translated by T. K. Wiewiorowski. *Tulane Drama Review* 11, no. 3 (1967): 60–65.

Guber, Rosana. *¿Por qué Malvinas?* Buenos Aires: Fondo de Cultura Económica, 2001.

Hayner, Priscilla B. *Unspeakable Truths: Transitional Justice and the Challenge of Truth Commissions*. 2nd ed. New York: Routledge, 2011.

Heddon, Dierdre. *Autobiography and Performance*. Basingstoke, England: Palgrave Macmillan, 2008.

Hernández, Paola. "Biografías escénicas: *Mi vida después* de Lola Arias." *Latin American Theatre Review* 45, no. 1 (Fall 2011): 115–128.

———. "Remapping Memory Discourses: *Villa* and *Discurso* by Guillermo Calderón." *South Central Review* 30, no. 3 (Winter 2013): 60–75.

Hirsch, Marianne. *Family Frames: Photography, Narrative and Postmemory*. Cambridge, Mass.: Harvard University Press, 1997.

———. "The Generation of Postmemory." *Poetics Today* 29, no. 1 (2008): 103–128.

———. *The Generation of Postmemory: Writing and Visual Culture after the Holocaust*. New York: Columbia University Press, 2012.

———. "Surviving Images: Holocaust Photographs and the Work of Postmemory." *Yale Journal of Criticism* 14, no. 1 (2001): 5–38.

Holzapfel, Tamara. "*Pueblo rechazado*: Educating the Public through Reportage." *Latin American Theatre Review* (Fall 1976): 15–21.

Huyssen, Andreas. *Present Pasts: Urban Palimpsests and the Politics of Memory*. Stanford, Calif.: Stanford University Press, 2003.

———. *Twilight Memories: Marking Time in a Culture of Amnesia*. New York: Routledge, 1995.

Inter-American Commission on Human Rights. *Situación de los derechos de la mujer en Ciudad Juárez, México: El derecho a no ser objeto de violencia y discriminación*. Washington, D.C.: General Secretariat, Organization of American States, 2003.

Irmer, Thomas. "A Search for New Realities: Documentary Theatre in Germany." *The Drama Review* 50, no. 3-T191 (Fall 2006): 16–27.

Isherwood, Charles. "Review: From Chile, *Escuela*, a Drama about Education." *New York Times*, January 17, 2016.

Ivatts, Sophie. "Guillermo Calderón on Theatre, Politics, and Pinochet's Legacy." *Pulsamerica*, October 2011. http://www.pulsamerica.co.uk/2011/10/19/guillermo-calderon-on-theatre-politics-and-pinochet's-legacy/.

Jackson, Shannon. *Social Works: Performing Art, Supporting Publics*. New York: Routledge, 2011.

Jaroslavsky, Sonia. "Capturar la teatralidad." *Teatro: Revista del Complejo Teatral de Buenos Aires* 29, no. 95 (August 2008): 70–79.

Jelin, Elizabeth. *State Repression and the Labors of Memory*. Translated by Judy Rein and Marcial Godoy-Anativia. Minneapolis: University of Minnesota Press, 2003.

Kiderlen, Meret. "Experimentar con lo real: Entrevista a Vivi Tellas." *telondefondo: Revista de Teoría y Crítica Teatral* 3, no. 5 (July 2007). http://www.telondefondo.org.

Kuhn, Annette. *Family Secrets: Acts of Memory and Imagination*. London: Verso, 2002.

Lagarde y de los Ríos, Marcela. *Por la vida y la libertad de las mujeres: Fin al feminicidio*. Mexico City: Congreso de la Unión, Cámara de Diputados, LIX Legislatura, Comisión Especial para Conocer y dar Seguimiento a las Investigaciones Relacionadas con los Feminicidios en la República Mexicana y a la Procuración de Justicia Vinculada, 2005.

———. "Preface: Feminist Keys for Understanding Feminicide." In *Terrorizing Women: Feminicide in the Americas*, edited by Rosa-Linda Fregoso and Cynthia Bejarano. Durham, N.C.: Duke University Press, 2010.

Lamadrid Guerrero, Geraldine. "Informe sobre *El puro lugar*: Recuento y preguntas." *Revista Conjunto*, no. 183 (2017): 2–13.

Landsberg, Alison. *Prosthetic Memory: The Transformation of American Remembrance in the Age of Mass Culture*. New York: Columbia University Press, 2004.

Larios, Shaday. "Teatro de objetos documental: Derivaciones del teatro de objetos hacia lo documental." *Titeresante*. http://www.titeresante.es/2016/08/teatro-de-objetos-documental-derivaciones-del-teatro-de-objetos-hacia-lo-documental-por-shaday-larios/.

Larrabure, Manuel, and Carlos Torchia. "The 2011 Chilean Student Movement and the Struggle for a New Left." *Latin American Perspectives* 204.42, no. 5 (Fall 2015): 248–268.

Laub, Dori. "Truth and Testimony: The Process and the Struggle." In *Trauma: Explorations of Memory*, edited by Cathy Caruth, 61–75. Baltimore: Johns Hopkins University Press, 1995.

Laufenberg, Marin. "Tempering Trauma with Humor in Argentine Post-dictatorship Theatre: Laughing to Recover, Reimagine, Rebuild." PhD diss., University of Wisconsin, 2017.

Lazzara, Michael. *Chile in Transition: The Poetics and Politics of Memory*. Gainesville: University Press of Florida, 2006.

Lehmann, Hans-Thies. *Postdramatic Theatre*. Translated by Karen Jürs-Munby. London: Routledge, 2009.

Lejeune, Philippe. *On Autobiography*. Foreword by Paul John Eakin. Translated by Katherine Leary. Minneapolis: University of Minnesota Press, 1989.

León, Federico. *Las ideas*. Video, 2015, 60 min.

León, Luis D. "Metaphor and Place: The U.S.-Mexico Border as Center and Periphery in the Interpretation of Religion." *Journal of the American Academy of Religion* 67, no. 3 (1999): 541–571.

Lingenti, Alejandro. "Vivi Tellas, el nombre de la vanguardia teatral." *La Nación*, February 22, 2020. https://www.lanacion.com.ar/espectaculos/vivi-tellas-el-nombre-de-la-vanguardia-teatral-nid2335046.

Lorenz, Federico. *Malvinas: Una guerra argentina*. Buenos Aires: Editorial Sudamericana, 2009.

———. "Testigos de la derrota Malvinas: Los soldados y la guerra durante la transición democrática argentina, 1982–1987." In *Historizar el pasado vivo en América Latina*, edited by Anne Perotin-Dumon, 3–63. Buenos Aires: Edhasa, 2007.

———. *Unas islas demasiado famosas: Malvinas, historia y política*. Buenos Aires: Capital intelectual, 2013.

Luna, Alfadir. Interview by Bernard Vienat. *Vorticidad*. https://vorticidad.org/artist/alfadir-luna-2/. Accessed August 20, 2018.

Madison, D. Soyini. *Acts of Activism: Human Rights as Radical Performance*. Cambridge: Cambridge University Press, 2010.

Maguire, Geoffrey. *The Politics of Postmemory: Violence and Victimhood in Contemporary Argentine Culture*. Basingstoke, England: Palgrave Macmillan, 2017.

Malzacher, Florian. "Dramaturgies of Care and Insecurity: The Story of Rimini Protokoll." In *Experts of the Everyday: The Theatre of Rimini Protokoll*, translated by Daniel Belasco Rogers, Ehren Fordyce, Geoffrey Garrison, Mat Hand, Sophia New, and Walter Sutcliffe; edited by Miriam Dreysse and Florian Malzacher. Berlin: Alexander Verlag, 2008.

Martin, Carol. "Bodies of Evidence." In *Dramaturgy of the Real on the World Stage*, edited by Martin. Basingstoke, England: Palgrave Macmillan, 2010.

———, ed. *Dramaturgy of the Real on the World Stage*. Basingstoke, England: Palgrave Macmillan, 2010.

———. "The Theatrical Life of Documents." *Peripeti* 21 (2014): 24–34.

Megson, Chris. "Half the Picture: 'A Certain Frisson; at the Tricycle Theatre." In *Get Real: Documentary Theatre Past and Present*, edited by Alison Forsyth and Chris Megson. Basingstoke, England: Palgrave Macmillan, 2009.

———. *Theatre of the Real*. Basingstoke, England: Palgrave Macmillan, 2013.

Méndez, Mercedes. "Primer film de la talentosa directora teatral Lola Arias y su personal visión de Malvinas." *Revista Ñ, Clarín*, August 31, 2018. https://www.clarin.com/revista-enie/escenarios/espacio-urbano/lola-arias-personal-vision-malvinas_0_ryff4gwPm.html.

"Mexican Gov't Agency Says 1968 Massacre Was a 'State Crime.'" *AP News*, September 25, 2018. https://www.apnews.com/8909ad7d01f4490bafd7899bb4e4cdb5.

Mexico Calls Student Massacre Ahead of '68 Olympics a 'State Crime,'" *Democracy Now!* (2018), accessed December 12, 2018. https://www.democracynow.org/2018/9/28/headlines/mexico_calls_student_massacre_ahead_of_68_olympics_a_state_crime.

Michels, Patrick. "The Strangers Next Door." *The Observer*, April 11, 2016. https://www.texasobserver.org/the-strangers-next-door-amarillo-refugees/.

Miller, Lynn C., Jacqueline Taylor, and M. Heather Carner. *Voices Made Flesh: Performing Women's Autobiography*. Madison: University of Wisconsin Press, 2003.

Miller, Nancy K., and Jason Tougaw, eds. *Extremities: Trauma, Testimony and Community*. Urbana: University of Illinois Press, 2002.

Monárrez Fragoso, Julia Estela. *Trama de una injusticia: Feminicidio sexual sistémico en Ciudad Juárez*. Tijuana: El Colegio de la Frontera Norte, 2009.

Montez, Noe. "Performing Public Memorialization of the Malvinas War." In *Memory, Transnational Justice, and Theatre in Postdictatorship Argentina*, 147–179. Carbondale: Southern Illinois University Press, 2017.

Moulián, Tomás. *Chile actual: Anatomía de un mito*. 3rd ed. Santiago de Chile: LOM, 2002.

Olin, Margaret. *Touching Photographs*. Chicago: University of Chicago Press, 2012.

Opazo, Cristián, and Carlos Benítez. "A Little Respect: Mateluna de Guillermo Calderón." *Revista Conjunto* no. 185 (October–December 2017): 8–15.

"Otorgaron la prisión domicialiaria al apropiador de Juan Cabandié," Sociedad, *Perfil*, June 30, 2018. https://www.perfil.com/noticias/sociedad/otorgaron-la-prision-domiciliaria-al-apropiador-de-juan-cabandie.phtml.

Page, Philippa. *Politics and Performance in Post-dictatorship Argentine Film and Theatre*. Woodbridge, England: Tamesis, 2011.

Paley, Julia. *Marketing Democracy: Power and Social Movements in Post-dictatorship Chile*. Berkeley: University of California Press, 2001.

Parrini, Rodrigo. "Figuras del límite: documentos, etnografías y teatro." *Investigación Teatral: Revista de Artes Escénicas y Performatividad* 9, no. 13 (Apr.–Sept. 2018): 14–34.

Pastrana, Myrna. *Cuando las banquetas fueron nuestras*. Mexico City: Ficticia, 2011.

Pauls, Alan. "Biodrama." In *Diccionario del pensamiento alternativo*, edited by Hugo E. Biagini and Arturo A. Roig. Buenos Aires: Editorial Biblos, 2008.

———. "Kidnapping Reality: An Interview with Vivi Tellas." Translated by Sarah Townsend. In *Dramaturgy of the Real on the World Stage*, edited by Carol Martin, 246–258. Basingstoke, England: Palgrave Macmillan, 2010.

———. "La bestia humana." *Radar* (blog), *Pagina 12*, May 7, 2003. https://www.pagina12.com.ar/diario/suplementos/radar/9-655-2003-03-16.html.

———. "La ciudad y sus dobles." *Radar* (blog), *Página 12*, November 21, 2010. https://www.pagina12.com.ar/diario/suplementos/radar/9-6628-2010-11-25.html.

Perera, Verónica. "Testimonios vivos, dramaturgia abierta: La guerra de Malvinas en Campo minado de Lola Arias." *Anagnórisis: Revista de investigación teatra*l, no. 6 (December 2017): 299–323.

Pérez, Mariana Eva. "Their Lives After: Theatre as Testimony and the So-Called 'Second Generation' in Post-dictatorship Argentina." *Journal of Romance Studies* 3, no. 3 (Winter 2013): 6–16.

Phelan, Peggy. *Unmarked: The Politics of Performance*. London: Routledge, 1993.

Pinter, Harold. "Death." *Times Literary Supplement*, August 22, 2011. https://www.the-tls.co.uk/articles/public/harold-pinter-death-2-2/.

Pottlizer, Joanne. "Forgetting Filled with Memory." *Theater* 43, no. 2 (2013): 57–63.

———. "A Serious Man of the Theatre." *Edinburgh International Festival Program*, August 2010, 6–12.

Prieto Stambaugh, Antonio. "Memorias inquietas en el teatro del unheimlich: *El Puro Lugar*." *Telecápita* (blog), 2016. https://telecapitarevista.org/2016/09/24/memorias-inquietas-en-el-teatro-del-unheimlich-el-puro-lugar/.

Primer Tribunal de Conciencia sobre la violencia y discriminación hacia las mujeres. Casos: Cd. Juárez y Chihuahua. Chihuahua, Mexico: La Gota Editorial, 2004.

Puga, Ana Elena. *Memory, Allegory, and Testimony in South American Theater: Upstaging Dictatorship*. New York: Routledge, 2008.

Rancière, Jacques. *The Emancipated Spectator*. Translated by Gregory Elliott. London: Verso, 2009.

Revista Gente. Special issue, no. 879 (1982).

Richard, Nelly. "Sitios de la memoria, vaciamiento del recuerdo." *Revista de Crítica Cultural* 23 (2001): 10–13.

Ridout, Nicholas. *Stage Fright, Animals, and Other Theatrical Problems*. Cambridge: Cambridge University Press, 2006.

———. "Welcome to the Vibratorium." *Senses and Society* 3, no. 2 (2008): 221–231.

Ripp, Alexandra. "Remembering the Coup: Chilean Theatre Now." *Performing Arts Journal*, no. 108 (2014): 87–101.

Roach, Joseph. *Cities of the Dead*. New York: Columbia University Press, 1996.

Rojo, Sara. "Teatro politico actual: La dramaturgia de Guillermo Calderón." *Meridional: Revista Chilena de Estudios Latinoamericanos*, no. 5 (October 2015): 109–129.

Sánchez, José A. *Practising the Real on the Contemporary Stage*. Translated by Charlie Allwood. Bristol: Intellect, 2014.

Santillán, Juan José. "Cómo poner la vida sobre el escenario." Espectáculos, *Diario Clarín*, July 31, 2008. https://www.clarin.com/espectaculos/poner-vida-escenario_0_SkMztunCatg.html.

Schechner, Richard. *Between Theatre and Anthropology*. Philadelphia: University of Pennsylvania Press, 1985.

———. *Performance Studies: An Introduction*. New York: Routledge, 2002.

Schneider, Rebecca. "New Materialisms and Performance Studies." *TDR: The Drama Review* 59, no. 4 (Winter 2015): 7–17.

———. "Performance Remains." *Performance Research* 6, no. 2 (2001): 100–108.

———. *Performing Remains: Art and War in Times of Theatrical Reenactment*. London: Routledge, 2011.

Schweitzzer, Marlis, and Joanne Zerdy. "Introduction: Object Lessons." In *Performing Objects and Theatrical Things*, edited by Marlis Schweitzzer and Joanne Zerdy. Basingstoke, England: Palgrave Macmillan, 2014.

Sedgwick, Eve Kosofsky. *Touching Feeling: Affect, Pedagogy, Performativity*. Durham, N.C.: Duke University Press, 2003.

Seear, Mike. *With the Gurkhas in the Falklands: A War Journal*. Barnsley, South Yorkshire, England: Pen and Sword Books, 2017.

Seigworth, Gregory J., and Melissa Gregg. "An Inventory of Shimmers." In *The Affect Theory Reader*, edited by Gregg and Seigworth, 1–29. Durham, N.C.: Duke University Press, 2010.

Sikkink, Kathryn, and Carrie Booth Walling. "The Impact of Human Rights Trials in Latin America." *Journal of Peace Research* 44, no. 4 (July 2007): 427–445.

Smith, Sidonie, and Julia Watson, eds. *Interfaces: Women/Autobiography/Image/Performance* Ann Arbor: University of Michigan Press, 2002.

Sofer, Andrew. *The Stage Life of Props*. Ann Arbor: University of Michigan Press, 2003.

Somma, Nicolás M. "The Chilean Student Movement of 2011–2012: Challenging the Marketization of Education." *Interface* 4, no. 2 (November 2012): 296–309.

Sontag, Susan. *Regarding the Pain of Others*. New York: Picador, 2003.

Sosa, Cecilia. "*Campo minado / Minefield*: War, Affect and Vulnerability—a Spectacle of Intimate Power." *Theatre Research International* 42, no. 2 (July 2017): 179–189.

———. "Cuéntame tu vida." *Radar* (blog), *Página 12*, October 17, 2004. http://www.pagina12.com.ar/diario/suplementos/radar/9-1748-2004-10-17.html.

———. "La máquina del tiempo." In *Acercamientos de lo real: Textos y escenarios*, edited by Óscar Cornago. Buenos Aires: Ediciones Artes del Sur, 2007.
———. "Los niños que fuimos." *Radar* (blog), *Página 12*, October 7, 2012. https://www.pagina12.com.ar/diario/suplementos/radar/9-8291-2012-10-07.html.
———. *Queering Acts of Mourning in the Aftermath of Argentina's Dictatorship*. Woodbridge, England: Tamesis, 2014.
Stephenson, Jenn. *Insecurity: Perils and Products of Theatres of the Real*. Toronto: University of Toronto Press, 2019.
Stern, Steve J. *Remembering Pinochet's Chile: On the Eve of London 1998*. Durham, N.C.: Duke University Press, 2004.
Stoll, David. *Rigoberta Menchú and the Story of All Poor Guatemalans*. Boulder, CO: Westview Press, 1999.
Swindells, Julia. *The Uses of Autobiography*. London: Taylor & Francis, 1995.
Taylor, Diana. *The Archive and the Repertoire: Performing Cultural Memory in the Americas*. Durham, N.C.: Duke University Press, 2003.
———. *Disappearing Acts: Spectacles of Gender and Nationalism in Argentina's "Dirty War."* Durham, N.C.: Duke University Press, 1997.
———. *Performance*. Durham, N.C.: Duke University Press, 2016.
———. "Performing Ruins." In *Telling Ruins in Latin America*. Edited by Vicky Unruh and Michael Lazzara, 13–26. New York: Palgrave Macmillan, 2008.
———. "Trauma, memoria y performance: Un recorrido por Villa Grimaldi con Pedro Matta." *e-misférica* 7, no. 2 (Winter 2010). https://hemisphericinstitute.org/en/emisferica-72/7-2-essays/e72-essay-trauma-memoria-y-performance-un-recorrido-por-villa-grimaldi-con-pedro-matta.html.
Taylor, Paul. "*Minefield*, Royal Court London: Unforgettably Potent." Review of *Minefield / Campo minado*. *Independent*, June 6, 2016. https://www.independent.co.uk/arts-entertainment/theatre-dance/reviews/minefield-royal-court-london-theatre-review-unforgettably-potent-a7067196.html.
Teatro Línea de Sombra (TLS). *Amarillo*. Unpublished MS.
———. *Baños Roma*. Unpublished MS.
———. *No Negociable: Mantequilla Nápoles (en), Baños Roma (con) Teatro Línea de Sombra*. Fanzine.
Tellas, Vivi. *Biodrama / Proyecto Archivos: Seis escenarios documentales de Vivi Tellas*. Edited by Pamela Brownell and Paola Hernández. Córdoba: Papeles Teatrales, 2017.
———. "Comienza el Biodrama." Press release, Complejo Teatral de Buenos Aires, April 9, 2002.
———. "Intimidad." www.archivostellas.com.ar (currently accesssible only within Argentina).
———. *Proyecto Museos*. Buenos Aires: Libros del Rojas/Universidad de Buenos Aires, 2002.
———. "Vidas prestadas." *Radar* (blog), *Página 12*, August 24, 2008. https://www.pagina12.com.ar/diario/suplementos/radar/9-4788-2008-08-30.html.
Thompson, Jennifer Joan. "Dramaturgies of Democracy: Performance, Cultural Policy, and Citizenship in Chile 1979–Present." PhD diss., CUNY–Graduate Center, 2019.
Till, Karen. *The New Berlin: Memory, Politics, Place*. Minneapolis: University of Minnesota Press, 2005.

Tompkins, Joanne. "The 'Place' and Practice of Site-Specific Theatre and Performance." In *Performing Site-Specific Theatre: Politics, Place, Practice*, edited by Anna Birch and Joanne Tompkins, 27–60. New York: Palgrave Macmillan, 2012.

Trastoy, Beatriz. "El lugar del otro: Interferencias y deslindes entre discurso crítico y práctica escénica contemporánea." *Orbis Tertius* 11, no. 12 (2006): 1–11.

Valencia, Sayak. *Gore Capitalism*. Translated by John Pluecker. South Pasadena, Calif.: Semiotext(e) Intervention Series, 2018.

Vázquez, Juan Manuel. "Una vez me puse los guantes con Alain Delon." Deportes, *La jornada*, July 25, 2009. http://www.jornada.unam.mx/2009/07/25/deportes/a36n1dep.

Verzero, Lorena. "Representaciones afectivas/efectivas en Lola Arias: 'La memoria también puede funcionar como un campo minado.' " *Revista Conjunto*, no. 185 (2017): 32–41.

Villegas, Juan. "El teatro chileno de la postdictadura." *Inti: Revista de literatura hispánica* 1, no. 69 (2009): 189–205.

———. *Historia multicultural del teatro y las teatralidades en América Latina*. Colección teatrología, dir. Osvaldo Pellettieri. Buenos Aires: Galerna, 2005.

Violi, Patrizia. "Trauma Site Museums and Politics of Memory: Tuol Sleng, Villa Grimaldi and the Bologna Ustica Museum." *Theory, Culture and Society* 29, no. 1 (January 2012): 36–75.

Vitullo, Julieta. *Islas imaginadas: La Guerra de Malvinas en la literatura y el cine argentinos*. Buenos Aires: Corregidor, 2012.

Ward, Julie Ann. *A Shared Truth: The Theater of Lagartijas tiradas al sol*. Pittsburgh: University of Pittsburgh Press, 2019.

Weiss, Peter. "Fourteen Propositions for a Documentary Theatre." *World Theatre* 17, nos. 5–6 (1968): 375–389.

Weizman, Eyal, et al. "The Enforced Disappearance of the Ayotzinapa Students." Forensic Architecture, accessed July 16, 2020. https://forensic-architecture.org/investigation/the-enforced-disappearance-of-the-ayotzinapa-students.

Werth, Brenda. "A Malvinas Veteran Onstage: From Intimate Testimony to Public Memorialization." *South Central Review* 30, no. 3 (Fall 2013): 83–100.

———. "*Mi mamá y mi tía*: El arte de crear mundos íntimos." In *Biodrama / Proyecto Archivos: Seis documentales escénicos*, edited by Pamela Brownell and Paola Hernández. Córdoba: Papeles Teatrales, 2017.

———. *Theatre, Performance, and Memory Politics in Argentina*. New York: Palgrave Macmillan, 2010.

White Book of the Change of Government in Chile: 11th September 1973. Santiago, Chile: Empresa Editora Nacional "Gabriela Mistral," 1974.

Willett, John. *The Theatre of Erwin Piscator*. New York: Holmes & Meier, 1979.

Williams, Paul. *Memorial Museums: The Global Rush to Commemorate Atrocities*. Oxford: Berg, 2007.

Willson, William Moss. "Just Don't Call Her Che." *New York Times*, January 28, 2012. https://www.nytimes.com/2012/01/29/opinion/sunday/student-protests-rile-chile.html.

Ybarra, Patricia A. *Latinx Theater in the Times of Neoliberalism*. Evanston, Ill.: Northwestern University Press, 2018.

INDEX

Numbers in italic indicate illustrations.